Biblical Counseling Manual

Adam Pulaski

Order this book online at www.trafford.com
or email orders@trafford.com

Most Trafford titles are also available at major online book retailers.

Print information available on the last page.

ISBN: 978-1-4120-3879-9 (sc)

Unless otherwise noted, Scripture quotations are from the Holy Bible, King James Version.

Disclaimer: Those organizations from whom we have drawn materials and approaches to Biblical Counseling have not necessarily endorsed not approved this program.

Trafford rev. 09/13/2024

North America & international
toll-free: 844-688-6899 (USA & Canada)
fax: 812 355 4082

This book is dedicated to Ruth, Amy and Zachary.

Table of Contents

Foreword

In 1978, I began seeking biblical resources to help work out some personal problems. This I found in a Christian bookstore where I picked up a book titled "Competent to Counsel" by Jay E. Adams, which opened my eyes to the possibility that I could with confidence counsel myself as well as help others. This led me in June of 1979 to the Biblical Counseling Foundation located then in Arlington, Virginia, where I spent three plus years training as a Biblical Counselor.

My training continued as I began teaching a biblical counseling course to various groups in 1980 through 1984. From 1984 until the present (2004) I continue in the capacity of teaching and counseling at a local church in Silver Spring, Maryland..

During this period of time, I was led to counsel in numerous and varied problem areas. From experiences gained, I accumulated a repository of handouts and worksheets to facilitate and keep the counseling session biblical, to maintain a focus on God's word, and to provide resource material to assist disciples to counsel themselves

This is what appealed to Steve. After attending my 22-week course in 1996, Steve Lihn, who was in the final stages of obtaining his doctorate degree from University of Maryland, suggested that this program should be put on the internet. We used the acronym "BCOL" for this undertaking, which stands for Biblical Counseling On-Line. It took the summer of 1997 through 1998 to accomplish this feat. This cyberspace ministry proved to be very beneficial to the global body of Christ. It has recorded thousands upon thousands of hits and many requests for information from all over the world.

This prompted us to transform the online materials into a book form, available both electronically and in paper print, so that the greater christian community can benefit. Since the winter of 2002, Steve and I worked together to accomplish this conversion.

We trust that our findings will provide the insights and the tools necessary to help one effectively and succesfully become an overcomer in this battle zone called life.

Many are tossed about by the winds of the world's philosophies and arguments. But our battle is to be led by the Holy Spirit in applying God's wisdom and truth to the challenges of life. The Bible provides all the instruction that one needs on how to live this victorious life in the midst of obstacles, of temptations, of trials and varied difficulties (**Rom. 8:4-9**). Thus, anyone born of the will of God, who has received Christ as Lord and Savior, is equipped and qualified to engage in this battle of wisdom (**2 Tim. 3:16-17**).

Our Lord directs us in **Matthew 28:18-20** to make disciples: to baptize them in the name of the Father, of the Son, and of the Holy Spirit, and to teach them to observe and live by God's commandments. This is the responsibility of the body of Christ who are to be equipped to accomplish this mission. **1 Cor. 1:30**; **3:16**; **Rom. 15:14**; **Gal. 6:1-5**; **Eph. 1:17-23** and **Col. 1:10-12** confirm that wisdom resides within us, that we are to grow in this wisdom, and to inform, instruct and restore others to the light of His word.

Accordingly, the purpose of this manual is to provide a basic approach, and the tools to establish a foundation to assist one to deal progressively with his own problems from a biblical perspective. And then to teach and counsel others to live by God's commandments; thereby, fulfilling our Lord's directive to make disciples of all nations (**Matt. 7:5**; **22:36-40**).

Adam Pulaski

March, 2004

How to View and Use This Manual

Prerequisites

Matthew 28:18-20 commands us to make disciples, and to teach them all that the Lord commands. Thus, a disciple, a follower of Christ, is a student, ever learning to put-off the ways of the old self and to put-on the ways of the new self, Christ Himself (**Eph. 4:22-24**). All Christians by definition are disciples, ever learning, and are to teach themselves as well as others to follow Christ. Accordingly, the body of Christ is responsible to provide guidance, counsel, advice, forethought, information and instruction to one another (**Rom. 15:14**; **Gal. 6:1-5**; **Eph. 4:11-16**; **Phil. 2:12-13**).

Handicapped by a total lack of bible knowledge, I was woefully inadequate in every way to fulfill the above requirements. But a wise counselor advised me to start one day at a time, and not to go beyond my ability: for it is the Holy Spirit Who is the counselor, and the convictor—we are just witnesses to His word. As long as I relied on and proclaimed His word, I was okay.

Resources

Accordingly, over the years, I sought biblical support from anointed teachers to supplement, to complement, to equip, and to prompt me as a trainee to maintain and sustain a biblical focus during teaching, advising, and counseling sessions, and to provide written biblical resources as homework assignments and study material to reinforce biblical truths.

The manual and worksheets are the result of these efforts. Each sheet is complete in itself with verses and comments, and suggested homework assignments to assist and guide a trainee as well as a mature disciple to maintain a biblical focus. Likewise, each chapter may be viewed as a separate unit and complete in itself. Accordingly, the teacher/advisor/counselor may review and study the appropriate chapter and individual worksheets to prepare himself beforehand for each discipling session. During the session and subsequent sessions he may use one particular worksheet as a focal point for discussion purposes, supplemented by other pertinent sheets which may be provided as homework for the student to study.

Case Study

For example, a 19 year old christian lad is addicted to pornography and masturbation. These symptoms may or may not be directly addressed. Our responsibility as teachers/advisors/counselors is to relate him to the source of his help, the Holy Spirit.

Underlying our approach in all our endeavors, as we see it—bearing in mind that most, if not all, problems in life, the lack or absence of peace and joy—are due to basically four factors, the root issues that lead to the solution:

1. (**Matt. 22:36-40**; **John 14:21,27**) Major problem is failure to love God and neighbor by not living according to His commandments. Thus, the first and key step is to underline and reinforce daily devotions, bible study, christian friends and activities in order to get the focus off self and on to God and others. The worksheets **Section 8.2, "Prerequisite to Biblical Change"**, **Section 15.9, "Union With God"**, the **"Soul Dynamics"** series (**Chapter 4, 5**) and **Chapter 6, "Christian Growth Series, Part A"** may be appropriately used for discussion purposes and homework assignments.

2. (**Luke 9:23-24**; **Rom. 6:11**; **Eph. 4:22-24**; **Heb. 5:13-14**) The old way of thinking and doing must be identified and eradicated; and God's way of thinking and doing must be emphasized and practiced on a daily basis. The key here is to develop a sensitivity to sin, to hate sin—not to hate self but the selfish core, and allow the new self to emerge and to concentrate on a new way of thinking and doing, developing an attitude of self donation. The worksheets **Section 7.14, "Mind Control"**, **Section 10.10, "Breaking Physical Habits"**, **Section 11.9, "Life Dominating Sins"** and **Chapter 5, "Soul Dynamics Series, Part B"** may be appropriate for discussions purposes and for homework assignments.

3. (**Matt. 5:23-24**; **6:14-15**) The cardinal principle of God's universe is forgiveness. Unless this issue is dealt with, spiritual healing and growth is impossible. Bitter root judgments must be dealt with such as: childhood abuses, absence of or lack of parental affirmation, sexual violations, addictions of various sorts, and similar situations. All offenses of the past and of the present are to be resolved biblically and on a daily basis. Therefore, selected worksheets of chapters 5, 10, 11 and 12 may be appropriate for discussion and homework assignments.

4. (**Rom. 5:1-5**; **8:29**; **2 Peter 1:1-12**) Set up plans to be separated from the world, the flesh and the devil. Worksheets in Chapters 6, 7 and 15 may be

appropriate for a plan of action. The objective is to dispose self to the purification of the intellect, the memories, the emotions, and the will through meditation (disciple speaking to God) and contemplation (God speaking to disciple). **Appendix A.12, "Anchor Posts", Section 5.4, "Transforming the Natural Self"** and other appropriate worksheets may also be useful for this purpose.

Sanctification

As we direct the disciple and emphasize these four factors, the root issues, and the suggested use of the "Anchor Posts" as a daily maintenance guide and support, as well as applying appropriate worksheets, the symptoms, the urges of sin, will fade, and the 'new self' will emerge.

As witnesses our job is simply to direct ourselves and others to the truth, and the truth will set us free. Free now to prepare ourselves to be perfectly dispossessed of all that is not of God. This opens up the human faculties to be infused and filled with God (**Matt. 5:48**; **6:10**; **Luke 14:26,33**; **Rom. 8:29**).

By the process of renewing his mind, daily being conformed to the image of Christ, the disciple unites his will with God's will and fulfills Christ's command in **Matthew 28** to establish His kingdom on earth of righteousness and peace and joy in the Holy Spirit.

Part I. Overview

Table of Contents

Chapter 1. Counseling Objectives

Table of Contents

1.1. Introduction

This manual is designed to teach one to approach circumstances, relationships, and situations of life from a biblical perspective and to experience victory and contentment in all of life's trials, testings and problems.

The essence of who we are is made of events and how we responded to those events. We are the sum of what we encountered in life and our reactions to those experiences. **Memory**, the recalling of the past, is our spirit gazing at the substance of our soul which, at times, directs our lives rather than the word of God. Thus, most of our problems are due to ignorance on how to biblically respond to life and to use life's adversities to our advantage as opportunities to grow and mature in Christ (**Rom. 8:28-29**).

These spiritual resources are available to those who are born by the will of God. Having accepted Jesus Christ as Savior and Lord, the believer is enabled by Holy Spirit to face life, to counter adversities, to grow in grace and strength, and to live in peace and joy (**John 1:12**; **John 3:16**; **John 14:27**).

The issue is the **self**, the soul of man. The self created by God, belongs to God. The self, tempted to be god without God, became enslaved by Satan (**Gen. 1:26-27**; **Gen. 2:7**; **Gen. 3:1-6**).

The living soul is what we will deal with...

- To set it free.
- To again be completely dependent upon God.
- To follow Him and to glorify Him.

Phil. 2:12-13; **2 Pet. 1:3-11** tell us to work out our salvation daily being conformed to the image of Christ. **The key is daily**, being God-conscious twenty-four hours a day. Either we are thinking God's thoughts or we defer to lower level thinking. There is no gray area. You are either for God or you are against Him (**Matt. 12:30**).

1.2. Preconditions in Biblical Counseling

Throughout the counseling session, the goal is to change the disciple/counselee's focus on the false self, a self of lusts and appetites, to a realization of his true self, a self in union with Christ. This is accomplished by a continuous process of judging self, one's own sins, not others; changing focus from self needs to one of accomplishing God's purposes for one's life by loving Him and others foremost; daily dying to the old man and putting-on the new man; and of maintaining a state of forgiving and reconciling throughout life. The ultimate goal now is for the counselee to be a disciple, to help and restore others to this same position whereas they, in turn, will do likewise.

False Self

All of life in the natural sphere conditions and inclines one to deal with life's experiences from a horizontal perspective, that is, to react from a self-protective and self-defensive posture, to insure one's survival in a competitive and fallen environment. This pronounced self-focus degenerates, in time, until life is characterized by guilt and shame, anger and bitterness, and fear: a life devoid of the Presence of God. Life becomes filled with the presence of self attempting to meet the needs of self by a fruitless search for the meaning of life in a world system energized by evil.

A person in this condition seeks relief by the fashions and customs of this world, by the lusts and appetites of the flesh, by justifying his own behavior, by placing the blame on others, by seeking peace and joy in things, people, and possessions. Emphasis is on what others have done or failed to do, and the remedy is to manipulate others and the circumstances of life by whatever human (fallen) resources are available. The focus is on self, to save self by using others, and the things of the world to fabricate a false sense of value and significance.

True Self

All that was done to us, what we have done to others, the failures, the ills, the violations of our persons, the brutalities, the perversions of life, rejections, death of loved ones, tragedies, loneliness, abandonment, Jesus paid the penalty for all these

3

sins, and provided the means to handle the tragedies of life. We do not need to deal with these violations and tragedies on our own. Christ is in us to work out our salvation daily (**Phil. 2:12-13**; **Gal. 2:20**; **2 Cor. 5:17**; **2 Cor. 5:21**; **Rom. 6:3-6**; **Ezek. 18:20**).

Being in Christ, we are new creatures and we are to deal with life now from a biblical perspective. Our problem is not with Satan, not with people, not with the circumstances of life, but our problem lies in our relationship with God. Our focus is to change from a concern about self, to a concern about God's glory and that is accomplished by our godly responses to others and to life in general (**Rom. 5:17**; **2 Cor. 5:21**).

1.3. Foundations of Biblical Counseling/Discipleship

Self Knowledge

When born from above, the human spirit is regenerated, and united with the Spirit of God. However, the soul remains the same as conditioned by life's experiences. Before we can advance in our spiritual life, we can advance only if we come to know ourselves as we really are, that is, as we appear before the Almighty God. What we have done to others, what others have done to us—our interpretations of and sinful reactions to these and other issues—are to be dealt with from a biblical perspective.

Deliverance

One cannot go back and reform the 'old man', and redo what was said and done. But as a new creation, citizens of heaven, we look at life now from the spiritual realm to the earthly. Being adopted as sons, our primary concern is in our relationship with God the Father, nothing else should matter. As the Father loves the Son, the Son loves the Father. As we are in Jesus, the sonship, we are to love as Jesus loves the Father. Participating and sharing in the triune love, our loving action becomes the means of our deliverance (**John 15:10**; **John 17:20-24,26**).

The answer to healing the soul lies here: loving God by obeying His commands (**John 14:21**). Accordingly, unresolved actions of the past are to be dealt with in the present, and in the spirit of repentance and reconciliation.

Sanctification

Sanctification is the work of the Holy Spirit; only He knows the heart and the motives. As a counselor, our basic function is to lead and encourage the disciple to rely on the Bible as the sole authority and rule for living, and to hear from and to know the Person of the Holy Spirit (**John 16:13**). To accomplish this, our aim is to work with the disciple to establish a biblical standard from which he can work out his salvation.

To this effect, the following guidelines are provided to assist the disciple to work and abide within a biblical framework.

- **Loving God by Obeying His Commands**

  Our problem is not with Satan, not with people, not with circumstances. But our primary concern lies in our relationship with God the Father. No matter what one's life is at the moment, we must hold ourselves accountable. We cannot blame others or the circumstances of life. People and circumstances are not to direct our lives (**Ezek. 18:20**). Reacting to life without reference to God's word, one becomes his own god. God is to be God. Allow God to have full command of your life. He will use the trials and tests of life to perfect you and conform you to His Son (**Rom. 8:28-29**; **James 1:2-4**).

- **Judging Self**

  The starting point is to develop a keen sensitivity to sin by not taking life for granted. We are inclined to be critical of others, to blame shift, to be self-defensive, to retaliate, to be malicious, and similar sinful actions (**Matt. 7:5**; **Rom. 2:2**).

  How we respond to offenses and irritations of life reveals the spirit that is in us. Be aware, and ask God for His grace to be conscious of and sensitive to one's own spirit: then by His grace we establish plans to respond to offenses in a manner to restore ourselves and others (**Gal. 6:1-4**; **Eph. 4:22-24**).

- **Forgiving and Reconciling**

  Many souls are wounded by bitter roots: parental/child relationships, abuses of all kinds, disappointments, betrayals, and such, which paralyzes and poisons the spirit. Put the offender and the offense in God's hands; let Him judge the person and the situation. Get oneself free from the offender and offense by asking God for the grace to forgive and be reconciled. Forgiveness is an act of the will, to please the Father—it is not an option (**Matt. 5:23-24**; **Matt. 6:14-15**; **Heb. 12:15**; **1 Pet. 2:23**).

- **Daily Devotions**

  We are either in the flesh or the spirit: there is no gray area. We need the daily infusion of God's word to keep us in the spirit moment to moment. We are to be God-conscious, practicing His Presence twenty-four hours a day (**Ps. 1:1-3**; **2 Cor. 10:3-5**).

- **Daily Meditations**

  Recollections of the past stimulate memories and unresolved issues which, in turn, prompt spontaneous mood swings and reactions. As we meditate on God's word, we participate in the purification process of regenerating our intellect, our memories, our emotions, and our will to be integrated with God's will. By His grace, we are enabled to refashion the integrity of our inner life, preparing ourselves to be acutely sensitive to the promptings of the Holy Spirit (**Josh. 1:8**; **2 Cor. 7:1**; **James 1:21**).

Objective

We begin a life of reversals. The issues of the past are dealt with in the present, in a biblical manner. The daily offenses and irritations of life are confronted and dealt with as directed by the Holy Spirit. The self is dethroned… God is enthroned. The stage is set for the drama of being conformed to the image of Christ by practicing...

> … loving God.
> … judging self.
> … forgiving and reconciling with one another.
> … conducting daily devotions.
> … engaging in daily meditations.

We trust that the proposed guidelines as amplified and elaborated upon in the manual may prove beneficial to equip the children of God: to walk out of darkness into His marvelous light; to establish God's kingdom and will on earth; and to be a fit disciple of Christ (**2 Cor. 3:18**; **Matt. 28:18-20**).

6

1.4. Essential Considerations

Overcomers

First step is to judge self, not others. We are accountable for our own actions, and not the actions of others, that is, we are to develop a sensitivity to our own sin, and to respond to the present situation as a new creature in Christ (**Matt. 7:5**; **1 Pet. 3:9**; **Ezek. 18:20**).

- **Thought 1**

  Since the 1st Adam failed to overcome Satan, Satan is allowed to remain on earth for us to finish the job. Man opened the door for Satan to reign on earth, it is up to man to put him under foot. Jesus condemned sin in our corrupt nature to deal with the sin issue. Reckoning ourselves dead to sin but alive to God in Christ Jesus, we are now emboldened to confront and subdue Satan.

  Looking one level deeper, it is our responses to the temptations, the emotions of sin, that impact upon our senses and into our thought processes. This is what we resist and overcome: the evil tendencies that dwell within. Submitting to God, we are now enabled to resist and say 'no' to these emotions, and say 'yes' to the Holy Spirit. At this point we become overcomers by giving no foothold to the enemy in our thoughts, speech and actions: but instead we subdue and put him under foot as initially commanded (**Gen. 1:28**; **Eph. 4:22-24,26**; **James 4:6-8**; **Rev. 3:21**).

God Lovers

All that was done to us, and all that we have done to others, the pains and sorrows of life, God will intervene and rearrange all things to our advantage provided we do two things: obey His commandments, and live according to His purposes for our lives by being conformed to His Son (**Luke 9:23-24**; **Rom. 8:28-29**; **Col. 1:10**).

Therefore, we are to change our focus from self to God, by loving Him in our minds, our emotions, our memories, and our wills. Our biblical responses to our neighbors and to the offenses of life provide the evidence that we are loving God (**John 14:21**; **1 Pet. 3:9-15**; **Matt. 22:36-40**; **Luke 6:27-38**).

- **Thought 2**

We judge ourselves by the 'love' factor. The first thing that love is, is patience. Impatience separates us from God, from self, from neighbor. "Impatience is a form of self-indulgence, and has its roots in the sovereignty of self... This ego-centric attitude severs our link with God... Patience is a life centered in Christ. He who has patience abides in Truth. The impatient man submits to the bondage of the moment... And the ups and downs of life challenge the pursuit of constancy and perseverance... Holy patience embodies an ultimate act of our surrender to God, a status of consummate self-possession. Only in the measure that we have surrendered our inmost being to God, do we possess ourselves." (**Luke 21:19**). [Hildebrand1]

To the extent and degree we love as God loves determines the extent and degree we are overcoming Satan in this battle of wills (**1 Cor. 13:4-8**).

Word Knowledge

"**The Word of God** must abide in a person for a person to know God in a personal way. To 'abide' means that the word of God must not only be allowed to come into a person's mind and heart, it must be grasped and clung to. 'Abiding' means the Word of God...

- living, moving, ruling, and reigning in a person's life and heart.
- stirring and convicting, and challenging a person.
- leading to confession, repentance, growth, maturity.
- teaching love, compassion, forgiveness, goodness, and just behavior.
- causing one to believe and trust God's Son, Jesus Christ, as his Savior and Lord." (Quoted from [Leader1])

Goal

Our Lord took on flesh and bones—the human nature—that through the Cross, we may be translated from the earthly to the spiritual realm. No longer in the image of man after the fall, but now in the image of God as originally planned before the fall, we proceed to the 'high calling of Christ Jesus' (**Gen. 1:26**; **Rom. 6:3-6**; **Rom. 8:29**; **Phil. 3:12**; **Col. 1:13**).

Accordingly, it is our responsibility to attain to this level of being in our souls by identifying, locating, and eradicating the residuals of our fallen nature residing in our souls (**Eph. 4:22-24**). This is a lifelong process dedicated to purifying the intellect, the memories, the emotions, and the will to equip us to love as God loves (**2 Cor. 7:1**).

1.5. Summary

- Judge self in every encounter, being aware that my responses to life either glorify God or offend Him, and being continually sensitive to sinful reactions, not excusing, neither justifying self, nor blaming others. We are to restore self, to prepare self to be in a position to restore others.

- Daily put-off the old self and put-on the new self by biblically responding to life's irritations and offenses.

- Constantly sustain a state of forgiving and reconciling in the affairs of life, thus, allowing Jesus to live out His obedient life through us.

- Dispose self to the purification of the intellect, the memories, the emotions, and the will through meditation (you speaking to God) and contemplation (God speaking to you).

(**Gen. 1:28**; **Luke 9:23-24**; **Eph. 3:19**; **Col. 1:27**) As we are made of the earth, the first thing we are to dominate is the self: to put self under the complete influence of the Holy Spirit, to be a blessing upon this earth until we are filled with the fulness of God, to be clothed with the glory of God as in the days of the Apostles and Adam and Eve before the fall.

Chapter 2. Biblical Psychology: Approach to Problems

Table of Contents

2.1. Diagnosis

Feelings

(**Matt. 12:33-37**) We are the sum of what we encountered in life and our reactions to these events. Being conditioned by life's experiences, we are prone to react to life impulsively and instinctively rather than to respond on the basis of considered judgment. Such actions reveal a man's inner life—his focus—and who and what determines his peace and joy (**1 John 2:3-6**; **Matt. 5:44**; **Gal. 5:19-21**; **Col. 3:5-9**).

Our usual focus is on what others have done or failed to do. As we maintain a self-defensive and self-protective posture, we are inclined to judge, to condemn, to criticize, to blame shift, and similar reactions. This self focus is a breeding ground for anger, frustration, despair, bitterness, self-pity, and the like—a life of feelings. A feeling-oriented life is a fertile area in which Satan operates and upon which he feeds (**Gen. 4:7**).

Doing

(**John 14:21**; **James 1:22-25**) Thusly, the ungodly live by their senses. Their lives are directed by how and what they feel. This is what distinguishes a committed christian from the world: a christian lives by the will of God, not by feelings. However, there is nothing wrong with feelings in themselves until we act upon them. We are not to be directed or to live by feelings. We are to take stock and make note of our intents—the spirit that is being manifested: Then ask God for the grace to insure that we respond in a manner that honors and glorifies Him.

Regardless of how we feel we are to do what the word of God says to do. As we do to please the Father, godly feelings follow—the joy of the Lord. Living by the word, one serves God the Creator. Anything done without faith, without reference to God's word is sin (**James 4:17**; **Eph. 4:29**; **Rom. 2:6-9**; **John. 3:21**; **1 John 2:3**; **Prov. 1:22-31**; **Rom. 8:13**).

Root

(**2 Cor. 5:17**; **Jer. 17:9**) Our responses and reactions to life reflect our roots, the source of our being. Man's thoughts, speech and actions convey the character of these roots. Here we can identify the sin patterns and strongholds developed over the years that characterize the lifestyle and personality of the individual.

Category of root problems are many: hypocrisy, manipulation, lying, cheating, stealing, boasting, blame shifting, self-centeredness, self-protection, self-interest, anger, impatience, self-pity, lust, immorality, greed, malice, deceit, etc—a life characterized by self being on the throne of one's life.

Key

We establish godly roots by changing **I** to **We**, you in union with Christ. This begins with the new birth, followed by daily renewal of the mind. Thus life is confronted on the basis of God's word—the will of God. As we do the word, the Holy Spirit changes our roots which affect our feelings. This is a purification process. And we, in turn, begin to respond to life in a manner that glorifies God (**2 Cor. 10:3-5**; **Gal. 5:22-23**; **2 Pet. 1:3-8**; **Eph. 4:22-24**; **Col. 3:10**).

2.2. Approach to Solutions

Perspective

(**Isa. 55:8-9**; **Prov. 14:12**) We are to look at life from God's perspective, His view, not from our way, experiences, ideas, opinions, what others say, the world's philosophy or its psychology. The basic problem and the supreme challenge you will face in making Christ-honoring changes is dying to self. The biblical perspective concerning 'self' is exactly opposite to what the wisdom of this world proclaims (**Luke 9:23-24**).

Accordingly, to live biblically is to respond to life's challenges in a manner that pleases and honors God, no longer pleasing and gratifying self (**1 Cor. 3:19-20**; **1 John 2:15-17**; **1 John 2:20,27**; **1 Cor. 2:12-13**).

Hope

(**Heb. 6:18-20**) Hope is an anchor of the soul because it affects our mind and emotions. Christ within me, the Anointed One, breaks the yoke of life's pressures on me. And my job is to develop this inner image of Christ within me, that in Him,

I am more than a conqueror, never under but always over circumstances, no matter what I face in life.

To really believe this in the inner core of my being that all God's promises are mine depends upon my living in and by the living word of God (**John 16:33**; **James 1:2-4**).

- (**Ezek. 36:26-27**) God gave me a heart of flesh, put His Spirit within me, and gives me power to carry out His commands.

- (**1 Cor. 2:12-13**) Being a child of God, I receive revelation knowledge by the word of God in and through my human spirit.

- (**Rom. 8:28-29**) No matter what happens to me in life, when I call upon God He will intervene in my life. He will reach into my experiences, redeem my past, and cause things to work out for my benefit.

- (**1 Cor. 10:13**) God is the One who is faithful. As I put my faith in Him, He will bring me out successfully.

- (**Heb. 4:15-16**; **Heb. 7:25**) All I have to do is ask boldly, and God's Grace is available to me. The blood of Jesus Christ intercedes always, washing and cleansing from all senses of guilt and shame whether real or imaginary.

- (**Rom. 6:3-6**) My old human nature and all my past has been buried with Christ when I was baptized into His death. At the burial I was also raised with Him into the newness of life, freed from the power of sin, and free now to do acts of righteousness.

Change

(**Gen. 4:7**; **Eph. 5:14-16**) We must choose to change. We cannot afford to be careless or casual about our thinking, speaking and acting, nor can we take life for granted. God put us on this earth to actively replace evil with righteousness.

(**Matt. 7:1-5**; **1 Cor. 11:28-31**) Critical that I judge myself daily, that I am walking in the Spirit, responding to life God's way, then as a disciple of Christ I will be in the position to help restore others.

(**Rom. 12:1-2**) My total being belongs to the Lord for His use. This requires a total overhaul of my person, separating myself from my past, and the world's system and influences in order to be conformed to the ways of the Lord.

(**Eph. 4:25-32**; **Col. 3:5-17**; **Rom. 12:9-21**; **1 Pet. 2**; **1 Pet. 3**) Listed in these references are the basic put-offs and put-ons to guide and lead one to live a biblical lifestyle.

(**Rom. 8:29**; **1 John 3:8**) Examine self daily to see if I am living by God's standards for that day, being a blessing and destroying the works of the devil.

Work Out Your Salvation

(**Phil. 2:12-13**; **Ps. 1:1**; **John 15:5**) The enemy never stops working. This compels us to be completely dependent upon the Lord twenty-four hours a day: to be conscious of His Presence, and to be actively involved in the pursuit of establishing His righteousness in all of life's endeavors.

(**James 1:21-25**) Through the meditation process, we enable the Holy Spirit to change our inner man, the root, and from the godly root, our thoughts, our speech, and our actions. This continues until we experience the fulness of God and express His Presence wherever we go.

(**Eph. 4:22-24**; **1 John 2:3-5**) We are to identify areas that need changing, being specific to identify put-offs and appropriate put-ons.

Chapter 3. Counseling Process

3.1. Problem Area

We understand that biblical counseling looks at life's issues from the perspective of our 'feelings', 'doing' and 'root' levels. It is through these levels that we assess and evaluate the problem, the diagnostics.

Our 'feelings' tell us what is happening, but we are not to make decisions or live by those 'feelings'. This is what distinguishes a christian from the world. The world lives by 'feelings' but a christian lives by his will. And his will is based on the word of God which is the will of God. He is to do what God says to do regardless of his 'feelings'.

The 'doing' of God's word regardless of feelings is illustrated by God's commandment to love our enemies, do good to those who hate you, bless those who curse you, and pray for those who persecute you. This is all contrary to our natural feelings: but our true self in exercising God's command—the self in union with the Holy Spirit—transcends the natural and changes our feelings into compassion rather than retaliation.

The emphasis on the christian life is in the 'doing'. It is the 'doing' that changes our feelings as well as our 'root' level. As we do what God's word commands, the Holy Spirit changes our 'root' from selfishness and self-centeredness, conforming us to the image of the Lord Jesus Christ.

This lifelong process continues changing us from glory to glory as we simply obey God's word.

3.2. Solution

Accordingly, we are to view the problem from God's 'perspective', and His word provides the solution, the 'hope', and with hope are 'changes' that are necessary, and the 'practice' of these changes to work out our salvation and conform us to the image of Christ.

Depending upon your problem or situation, the following are provided to assist you in seeking a biblical solution.

1. **Orientation to Biblical Counseling**. A basic eight week training course to equip the student to address life's issues from a biblical perspective.

2. **Biblical Discipleship**. A five week program for new christians, teaching disciples how to grow and mature in Christ. This is suitable for individual counseling sessions and for group instructions.

3. **Strengthening Your Marriage**. A ten week program for the pre-marriage and the married.

4. **Life Studies**. These worksheets deal with an assessment of and a biblical approach to the various snares and traps that the enemy sets for the unwary and the uninformed.

The Life Studies are divided into three categories:

- **Guilt and Shame**, the past.
- **Anger and Bitterness**, the present.
- **Fear**, the future.

Accordingly, a disciple must grow in the knowledge that he is identified with Christ, that by the blood of our Lord, disciple's conscience is washed and cleansed of guilt and shame once and forever. Now he is to live the new life, empowered by the Holy Spirit, collaborating with God, to deal with his present, the daily offenses and irritations of life. Thus he is being fitted to establish God's kingdom and His will on earth, leaving the future in God's hands.

3.3. Counseling Tools

Use **Appendix A.7, "Problem/Solution Worksheet"** as a guide to gather basic information in order to evaluate the problem, and to provide a biblical approach.

The Life Studies, the various subject matter worksheets, and the forms listed in the **Appendix**, provide source material for individual and group discussion purposes as well as for homework assignments.

15

For an in-depth biblical understanding of the issues addressed in this manual, we recommend the following:

- **Self-Confrontation Manual** and **Handbook**, for the ministry of Biblical Discipleship/Counseling.
  By Biblical Counseling Foundation. [BCF1]

- **Strengthening Your Marriage**. By Wayne Mack. [Mack1]

- **The Healing Presence**. by Leanne Payne. [Payne1]

- **Restoring the Christian Soul Through Healing Prayer**.
  By Leanne Payne. [Payne2]

- **Bold Love**. By Dan Allender. [Allender1]

- **The Divine Conspiracy**. By Dallas Willard. [Willard1]

- **The Interior Castle**. By St Teresa of Avila. [StTeresa1]

- **Transformation in Christ**.
  By Dietrich von Hildeband. [Hildebrand1]

- **Collected Works of St. John of the Cross**.
  By Kieran Kavanaugh. [Kavanaugh1]

- **Healing the Culture**. By Robert J. Spitzer. [Spitzer1]

- **My Utmost for His Highest**. By Oswald Chambers [Chambers2]

You are given life so that Life may indwell you, Christ Himself, and you are to work out this life daily being conformed to His image. God's word is your authority, and the indwelling Holy Spirit is your power to enable you to be a blessing on this earth. Go now as you make a disciple of yourself, go and make disciples of others and fulfill Christ's command. Let a godly lifestyle be a living witness of Christ walking this earth in, as, and through you.

Preview **Appendix A.2, "Think and Do List"** and **Appendix A.4, "Victory over Sin Worksheet"**. Review **Josh. 1:8**; **Eph. 4:25-32**; **Rom. 12:9-21**; **1 Pet. 2** and **1 Pet. 3**.

Chapter 4. Soul Dynamics Series, Part A

Table of Contents

4.1. Living Soul

Perspective

(**Gen. 2:7**; **John 6:63**; **Rom. 8:16**; **Heb. 4:12**) Since soul and spirit can be divided, they must be different in nature. When God inbreathed into man, the breath of life became man's spirit, that is, the principle of life within him. When this Spirit came into contact with the body, the soul was produced. Hence, the soul is the combination of man's body and spirit. From this, man is called 'a living soul'.

Man was designated a living soul: for it was there that the spirit and body met and through which his individuality was known. It is the organ of man's free will by which man chooses to follow God or some other sources to guide and direct his life, goals, and purposes.

Hope

(**1 Cor. 15:44,45**; **Luke 1:46-47**; **John 16:13**) The first Adam, a living soul, lived through the body, and the body gives us world-consciousness. The spirit is that part by which we commune with God, by which we apprehend and worship Him. This spirit is called the element of God-consciousness. Thus, God dwells in the spirit, self dwells in the soul, while senses dwell in the body.

The spirit transmits its thought to the soul, and the soul exercises the body to obey the spirit's order. Since the soul lies between spirit and body, it is the medium by which the spirit or the body determines its character. Before the fall of man, the spirit controlled the whole being through the soul. It is the will in the soul which determines whether the spirit, the body, or even itself is to rule.

(**1 Cor. 3:16**; **1 Thess. 5:23**) God formerly dwelt in the temple, as the Holy Spirit indwells man today. As in the temple, God is present in the Holy of Holies and His Light shone on the Holy Place—the soul of man. The soul directs the body, the outer place. Before the fall, God's word, the Light, was directly linked to man's spirit. Before the fall, the soul was governed by the spirit. This is the order God still wants: first the spirit, then the soul, and lastly the body.

(**Ps. 51:10**; **1 Cor. 2:11**; **Mark 2:8**; **John 4:23**) Human spirit is not the same as the soul nor is it the same as the Holy Spirit. The human spirit has three functions: conscience, intuition, and communion. The conscience is the discerning organ which distinguishes right and wrong, not by influence of knowledge stored in the mind but rather by a spontaneous direct judgment. The intuition is the sensing organ of the human spirit. We really 'know' through our intuition; our mind really helps us to 'understand' through the medium of our imagination. The revelations of God and all the movements of the Holy Spirit are known to the believer through his intuition. Communion is worshipping God. Our worship of God and God's communications with us are directly in the spirit—the 'inner man'.

Change

(**Lev. 11:44**; **Lev. 17:11**; **1 Chron. 22:19**; **Prov. 19:2**; **Luke 1:46**; **Matt. 16:26**; **Luke 9:25**; **1 Cor. 15:44**; **Heb. 4:12**) The soul comprises the mind, intellect, memory, imagination, emotion and will. The soul is man's life, his natural life. The life of our present body is that of the soul. The soul is the organ of volition and the natural life. Thus, as humans we determine what kind of christian we become, whether spiritual or soulish. Before regeneration, whatever is included in life—be it self, life, strength, power, choice, thought, opinion, love feeling—pertains to the soul. Soul life is the life man inherits at birth. All that this life possesses and all that it may become are in the realm of the soul. Therefore, if we can distinctly recognize what is soulical, it will then be easier to recognize what is spiritual.

(**Gen. 1:24-26**; **Gen. 2:7**; **Ezek. 36:26-27**) Our spirit comes directly from God, it is God-given. Our soul is not so directly derived; it was produced after the spirit entered the body. God bestowed upon man sovereign power and gifts to the human soul. Thought, will, intellect and intention are among the prominent portions. The original purpose of God is that the human soul should receive and assimilate the truth and substance of God's spiritual life by a voluntary action. Man, thus, is given the choice of two trees: one tree germinates spiritual life, supernatural grace; the other develops soulish life, natural grace.

(**Gen. 3:1-6**; **Gen. 3:12-13**; **1 Tim. 2:14**; **1 Pet. 2:24**; **1 Cor. 3:18-20**) Eve by trying to answer Satan exercised her mind-disobedience to the spirit. Satan provoked her soulical thought first, then advanced to seize her will. Exercising soul in relation to the body brought forth the lusts and associated emotions. The intellect was the chief cause of the fall, the activity of the mind. Thus, become a fool that you may become wise (**Prov. 3:5-6**).

Work Out Your Salvation (Phil. 2:12-13)

Memory Verse(s):
   Col. 3:1-3

Devotion:
   BSAF on **Eph. 4:22-32**.

Put-Off/Put-On:
   Study **Ps. 119**. For each set of 8 verses, summarize and meditate on one principle to live by for each set. Visualize and dwell upon the truths revealed—a meditation process. You are a spiritual being and as such to live solely by the Spirit of God through the word of God—rest in and allow God to speak to your spirit—a contemplation process. By faith, the word is anointed, and the anointed word connects the natural with the supernatural: Through us God establishes His Kingdom on earth. We are the salt and light, to shine into the deep darkness of this world, that is, God's light in our spirit, to our soul, then through the body to the world.

   Review **Section 15.7, "Center of the Soul"**.

Reference: See [Nee1]. For a comprehensive understanding of personhood and of the life principles we are to exercise to impact our culture, see [Spitzer1].

4.2. Sins of the Flesh/Self of the Flesh

Perspective

(**Rom. 7:14,17-18**; **Rom. 6:6,11,14**) 'Sin' here is the power of sin and the 'me' here is acknowledged as the 'self'—the soul. Our old self was crucified with Christ. Man is not required to do anything. He only need consider this an accomplished fact. He reaps the effectiveness of the death of Jesus in being wholly delivered from the 'power of sin'. However, the self remains and we are to take up the cross for denying self—the residuals of the old life that still remain in the mind, memory, emotion and will. To wholly conquer sin the believer needs to deny the self (**Rom. 6:11**), not for just a moment, but for an entire lifetime. Only on the cross did Jesus bear our sins; yet, throughout His life the Lord 'denied' Himself (the appeal to self preservation). The same must be true of us.

(**Gal. 5:17-24**) Verse 17 stresses the 'self' (sinful nature) of the flesh while verse 24 stresses the 'sin' of the flesh. Thus, the cross of Christ deals with sin and the Holy Spirit through the cross treats of self. The self of the flesh—the life of feelings, of senses—seeks self-centered purposes and fulfillment: the tree of good and evil.

This is the issue, the battle zone. Man was placed on earth not to meet his own needs but to serve and accomplish God's purposes: the tree of life, living by supernatural grace. Thus, the Holy Spirit is the power in man to overcome the pull of the senses, the memories and emotions that tempt, in order to say 'no' to the old way, and to say 'yes' to God, the new way. He is enabled to do what God's word says to do regardless of any feelings to the contrary. Thus, sin is dealt with once and forever at the cross. Therefore, our job is not to deal with sin directly but with the inordinate sensuality and corrupted imaging that usually follows. This is the battle: to keep our thoughts, our memories, our reasonings, and our imaginations pure and holy. Here we "fight the good fight of faith." Accordingly, be aware that reason knows by the faculty of the imagination; that affection feels by the faculty of sensuality. Both faculties are to be monitored and bounded: to be subject to constant vigilance, to insure that they are tempered and exercised in moderation in order to be kept pure and holy.

(**Luke 9:23-24**; **Rom. 8:5-8**) Christ delivers the believer completely from the power of sin through the cross, so that sin may not reign again. By the Holy Spirit who dwells in the believer, Christ enables the believer to overcome self daily and obey Him perfectly. Liberation from sin is an accomplished fact; denial of self is to be a daily experience.

(**Acts 9:17-18**; **Rom. 7:15-24**; **1 Cor. 3:1-3**; **James 1:2-4**; **1 Pet. 4:12-13**) Biblical regeneration is a birth by which the innermost part of man's being, the deeply hidden spirit, is renewed and indwelt by the Spirit of God. We need to progress from mental knowledge of God's truth to its being revealed in our inner man by the Holy Spirit. This truth is the realization that all believers will be filled with the Holy Spirit at the moment of belief and baptism. It takes time for the power of this new life to reach the outside, from the center of our being to the circumference. New believers still walk in the realm of inordinate sensuality and vain imaginations. It takes tests and trials to reveal and identify the carnal aspects of these faculties. All of this is to be refined by fire in order to bring man into the spiritual realm.

Change

(**Rom. 6:7**; **Gal. 5:17-24**) We become flesh by being born of it. The only way to get rid of it is for the flesh to die. The flesh is not to be conquered, it is to die. The flesh, the root of the tree, must be put to death. In Christ, the believer is delivered from the rule of the flesh. By the cross, he can walk according to the Spirit and no longer according to the flesh. Therefore, do not look at your unwholesome experiences, your sin patterns and sinful reactions which continue: but the word says you "have been crucified with Christ." Do not listen to or look at your experiences, but listen to what God says to you. Act upon this truth and you shall see that the flesh is dead, indeed.

(**Gal. 2:20**; **Rom. 6:6**) At the moment Christ was crucified, our flesh also was crucified. And it was the Lord Jesus Christ who took us to the Cross at His Crucifixion. Therefore, we are not to walk according to our experiences, feelings and sight but according to faith in the word of God.

> Note: (**Rom. 8:4-9**; **Eph. 2:2**; **Phil. 2:12-16**) There are two selves: the false self and the true self. The 'false self' is that of the flesh and its bodily appetites, stimulated by externals and circumstances of life, the feelings thereof of which you are no longer to live by or permit to direct your life. The 'true self' is the regenerated human spirit now in union with the Holy Spirit which lives by supernatural grace existent in the word and will of God. You must choose to live by one or the other. By your choice, you determine who energizes your life.

21

(**Rom. 8:13**; **Gal. 5:16**; **Rom. 6:12-13**) When wicked lusts are aroused or any sins of the flesh are stimulated, it is the power of the Holy Spirit who administers the death of the cross to whatever needs to die. In view of the fact that the believer's flesh was crucified with Christ on the cross, he does not need today to be crucified once again. Thus, by appropriating the cross the babe in Christ will be liberated from the power of the flesh and will be united with the Lord in resurrection life.

(**Rom. 7:15-24**; **Rom. 8:23**; **1 Cor. 15:22-23**; **1 Cor. 15:42-44**) No matter how much our inner mind may serve God's law, one's flesh always serves sin's law. As long as we live in the body, we must be alert daily lest the flesh break forth with its wicked deeds. You cannot take life for granted. Accordingly, examine yourself continuously: for you are either walking in the Spirit or in the flesh, there is no gray area.

Work Out Your Salvation (Phil. 2:12-13)

Memory Verse(s):
> **Phil. 3:10**

Put-Off/Put-On:
> Review **Col. 3:4-17**, list your failures, work through these failures in the power of the Holy Spirit. Put-on Christ's clothing, and see self being conformed unto His image as you become a blessing in this dark world which needs to see your light (**Eph. 6:10-17**; **Phil. 1:28**; **Rev. 16:15**). Review **Section 15.9, "Union with God"**.

4.3. Dividing of Spirit and Soul

Perspective

(**Heb. 4:12**; **2 Tim. 1:7**; **Matt. 10:38-39**) The call of the cross of the Lord Jesus is to beckon us to hate our natural life (the selfish core), to seek to lose it and not keep it. Our Lord wants us to sacrifice self and be yielded wholly to the working of the Holy Spirit. If we are to experience afresh His true life in the power and guidance of the Holy Spirit, we must be willing to present to death every opinion, labor and thought of the old soul life.

Hope

(**Ps. 25:20-21**; **Isa. 53:12**; **Luke 23:46**; **1 Pet. 4:19**) Self-pity, self-love, fear of suffering, withdrawal from the cross are manifestations of the old soul life: for its prime need and motivation is self preservation. When we choose to commit our souls to His keeping and not follow our desires, God will fulfill His purposes in and through us to establish His Kingdom on earth. Jesus poured out His soul to death and gave His Spirit to the Father. We are to do the same by putting our trust in His promises and to wait on God to fulfill us.

(**Heb. 4:12-16**; **Luke 2:35**; **Matt. 10:38-39**) By His word and the indwelling Holy Spirit, the christian is enabled to differentiate in experience the operation and expression of the spirit as distinct from those of the soul. The High-Priestly ministry of the Lord Jesus in this case fulfills His work as High Priest with respect to our spirit and soul, splitting apart the soul and spirit by the word of God which is the sword of the Spirit.

The sword pierced Mary's soul for she was required to let go of Him 'Her Son', to relinquish all her authority and demands upon Him. Mary must deny her natural affections, and so do we. As Jesus poured out His soul to death but committed His Spirit to God, we must do the same. Then we shall know the power of His resurrection and shall enjoy a perfect spiritual way in the glory of resurrection (**Phil. 3:10**).

Change

(**Ps. 25:20-21**; **Rom. 6:11-12**; **1 Pet. 1:22**; **Luke 9:23-24**; **Gal. 5:16-17**) We must know the necessity of having the spirit and soul divided. We are to ask God to do His work, the separation of our spirit from our soul. Our responsibility is to yield daily to specific situations as we stand on **Rom. 6:11** bearing the cross and living according to the Spirit.

(**Rom. 12:1-2**) To lie on the altar is what we must do. Everything that belongs to emotions, sensations, mind and natural energy would be separated one after another from the spirit so as to leave no trace of fusion.

(**Mark 15:38**) Curtain that remains is our soulish, natural life. We are to commit our soul life to death in order that the Lord who dwells in the Holiest may finish His work. As the work of the cross works thoroughly enough in us the Lord shall indeed integrate the Holiest and the Holy within us just as He did centuries ago: renting the curtain by His might so that the Holy Spirit might flow out from His glorious body, filling our soul completely with His Presence.

(**2 Chron. 7:1-2**; **Heb. 10:39**; **1 Pet. 1:9**; **Eph. 6:6**; **Matt. 6:25**; **1 Pet. 4:19**; **Luke 1:46**; **Matt. 6:33**) Our mind, emotion, memory, imagination, and will shall be filled by Him. What we know by faith, we shall know and experience in the soul. The cross works toward the surrender of the soul's independence so that it may be reconciled completely to the spirit. We obtain the life of the word from the word of life. Though the organs of the soul still remain, these organs no longer function through its own power; rather, they operate by the power of God's word. A soul under the rule of the Holy Spirit never fears, never worries because self-consciousness and self-centeredness are eliminated as believers lose their self in God. Instead of suffering anxiety we can restfully seek God's Kingdom and righteousness. We know if we care for God's cares that God will take care of our cares.

Work Out Your Salvation (Phil. 2:12-13)

Memory Verse(s):
>   **Heb. 4:12**; **Phil. 3:10**

Put-Off/Put-On:
>   Review **Rom. 5:1-5**; **Rom. 12:9-21**; **Col. 3:5-17**; **2 Pet. 1:3-11**.
>   Make a list of your sins and failures to live by God's standards.
>   Set a plan of action to live by God's word. Prepare **Appendix A.4,**
>   **"Victory over Sin Worksheet"** or **Appendix A.8, "Freedom**
>   **from Anxiety"** to accomplish God's goals for your life.

4.4. Union with Christ

Perspective

(**John 3:16**; **Rom. 8:14**; **1 Cor. 6:17**; **1 Cor. 15:45**; **Titus 2:5**) Faith in Christ makes one a regenerated believer. Obedience to the Holy Spirit makes one a spiritual believer. The risen Lord is the life-giving Spirit. His union with the believer is a union with the believer's spirit. The soul, the seat of man's personality, belongs to the natural. All it can and is to be is a vessel for expressing the fruit of the union between the Lord and the believer's inner man. Nothing in man's soul partakes of the Lord's life; it is solely in the spirit that such union is effected.

Hope

(**Rom. 6:5**; **Rom. 1:4**; **1 Pet. 3:18**; **Rom. 7:4,6**) Because the Lord Jesus was raised from the dead according to the Spirit of Holiness and was made alive in the Spirit, we too, are alive when united with Him in resurrection, and alive and united with Him in His resurrected Spirit. Henceforth, we are dead to everything pertaining to ourselves and alive to His Spirit alone. This requires faith being identified with His death: we lose the sinful and natural in us once we identify with His resurrection. We are united with His resurrected life, so that we serve now in the new life of the Spirit, the supernatural.

(**Col. 3:1-3**; **Eph. 1:2-4**) The Lord is the life-giving Spirit. Being joined to him, we are filled with life and nothing can limit that life. Dwelling upon God's word gives us the knowledge of God's will and mind: continuing to meditate on this provides a rich inflow of the Lord's vitality and nature. No longer swayed by emotion, we put under foot all that is earthly enabling us to discern everything with the transparent sight of heaven.

(**John 16:13**; **1 Cor. 3:16**; **Eph. 1:13-14**; **Eph. 3:16**; **James 4:5-8**) God's indwelling Presence teaches, guides and communicates the reality of Christ in the human spirit. The human spirit is strengthened by acting on God's word when confronted with daily tests and temptations, yielding to the Lord and forsaking any doubt: willing to believe with prayer that He will flood their spirit with His power. Thus, the strengthened spirit gains dominion over the soul and body, and therefore, serves as a channel for the life of the Spirit to be transmitted to others.

Change

(**Rom. 8:4-6**; **Gal. 3:14**) To live by the spirit means to walk according to intuition. It is to have all one's life service and action in the spirit, ever being governed and empowered by it: this is the christian's daily task. Such a walk by the spirit requires reliance and faith. Working in our innermost depth, the Holy Spirit expresses Himself through our spirit's delicate sensibilities.

(**Gal. 5:16-18**) Walking after the spirit involves both the initiation of a work by revelation and execution of it through the Lord's strength. If we follow intuition instead of thought, opinion, feeling or tendency, we will end well: for we rely on the Spirit's power and not on our talent, strength or ability.

(**1 Thess. 5:23**; **Rom. 8:9-14**) Paul describes the authentic condition of the spiritual man...

1. He has God dwelling in the spirit, sanctifying him totally.
2. Man does not live by soul life. His every thought, imagination, feeling, idea, affection, desires and opinion is renewed and purified by the Spirit and brought into subjection to his own spirit. He no longer operates independently.
3. He still possesses his body; yet, physical numbness, pain, and demand do not impel the spirit to topple from its ascended position. Every member of the body becomes an instrument of righteousness.

In conclusion, a spiritual man is one who belongs to the Spirit. The whole man is governed by the inner man, and, all the organs of his being are subject completely to it.

Work Out Your Salvation (Phil. 2:12-13)

Memory Verse/Devotion:
> **John 16:13**. BSAF on **1 Cor. 2**.

Put-Off/Put-On:
> In prayer, ask the Lord to reveal to you areas where you are controlled and conditioned by your soul life, that is, thoughts, speech, and actions that are not based on godly principles. To help in this, read **Rom. 12:9-21**; **Eph. 4:22-32**; **Col. 3:5-16**. Review **Section 5.4, "Transforming the Natural Self"**.

Chapter 5. Soul Dynamics Series, Part B

Table of Contents

5.1. Cleansing and Purifying the Soul

Divisions

Dividing our soul from our spirit is the working out of **Heb. 4:12**. The word of God, the Spirit of God, gradually penetrates through the levels of our soul: the mind, the imagination, the memory, the emotions, the will, down to the innermost hidden depths. Here in the depths, we don't see those things that are in conflict with the Lord:

> Our reason, our hopes, our affections, our views, our zeal, our culture, our creeds, our churchism, our senses, our religious experiences, and our spiritual comforts.

These are some of our belief systems that often feed our pride, our ego and our self-life and, thus, must be exposed and uprooted (**Jer. 17:9**).

Values

Such habits and self-centered ways form our attitudes and perspectives and responses to life. This is the conditioning of our human nature which comes from our upbringing, from the influences of others in our lives, from our preconceived value systems, from our habits, and from our self-oriented thought processes (**Luke 9:23-24**).

Human Nature

Our 'humanness' will never go away, it will always be there. This is called the 'flesh'. This must be dealt with, exposed and crucified at the cross, before we can enter the Holy Place of our hearts where God is to dwell. Thus, the self and the sin must be continually dealt with on a daily basis in order to be filled with the 'fulness of God' and to bear much fruit for the Kingdom (**Eph. 3:14-23**).

We are hindered from a life of freedom in the Spirit because of what we think and perceive down deep. What we 'believe' is what we will normally 'do'. If we want to change our behavior, we must discover what untruths we are believing (**John 8:32-36**).

Roots

What we believe is based on our 'root systems', i.e., all of our preconceived belief systems, our secret habits, our hidden motives and all of our self-centered ways. In other words, this can be identified as our 'human nature': our natural self-orientation, self-reliance and self-love: all our natural habits that do not reflect the Presence of God within. God wants to expose and eliminate these distortions because they often become the 'roots' of our sin (**Matt. 12:34-37; John 12:24-26**).

Pure In Heart

(**Matt. 5:8**) "Blessed are the pure in heart, for they shall see God." Purity is the result of continued spiritual harmony with God, i.e., we have to grow in purity. This is reflected by our inner life as conditioned by life's experiences and nurturing, and our 'outer life', contact with other people and responses and reactions to the world, the flesh and the devil. These are to be dealt with by the constant renewing of the 'spirit of the mind' to remove the spots and stains of life. If the outer level of our spiritual life with God is impaired to the slightest degree, we must put everything aside until we make it right. Spiritual vision depends on our character. It is 'the pure in heart' who 'see God' and sees life as God perceives it.

Application

The principles of **Luke 9:23-24**; **Eph. 4:22-24**; **Matt. 22:37-40** guide our lives to purify our hearts and direct our behavior. We die to our self-orientation by judging and evaluating a feeling-oriented life. And we respond to life on the basis of our will, and our will based on God's word. Our mind is the focal point as we change a self-focus to a God-focus. The evidence of a godly focus is proved by our biblical responses to others and to the circumstances of life.

Accordingly, we place ourselves under the influence and domain of the Holy Spirit who, on the basis of our biblical responses to life, changes our root and belief systems to conform us to the image of Christ. Our soul is to be the same as the soul of Christ: His soul is to be our soul.

Specifics

Matt. 7:5 states that the process of change begins with developing an acute sensitivity to sin. We judge ourselves first, not others, to see if we are living as new creatures before God. As we do, we will place ourselves in the position to help restore others. Therefore, we examine ourselves according to God's truth as revealed in **Matt. 5:43-46**; **Rom. 2:1-10**; **Rom. 5:1-5**; **Rom. 12:1-21**; **Eph. 4:17-32**; **Col. 3:1-17**; **1 Pet. 3:9-18**; **2 Pet. 1:3:11**.

As we examine ourselves daily, putting-off the old man and putting-on the new man, a process of simple obedience to the word of God, the doing of the word of God, the Holy Spirit will change our root and belief systems to be in accord with the image of Christ.

This is a lifetime process. Our job is to be faithful on a daily basis putting-off and putting-on. The Holy Spirit will do the rest: enlighten, enable and empower us to love God with all our heart, mind, and soul; and love our neighbor as ourselves (**Matt. 22:37-39**).

(**Rom. 6:3-11**; **Gal. 2:20**; **1 Pet. 4:1-2**; **2 Pet. 1:3-10**) We are made "partakers of the divine nature" receiving and sharing God's own nature through His promises. Then we have to work that divine nature into our human nature by developing godly habits. Gradually we begin to view life, no longer from the fleshly or carnal perspective, but from the spiritual: **being and doing God's will on earth**.

Work Out Your Salvation (Phil. 2:12-13)

Memory Verse(s):
      1 Cor. 2:12-13

Put-Off/Put-On:
    Review **Matt. 5:14-7:29**, make a list of your sins, and attitude distortions. Make plans to change attitudes and behavior via **Appendix A.4, "Victory over Sin Worksheet"**. To help remove those sin barriers that keep you from developing the mind of Christ, here are some major areas to be considered:

1. (**Matt. 5:21-26**) **Anger, Bitterness, Contempt**. Unless this is dealt with, our christian walk is crippled at the start. Jesus came to save not to condemn. We are to do the same.

2. (**Matt. 5:27-32**) **Obsessive Lust**. Keep your eyes single and pure. Women are the guardians of our culture. They are endowed with a natural reverence

for that which is sacred. Make plans to break from the spirit of the world, the flesh, and the devil regarding the issue of sensuality.

3. (**Matt. 5:32-37**) **Verbal Manipulation**. Don't force others to accept your opinions or position.

4. (**Matt. 5:38-48**) **Payback/Revenge**. Our job is to be reconciled to God, to self, and to others. Mercy is the postponement of judgment. As God does with us, do likewise. Restore and be reconciled to all of life: and be free.

5. (**Matt. 6:1-18**) **Seeking Approval and Acceptance of Man**. Develop the interior life, view life from God's perspective. You are already accepted and approved in Christ. Free self from self-righteous focus by exercising your talents and gifts for the benefit of others.

6. (**Matt. 6:19-34**) **Wealth and Greed**. Depending on and trusting in the externals of the world system (mind of the flesh) rather than trusting in God leads to frustration and despair. As a co-heir with Christ, a citizen of heaven, you already own the cattle on a thousand hills. Act accordingly, for we are to live by God's economy (**2 Cor. 8:9**).

7. (**Matt. 7:1-12**) **Criticism/Condemnation**. Our natural inclination is to judge and a penchant for condemnation engineering. Judge yourself first for condemning, then you will be in the position to help restore others. As God's ambassadors, we are here, not to compete, but to help complete one another.

8. (**Matt. 7:13-26**) **Doing and Not Just Hearing**. Active listening and doing of the word is the key. Severe warnings are issued to the passive, lazy and self-indulgent. Unless we develop the interior life, the heart level, daily practicing the Presence of the Lord, our house will crumble. Judge self daily to assure that you are living by the Kingdom rules of the beatitudes. Therefore, exercise dominion of self in, as, and through Christ: be on top in all of life's endeavors.

5.2. Sin, Self, Suffering

Perspective

(**Isa. 6:5**; **Luke 5:8**; **Jer. 17:9**) Until we see ourselves through God's eyes, we really don't know ourselves. The more God enables us to see ourselves, the more we'll realize we cannot live without Him. We cannot be intimate with God except as we come to know ourselves as we really are.

(**Ps. 139:23-24**; **Prov. 21:2**) Thus, there are impurities inside of us that rule us without our knowledge. These ambitions, hopes, dreams, desires, expectations and presumptions are preconceived belief systems upon which we build our lives separate from God. It is vital that we allow God to reveal them to us, so that we can recognize and surrender them to Him. Only God can see and know our hearts. He alone knows our true motives and intents. His views are all that matters!

Death to Sin/Deeper Death to Self

(**Rom. 6:3-11**; **Eph. 4:22-24**) Buried with Christ, we are dead with Him to sin but alive to God in Christ Jesus and thus empowered to live the virtuous life. Jesus took care of the sin issue, but now it is up to us to deal with our own immorality. The residuals of sin remain in our soul—the mind, the emotions, the will: the organs of the self. The thinking, the speaking and the acting are our responsibility to insure that we are being conformed to the image of Christ.

(**Luke 9:23-24**; **1 John 5:21**) To take up the cross and follow Jesus involves the interior crucifixion of self-love, self-confidence, self-reliance, self-trust, self-will, self-pity, self-grasping, self-seeking, self-preservation, and self-esteem.

(**Phil. 2:12-13**; **Prov. 3:5-6**) God wants all our self-interest, pettiness, spite, revenge, cruelty, foolishness, egotism, possessiveness, addictions and selfishness removed. These self-centered ways not only affect our communications with God, they also affect our communications with others. We must become detached from all our self-centered thoughts, hopes, plans, preferences, sorrows, successes, failures and comforts: dead to all desires but those of God. Until these things are purged from our soul, we cannot have the union with Him as intended from the beginning.

Obedience Through Suffering

(**Rom. 8:12-29**) We are naturally conditioned by the world's influences to pursue a course of self-preservation, self-protection and self-interest: a course of avoidance of suffering (taking the easy way out) leading to destruction. God 'foresaw' the sin of man, but instead of destroying all of mankind, God used the suffering caused by sin to conform us to the image of Christ. If we refuse to suffer, we will not be conformed. The 'true self' is wholly identified with Christ. No longer self-conscious but God conscious, ready to give self to God and to others. This is a dying process, which involves pain and suffering. By dying we gain eternal life.

Predestined/Conformed

(**Heb. 5:1-10**; **Rom. 8:29**; **Rom. 12:1-2**; **Eph. 1:4-5**) Jesus learned obedience through what He suffered which was predestined. Likewise, our goal is to follow the same predestined path and be 'conformed to his likeness'.

Conformation Process

(**2 Tim. 1:9**; **1 Pet. 1:2**; **1 Thess. 1:4-6**) God has laid out a 'predestined' path in order for man to enter heaven and there is no other way God will allow us to enter. The predestined path includes ...

> ... Suffering (**Rom. 8:18-28**; **Acts 14:22**);
> ... Maintaining faith in spite of not being able to see God or when life appears too hard (**Rom. 4:18-25**; **Heb. 11:1-40**; **1 Pet. 1:6-9**);
> ... Obedience in spite of sin and concupiscence (**Rom. 7:7-25**; **Rom. 8:1-17**);
> ... Perseverance in spite of harsh treatment and ridicule (**James 5:1-12**; **1 Pet. 3:8-4:19**);
> ... Submission to authority (**Rom. 13:1-8**; **1 Pet. 2:13-25**);
> ... Loving your enemies and praying for those who persecute you (**Matt. 5:43-48**; **1 John 3:11-4:21**);
> ... Repenting of sin (**Acts 2:3, 8-41**);
> ... Charity and giving riches to the poor (**Matt. 19:16-26**);
> ... Self-denial and shunning the world and its lusts (**1 John 2 :15-17**).

Following this path (instead of allowing sin and suffering to destroy us), God will take the sin, the pain, the suffering, the good as well as the bad, all the things of life, to perfect us, to conform us to His Son who overcame the world. Thus, we, in Him, cannot lose for winning, being 'more than a conqueror' in Him who loved us.

True Selfhood

(**Matt. 10:39**; **1 Thess. 4:3**; **Gal. 2:20**) Christ must become the center of our thought, our yearnings, and our will. Saints do die to themselves in the sense of being absorbed by their love of Christ, losing themselves in Christ. Only in this way will they find their true selfhood: the self as intended by God.

True self-surrender consists in giving ourselves to Christ absolutely: in a spirit of loving adoration; in our full renunciation of sovereignty; in our becoming empty with regard to all things. We set a course of action to be separated from the world, the flesh and the devil. In true self-surrender, we experience ourselves being possessed by God. Thus, the only gift we can offer God is the gift of the 'right to our selves'. As we do God will make a holy experiment out of us (**Rom. 12:1**).

Abandonment

(**John 6:69**) Supernatural life as a whole requires us to depart from all that was natural and comfortable. Our abandonment of self is an indispensable condition of the full unfolding of supernatural life. To be perfected by and lost in what is greater than ourselves comes to us as a gift of God. But we must receive it should it be granted, and allow grace to elevate us above ourselves.

Paradise Regained

(**John 15:16**; **Eph. 4:24**; **1 Pet. 2:9**) Now the new man is renewed unto knowledge according to the image of Him who created him in order to 'declare his virtues, who hath called you out of darkness into his marvelous light'.

Work Out Your Salvation (Phil. 2:12-13)

Memory Verse(s):
> **Heb. 2:10**

Put-Off/Put-On:
> Review **Appendix A.5, "Dying to Self"**, and list in priority the old self sin patterns that are to be dealt with. Use **Appendix A.4, "Victory over Sin Worksheet"** to work out the healing of the soul process.

5.3. The Spirituality of Abundance

All shall be well, and all shall be well, and all manner of things shall be well.

— Julian of Norwich

Confidence in God

Julian's spirituality is filled with hope and confidence in the God "who loves us and delights in us", the God who "will make all things well", the God who created us to live fully the life we have been given.

Thus, this is a response to live life based on what we have rather than on what we lack. What we have is that the God of life is at the center of our existence. I will have everything I need to live fully this moment in time. This view also means that because the God of Abundance continues to be active in my life, "all shall be well, and all manner of things shall be well."

Despite the pains of life, the sorrows, the disappointments, the deceit and corruption of the world, the hatred and violence, the hunger and war, God is still in charge, and He "shall make all things all well."

We are not to be blind or deny the dark realities of life, whether in the worldwide community or in our own personal lives. But we need to name the brokenness and the evil in ourselves and around us, and to own and claim our part in it. Then we can respond in faith and live in hope that the God of Abundance will truly resolve and fill our hearts.

Abundance means believing in God's promises as spoken through the prophet Jeremiah: "For surely I know the plans I have for you, says the Lord, plans for your welfare and not for harm! Plans to give you a future full of hope. When you call me and when you pray to me, I will listen to you. When you look for me, you will find me. Yes, when you seek me with all your heart, you will find me, and I will change your lot" (**Jer. 29:11-14**).

Abide in God

These words offer us hope and the promise of blessing, despite and in the midst of suffering. They call us to live with eyes, ears, and hearts attentive to God's abiding presence in our lives. They call us to choose life or death: to dwell on God's promises or to dwell on the circumstances of life:

"I have set before you life and death, the blessing and the curse. Choose life then that you and your descendants may live. For that will mean life for you, a long life for you to live" (**Deut. 30:19-20**).

John 10:10 states that Jesus came to give us an abundant life. To choose life is to look at life while focusing on what life offers me, instead of getting stuck on what I lack. It means looking at what I know instead of dwelling on doubts and questions. Live with the questions, and, in time, the answers will come.

Living fully means choosing to live consciously the reality of every moment, every event, and every encounter with the conviction that each is a gift from my loving God. I will lack nothing because I know I will have enough because the God of Abundance will always be there going through it with me (**Isa. 43:1-5**).

Reference:

Abstract from [Julian1]. See also "Julian of Norwich" on CCEL. (URL: http://www.ccel.org/j/julian/)

5.4. Transforming the Natural Self

Perspective

(Gen. 1:26-28,31; Gen. 2:3,7; 1 Cor. 15:47) Man was made before sin entered, and he was made of dust and divinity, his fundamental nature. Made of the dust of the ground is man's glory because in it man was to manifest the image of God. Sin is not in 'matter', it was never planted. Sin is not part of human nature as God designed it. Sin is not a 'disease', but a rebellion against God.

In **John 6:56-58** Jesus says we should let the very corpuscles of our blood, every nerve and cell of our flesh, exhibit the new life that has been created in us. And to complete what the first Adam failed to do: that is to transform the natural into the spiritual through obedience.

Hope

(1 Cor. 6:19-20) Our temple is a fleshly one, not a spiritual one. But being born-again and becoming identified with the death of Christ, we exhibit His life in our mortal flesh. The life of the Son of God is born in us; therefore, the perfection of that life enables us not only to know what the will of God is, but to carry out His will in our mortal body.

(Exodus 33:20; Rom. 6:23; Eph. 2:1) We became subject to death not because we are finite beings but because of sin. Whenever we touch sin, death is the result. No one can see God and live, yet we do see God and live, but only by going through death. When we are born-again, we are also experiencing death. For to be born-again we must die—die to our claim to our right to ourselves. As we do, we receive the gift of eternal life, which is "the gift of God in Jesus Christ Our Lord."

(Gen. 3:12-15) Adam and Eve did not blame themselves, both evaded the moral truth. They admitted but did not confess. Either we refuse to say we have sinned or we admit we have sinned and refuse to let God save us.

(Rom. 16:20; James 4:6-8; 1 John 1:9; Gen. 3:15) Whenever the conviction of sin comes, we must pull it out into the light and confess it. When we realize the shame of sin and accept God's forgiveness, an inwrought energy replaces the energy spent in the sin. That energy is recovered in "the fruits of repentance." Man must deal with Satan because man is responsible for his introduction into this world. It is man, through redemption, who is to overcome Satan. And to do that which would exhibit the perfect fulfillment of His prophecy regarding the serpent.

(**Gen. 6:5**; **Jer. 17:9**; **Matt. 15:19**; **1 Cor. 2:9-16**; **Eph. 4:22-24**) Whenever we choose to disregard God, we are acting out of our depravity. We can never rest on the assumption that now that I am saved and sanctified, all that I choose and think are sure to be right. Not by any means. If our choices and our thinking do not spring from a determined recognition of God, we are depraved no matter what our spiritual experience has been.

We transform the natural into the spiritual by daily putting-off and putting-on: to reflect on the word of God, to learn the art of biblical meditation, to know the mind of Christ, and to "apprehend all things" from His divine perspective.

Change

(**Gen. 6:8-9**; **2 Pet. 1:2-8**) The only thing that keeps back God's grace and favor is our sin and perversity. To walk with God as Noah is the 'trial' of faith. Spiritual character is only developed by standing loyal to God's character, no matter what distress the trial of faith brings—as with Noah, the flood and the destruction of mankind. God in His infinite mercy saves us by His judgment.

It is not judgment inaugurating salvation, but judgment that is salvation—with nations and with the human race. The natural life is un-moral and unspiritual. It is translated into the spiritual by obedience. We are to add to our lives all that character means. No one is born either naturally or supernaturally with character, it must be developed. Nor are we born with habits. We have to form godly habits on the basis of the new life God has placed within us.

(**Gen. 7:17,19,23-24**; **Gen. 8:10,15,18**; **Gen. 9:8**; **Luke 21:19**; **James 1:2-4**) Check the instincts, the impulses, the reactions to sight, sense and circumstances. But hold firm to God's covenant, His promises by faith, by the Word and by the Spirit. Noah exhibited the humility of patience. Patience is not the same as endurance, for the heart of endurance is frequently stoical; whereas the heart of patience sees intuitively and waits God's time in perfect confidence. Noah waited for God's time to leave the ark. When He will come is a matter of indifference. What matters is that we walk with Him as we wait.

(**Gen. 2:2-3**; **Gen. 9:6-12**; **Phil. 2:12-13**) All great blessings of God are finished and complete, but they cannot be ours until we enter into relationship with Him on the basis of His salvation. Sitting idle and waiting for God somehow to do something in us means we have no faith in Him. We have to go out of ourselves to enter into the covenant of God, just as God went out of Himself to enter into His covenant with man.

Work Out Your Salvation (Phil. 2:12-13)

Memory Verse(s):
> **2 Cor. 5:16-17**; **1 Pet. 4:1-2**

Devotion:
> BSAF on **Luke 21:19**; **Eph. 4:26,29**.

Put-Off/Put-On:
> Judge yourself by the following verses, and note areas where you failed to translate the natural self into the spiritual. Establish plans by working through **Appendix A.4, "Victory over Sin Worksheet"**, **Appendix A.2, "Think And Do List"**, **Appendix A.8, "Freedom from Anxiety"**, and/or **Appendix A.9, "Contingency Plan"** to be conformed to the image of Christ (**Eph. 4:25-32**; **Rom. 12:9-21**; **Col. 3:1-17**). This is a lifetime commitment.

Reference: [Chambers1]

Part II.a. Basic Study: Biblical Discipleship

Table of Contents

Reference: Throughout **Chapter 6,** *Christian Growth Series, Part A*, you will find relevant information from [BCF1] and [Leader1].

Chapter 6. Christian Growth Series, Part A

Table of Contents

6.1. Establish a Foundation for Biblical Discipleship

Perspective

(Isa. 55:8-9) We are to think God's thoughts after Him. Unless our thoughts are in agreement with His, they are to be discarded. Our ways, our habits and practices are to change. We are to be directed and guided by God's word and commandments regardless of our feelings or our opinions. We cannot mix our thoughts with His, else God's word becomes polluted. God's word is pure and cannot be mixed with carnal thoughts.

Hope

(Rom. 8:28-29; John 14:21) As we think God's thoughts and do what He commands, God enters and intervenes in our lives and into our situation. Regardless if we cause the problem or the problem is caused by others, if we respond God's way, He will turn the situation to our advantage. When necessary the Holy Spirit will make His presence known by giving a deep sense of His love and care, helping and giving confidence, forgiveness, and assurance—whatever the believer needs to be built up.

(1 Cor. 10:13; Eph. 6:10-12; Ps. 91:1-3) The devil operates only in the carnal which is common to man but we are spiritual. We don't fight him with reason, by will-power, by tangibles: for our weapons are not carnal but spiritual and are mighty to tear down the strongholds of the enemy. Thus, our trust and faith is in God and in Him when we face our temptations. God will see us through. He is our refuge, our fortress, our God in whom we trust. It is He who delivers us from the demons.

(**Heb. 4:14-16**; **2 Cor. 5:21**; **Heb. 9:14**; **Eph. 2:4-10**) Jesus went to the end of temptation, and far beyond it. He did not collapse for no man was ever tempted as He was. He suffered all of this to secure the ideal and perfect righteousness for us that we may be acceptable to His Father. Based on what Jesus did, we are given the right to enter the Throne room and receive the very help of God Himself: to enable us by His grace to confront any trial, to conquer and triumph over any situation and circumstance of life. God is able to do this because His Son, while on earth, suffered the same trials we do. He knows how to walk through and conquer, and we in Him are to do likewise.

Change

(**Eph. 4:22-24**; **Rom. 6:6**) You must exercise your own will to put-off the old man, the man you were before you accepted Christ. As you choose God's way, the emphasis now is to make new, readjust, change, turn around and regenerate your mind by God's word which becomes the very Presence of Christ in the believer. You have Christ's mind and you are to allow the Spirit of Christ to focus your mind more and more upon God and spiritual things. Becoming a new man, you can now begin life all over again. Your spirit has been recreated into the righteousness and holiness of the truth. This qualifies you to have fellowship with God, enabled to become obedient to God's will and devoted to His service.

(**Col. 1:10-11**; **1 John 1:7**) Becoming a new person means activity. It is not enough to 'know' God's will, possess wisdom and understanding—all this must be put into practice. We are to set our lives, our behavior and conduct after Christ: being fruitful in every good work. As we increase in the knowledge of God, His presence and power also increases to enable us to exercise every kind of endurance, patience, forbearance with joy.

Work Out Your Salvation (Phil. 2:12-13)

Memory Verses/Devotion:
>   **Matt. 7:1,5**. BSAF on **Eph. 4:22-32**.

Put-Off/Put-On:
>   Develop list of failures to love God's way. Use **1 Cor. 13:4-8a** as
>   a guide; or refer to **Appendix A.3, "Love is an Action"**. List two
>   or more recent incidents in which you were upset, irritated, and
>   assess if these are behavior patterns, or isolated incidents.

6.2. Explore Problems and Develop Sensitivity to Sin

Perspective

(**John 14:26**; **Eph. 5:18**; **Isa. 55:8-9**) At the point you choose to stop perpetuating self-interest and begin to consider the interest of others before your own, God's wisdom, strength and ability will enter into your spirit to do those things that are pleasing to God. Only in the power of the Holy Spirit are you able to live the abundant life. You cannot live according to God's design in your own way or by your own wisdom.

The Holy Spirit will help the believer through the trials of life by teaching him all things: the words and life of Christ, the Truth and the Life, the theory and the practice, the principles and the conduct of christian living, the morality and behavior of christian existence.

Hope

(**Heb. 4:16**; **James 1:5-8**; **James 1:22-25**; **Phil. 4:13**) It is a question of faith. You believe God's word, you respond to what God says (whether you feel like it or not). You turn over your intellect and will to God, allowing God to direct your faculties, your passions, and to refurbish your memory. God intervenes through you into the situation or circumstances to resolve the problem in God's way, and to reconstitute your very being in order to establish His kingdom and His will on earth.

(**Matt. 7:1-5**; **Gal. 6:1-5**; **2 Cor. 1:3-4**; **1 Cor. 11:28-31**) Practicing God's word begins with judging ourselves and removing sinful obstructions from our own lives. Since we have no righteousness of our own, our only worthiness is Jesus Christ. The only time we could be counted worthy would be when we are walking in constant fellowship with Him. This means that we are to be actively thinking upon and talking with him through confession, repentance, praise and request. Thus, our hope is in Him who brings us to fruition and fulfillment.

(**1 John 2:3-6**; **2 Pet. 1:3-11**; **John 16:33**; **John 15:10-11**) You must obey God's word consistently to grow increasingly into godliness and to realize true peace and joy. The Lord's joy and glory was doing the will of God and looking ahead to the joy and glory of eternity with His Father and His followers. Likewise, the joy of believers is the joy of Christ Himself reigning within their hearts. And this joy is fulfilled as believers study His word, His promises and His commandments.

Change

(Luke 17:10; **John 14:5**; **2 Cor. 5:15**; **2 Cor. 10:5**; **Col. 3:1-7**; **Col. 1:10)** In order to mature (grow up) in Christ, you must persevere in doing what is good in the Lord's sight: by being obedient to Scripture, disciplining your thought life, speaking in a manner that is helpful to others, and loving others in a biblical manner. Patience, kindness, goodness embodies the standard by which we are to live. We belong to Him totally. It is our duty as His ambassadors, to serve Him, to increase in the knowledge of Him, and to fulfill our roles as His disciples.

(Gen. 4:7; **Isa. 26:3**; **Luke 11:28**; **John 15:10-11**; **Matt. 7:21)** Your contentment in all situations is dependent upon your obedient response to God in your thoughts, words and actions. This brings forth a tranquility of mind, a purity of memory, a composure, a peace that is calm in the face of bad circumstances and situations. By obeying the Lord in your daily walk, a person becomes bound, woven and joined together with himself, with God, and with others. We are naturally inclined to maliciousness and to retaliation. Accordingly, as a constant, check yourself to determine what spirit you are manifesting in all encounters (**Luke 9:53-55**).

(1 John 1:9; **Matt. 3:8**; **2 Cor. 7:9-11**; **James 4:8-10**; **Eph. 4:31-32)** Confess your sins to the Lord and, when appropriate, confess sins to others whom you have offended. Honor the Blood that washed away your sins, by 'acting forgiven'. To fall into despair or self-pity is to honor the enemy. No matter how many times you fall into sin, honor the Cross and Blood of Christ by getting up, confessing, repenting, and starting over again.

Work Out Your Salvation (Phil. 2:12-13)

Memory Verse(s):
> **Luke 9:23-24**

Put-Off/Put-On:
> As a basic guideline, list your failures, formulate a specific plan to change, and begin to implement the plan. List, at least, two or more recent incidents in which you failed to be patient, to be kind, and to exercise goodness, were offended, or offending another. Complete columns 1-3 of **Appendix A.4, "Victory over Sin Worksheet"**. This will be your working data to complete column 4 at the next session.

6.3. Establish Biblical Structure for Change

Perspective

(**Rom. 5:3-5**; **2 Tim. 3:16-17**; **James 1:21-25**; **2 Pet. 1:2-4**) Effective and lasting biblical change is a continuing process. You are to obey the commands and guidelines in God's word for every area of your life (your thoughts, words and actions). As you stop (put-off) the old continuing pattern of sin and begin (put-on) the new practice of righteousness and holiness, you are renewed in the spirit of your mind.

(**Rom. 5:17**) Being justified, we are no longer defeated by trials and sufferings. To the contrary, by God's grace, we use problems as opportunities to grow in Christ. Working through pressure, oppression, afflictions, and distress, we develop endurance, fortitude, steadfastness, constancy, perseverance. Thus, patience stirs experience and this develops character, integrity, strength. Also experience stirs up hope. By enduring trials, we experience the presence and strength of God. When a justified man becomes stronger in character, he draws closer to God. The closer he draws to God, the more he hopes for the glory of God.

Hope

(**John 15:10-11**; **John 16:33**; **Matt. 6:33**; **1 John 2:3-4**; **1 John 3:22**) You are to walk in a manner worthy of God and to please Him in every area of your life. As you obediently respond to God's love, you become mature in the Lord and are blessed with peace and joy regardless of your feelings, other people or circumstances of life. The believer's hope, peace and joy is based upon the presence of God's Spirit who dwells within the believer. These virtues are activated when one biblically responds to life.

(**1 Cor. 6:19-20**; **1 Pet. 1:17-19**; **Luke 16:10-13**; **John 16:17**; **1 John 2:20,27**) You were purchased with the precious blood of Jesus, you wholly belong to Him. You are God's possession and a steward (managing servant) of all that the Lord has provided for you. The anointing of Christ is with you. God's wisdom, strength and ability are within you to exercise your particular talent and gifts to become a blessing to those about you. Christ in you, the hope of glory, the anointing of God is upon your flesh to do the things flesh cannot do.

(**Ps. 119:165**; **Matt. 5:3-12**; **John 14:27**) God's peace and joy are available to believers regardless of others, possessions or circumstances. We are to be dependent upon God. As we become so we will not be controlled by others but will be free to love others as God loves us. We are primarily accountable to God—not to self, spouse, parents or others.

Change

(**Eph. 4:22-24**; **Matt. 7:5**; **1 Cor. 11:28-31**; **Heb. 4:12**; **Rom. 6:12-13**; **2 Cor. 10:3-5**) To keep God's anointing flowing through you, you must daily put-off old sinful habits, identify them, judge yourself in the light of God's word, confess and repent and put them aside immediately. Do not take life for granted. You are God's ambassador on earth. You are His standard for the world to see.

(**2 Tim. 2:22**; **Titus 2:11-12**; **Gal. 5:16**; **Matt. 22:37**; **Col. 1:10**; **Rom. 8:29**) As we put-on the righteous deeds in the power of the Holy Spirit, we grow daily in the image of God. We become on earth, vessels reflecting and revealing the Spirit of God within to the world without as we destroy the works of the devil and establish God's righteousness on earth. We are to impact and to exercise moral influence over the world's system and institutions (**Gen. 1:28**; **Matt. 28:18-20**).

(**Prov. 10:12**; **Eph. 4:32**; **1 Pet. 3:8-9**) We begin the process by forgiving others biblically as necessary. We seek reconciliation and restoration in accordance with biblical principles, and seek ways to bless others. We do not retaliate, we eliminate stumbling blocks. Our Lord took care of sin at the cross. Our role is to destroy the structure—the scaffolding, the habit patterns—of sin embedded in our minds over the years (**Prov. 21:22**). We are to rebuild these structures until our faculties, our intellect, our passions, are placed solely under the rule and lordship of Jesus Christ.

Work Out Your Salvation (Phil. 2:12-13)

Memory Verse(s):
> **Eph. 4:29,31-32**

Put-Off/Put-On:
> Continue **Appendix A.4, "Victory over Sin Worksheet"** and begin to work on a biblical plan for any pattern of anger, bitterness and unwholesome speech. Review and as appropriate use **Appendix A.2, "Think and Do List"** to establish biblical patterns of thinking, speaking and acting. Place this information in column 4, and be specific in practicing new thought patterns: how you should speak, followed by concrete actions.

45

6.4. Establish the Practice of Righteousness

Perspective

(**Rom. 5:3-5**; **Rom. 12:1-2**; **Matt. 10:16-28**; **1 Pet. 3:13-17**) Do not be surprised at trials, even if they seem fiery. Rejoice in them because God uses them to reveal the spirit that is in you, and develop Christlike maturity. Be prepared to be reviled. If you should endure suffering for the sake of righteousness, you are blessed of the Lord. Renewing the mind is a constant process to free us from our own corruption of lusts and appetites; and to defend and protect ourselves from the fashions and customs of the world.

Hope

(**Eph. 5:15-16**; **1 Tim. 4:7-11**; **Heb. 5:14**; **Gal. 5:22-23**; **Heb. 13:20-21**) You must faithfully practice your daily responsibilities and discipline yourself toward godliness. As you continue to be a doer of the word, your senses will be trained to discern good and evil. Your growth is a sovereign work of God that is divinely linked to your living in a biblical manner.

(**Prov. 3:5-10**; **Ps. 55:22**; **Ps. 94:17-19**; **Jer. 29:11**; **Rom. 8:28-29**) God has promised to provide all the necessities of life as you seek to please Him. He is always available to help you and He is firmly in control of every aspect of your life. Living in a biblical manner, the believer is assured that God is arranging and re-arranging 'all things' for his good on a daily basis. Thus, hope is really faith extended into the future, living the divine life in the present.

(**Matt. 6:25,34**; **Luke 12:22-34**; **Matt. 6:33**; **Heb. 5:14**; **James 1:22-25**) Put-off self-centered concern about the future and put-on doing the Word. As you dwell on the things of God, He will protect and provide for you in all areas of your life.

God made man a spiritual being. As such, man is not to be preoccupied with making it on his own, taking care of oneself in this world, and fighting and struggling to make it through life. As a citizen of heaven, he works in partnership with God. He trusts and acknowledges God while doing all he can: plows and works, not looking back; and while working, trust the results to God. God says he will see to it that such a trusting person will always have the necessities of life.

Change

(**John 3:30**; **John 12:24-26**; **Matt. 20:26-28**; **Rom. 15:1-3**; **Col. 3:23-24**) Stop living to please self in daily situations, responsibilities and relationships. Regard others as more important than yourself by being a servant to God and others. The christian believer who truly lives and witnesses for Christ gives himself up to Christ. In Christ, as a bond-slave, he ministers to the needs of others.

(**Prov. 9:6**; **Prov. 14:16**; **Gal. 5:16-21**; **James 1:19**; **John 15:5**; **James 1:22-25**; **James 4:17**) List the circumstances or relationships in which you are (or have been) tempted to become angry or bitter. Develop a biblical plan for overcoming anger and bitterness in these situations. Formulate a contingency plan for dealing with anger and bitterness that may arise suddenly. What you comprehend, you will be conformed to, and this is what you will communicate.

(**Prov. 10:12**; **1 Cor. 13:4-8**; **1 Pet. 1:22**; **Eph. 4:32**; **1 Pet. 3:8-9**) Practice biblical love by forgiving others just as God has forgiven you. Do kind and tenderhearted deeds to the very individuals with whom you become irritated. Forbearance is giving what a person needs, not what he deserves.

Work Out Your Salvation (Phil. 2:12-13)

Memory Verse(s):
> **Heb. 5:14**

Put-Off/Put-On:
> Continue developing biblical patterns of submitting and continual dying to self through:

> 1. Considering others as more important than self, and
> 2. Serving others.

> Evaluate your deeds daily, determine areas where you are weak. Develop contingency plans to deal with and face possible stumbling blocks when they appear. These offenses (stumbling blocks) keep God's grace and His anointing from flowing through you. Look for data in areas of depression, fear and worry, anger and bitterness, interpersonal relationships, envy, greed and covetousness. Deal with specific problems via **Appendix A.6, "Problem Solving Worksheet"**, **Appendix A.4, "Victory over Sin Worksheet"**, **Appendix A.2, "Think and Do List"**, **Appendix A.8, "Freedom from Anxiety"**. See verses **Isa. 10:27**; **Isa. 61:1**; **Luke 4:18-19**; **James 4:6-8**.

6.5. Establish Pattern of the Mature Disciple

Perspective

(Eccl. 12:13-14; 1 Pet. 1:17; 1 John 4:11,19; Heb. 12:5-10; Phil. 2:12-13) Successfully facing and dealing with specific problems is only the beginning of living a godly life. Focus must remain on God's standards for continuing toward Christ-likeness. Accordingly, one must evaluate the whole of one's life constantly conforming to God's standards.

Hope

(Isa. 40:8; Acts 10:34-35; John 14:21; John 15:10-11; 1 John 3:22) God's standards are always consistent and are never subject to the whim of the moment. They are the same for all individuals, in all cultures, and at all age levels, regardless of personality or background. Keeping God's commandments, having reverence and awe of God, is the key to fruitfulness.

(Ps. 145:17; Jer. 29:11-17; Deut. 11:8-9; James 1:22-25) God's plan for you is for your benefit and has as His goal your maturity in Christ. If you keep God's commandments, He will bless you; otherwise, you will be subject to discipline.

(Matt. 11:28-30; Josh. 1:8-9; Ps. 103:1-5; Isa. 40:29-31; Eph. 1:13-14; Phil. 2:12-13) God's standards are not burdensome: for He will strengthen, uphold, and keep you from stumbling as you walk in His ways, cooperating with the changes He is accomplishing in your life.

Change

(Rom. 13:1-3; Rom. 13:12-14; Eph. 6:10-18) Put-off deeds of darkness, put-on the Lord Jesus Christ and make no provision for fleshly lusts. Put on the full armor of God to withstand the schemes of the devil.

(Rom. 5:3-5; Matt. 5:10-12; 1 Pet. 4:12-19; 1 Pet. 3:13-17) Do not be surprised at trials, even if they seem fiery. Instead, rejoice because God uses them to develop Christlike maturity in your life. Be prepared to be reviled and to suffer persecution. You will be blessed when you do.

(Gal. 5:22-23; Eph. 1:4; Eph. 4:1,17; Eph. 6:9; Col. 3:12-24; 1 Tim. 4:7-8; 2 Pet. 1:2-10) Establish and maintain biblical standards that will encourage you and your children toward godliness. Identify godly traits that need to be developed along with corresponding biblical responsibilities and activities which will demonstrate Christ-likeness.

Work Out Your Salvation (Phil. 2:12-13)

Memory Verse(s):
Gal. 6:14

Put-Off/Put-On:

Continually work on a biblical schedule (**Appendix A.11, "Scheduling Worksheet"**) to eliminate unprofitable activities, and in its place, add activities necessary to carry on God-given responsibilities.

Review the following questions to determine what activities need to be eliminated:

1. Is this profitable (**1 Cor. 6:12**; **1 Cor. 10:23**)?

2. Am I controlled by this in any way (**1 Cor. 6:12**)?

3. Is this a stumbling block in my life (**Matt. 5:29-30**; **Matt. 18:8-9**)?

4. Could this lead another to stumble (**Rom. 14:13**; **1 Cor. 8:9,13**)?

5. Does this edify (build up) others (**Rom. 14:19**; **1 Cor. 10:23-24**)?

6. Does this glorify God (**Matt. 5:16**; **1 Cor. 10:31**) ?

Chapter 7. Christian Growth Series, Part B

Table of Contents

7.1. Characteristics of a Christian

Perspective

(**Josh. 24:15**; **Deut. 11:26**) To be an overcomer and live a sanctified life, the choice is yours to either serve God or serve Satan. You cannot stay halted between two opinions. It's a question of life and death, blessings or curses.

Hope

(**John 1:12**; **John 5:24**; **Rom. 10:9-10**) To receive Christ is to receive power to become a child of God. The power to pass from death to life comes by confessing with your mouth that Jesus is the Lord of your life: that Jesus lived on this earth; that he died on the cross to pay the penalty for your sins; that He rose from the dead to give you eternal life. To receive this, to confess this, one commits himself to live totally for the Lord Jesus Christ.

(**Col. 1:10**; **2 Cor. 3:5**; **2 Cor. 4:4**; **Phil. 4:13**) Commitment means to progressively think, speak, and act according to God's principles, no longer by one's feelings or by one's past. One is committed now to bear fruit worthy of the

Lord: to do all things pleasing to Him, to study His word daily, and to gradually be strengthened by Him in order to live the Spirit-filled life on this planet.

Change

(Matt. 7:5; **Ps. 139:23-24**; **Gen. 1:26**; **Matt. 22:37-39**; **1 John 2:9-11**; **Gen. 4:7)** We can no longer blame others, circumstances, genealogy or people for our problems. Regardless of what others have done to you or what life has done to you, we are held accountable for our own actions before God. We always looked to others to change, but we must do the changing. The meaning of life is for God to live out His fullest in us and through us at the present moment in the areas of relationships and responsibilities. We are to develop our conduct and behavior in such a manner as to give glory to God.

(1 Tim. 4:7-8; **John 14:15,21**; **Phil. 4:8-9**; **Phil. 2:12-14)** We are to live obediently to God's word, by our will regardless of feelings. This takes discipline and practice, involving planning, scheduling and working out the plan. Change demands discipline in our thoughts and in our deeds. Out of the heart the mouth speaks. First comes a thought, then an idea, then action, then habit, then character and finally destiny. Thus, protect the gates of your heart by guarding what you see, what you hear and what you speak.

(Luke 9:23-24; **Eph. 4:15-32**; **Matt. 5:23-24)** We are born to die, and to die in order to live. Thus, life begins by denying self, putting-off our old habits and practices, and putting-on new habits and practices based on the principles of God's word. We learn to become a blessing instead of a curse: forgiving others instead of seeking revenge, forgiving offenses of the past, asking forgiveness of those we offended. Thus, we are to establish a consistent pattern of being reconciled to ourselves, to God, and to others.

Work Out Your Salvation (Phil. 2:12-13)

Memory Verses/Devotion:
> **Luke 9:23-24**. BSAF on **Eph. 4:22-32**.

Put-Off/Put-On:
> Judge yourself first on how you failed to live godly. Review **Rom. 1:18-32**; **Col. 3:5-17**; **1 Cor. 13:4-8**. Evil is not to be restrained but replaced by righteous thoughts and deeds. Accordingly, select one major sin pattern and work it out on **Appendix A.4, "Victory over Sin Worksheet"**.

51

7.2. Change is a Two-Factored Process

Perspective

(**Col. 3:1-7**; **Matt. 12:33-37**) We are the sum of what we encountered in life and our reactions to life. Being conditioned by life's experiences, we are prone to react to life impulsively and instinctively rather than to respond on the basis of considered judgment. Man's words and manner of speech reveal his inner life, where his focus is, and who and what determines his peace and joy.

We are to set our mind on things above, not below. The issue here is spirituality: the capacity to know, to experience, and to respond to God. As we do, the Holy Spirit empowers us to live and to work with Christ-likeness, dealing with our character (inner man) and conduct (outer man).

We are challenged to make Christ the center of our lives. All our faculties and passions (intellect, memory, emotions, will, and love, hope, joy, fear, sorrow) are to be at His disposal and direction.

Hope

(**Eph. 2:8-10**; **2 Cor. 5:17**) All man has to do is to believe what Jesus did for him on the cross. We were reconciled to God by the death of His Son. Man cannot earn merit or win salvation. He is to believe, confess, repent and by faith receive the gift of God's grace. His belief places his spirit in union with God's Spirit. Thus, he is empowered to do good works, to bear the fruit of his new nature.

(**Col. 1:15-21**) Christ lives in us to transform us personally. He wants to affect our individual jobs, our families, our communities, and our personal relationships. By faith in Christ and by our obedience Christ will reconcile all things within us: our minds and emotions, and our relationships with others. Thus, making us holy and blameless and above reproach in His sight.

(**Eph. 2:19**; **Phil. 3:20**; **Gal. 4:5-6**; **Matt. 12:50**) We are fellow citizens in a nation created by God. We have been adopted as children of God, and live in the same house with God and His family. Now, we have the privilege and responsibility to render service for the sake of God's family.

Change

(**Col. 1:10**; **Rom. 12:10-11**; **Gal. 6:2,10**) It is not enough to 'know' God's will or to possess wisdom and understanding. We are to put what we know into practice, so that our behavior and conduct reflects that of Christ. We must be committed to be fruitful in every good work and grow into the knowledge of God.

(**2 Tim. 2:19**; **John 10:14**; **Eph. 4:22**) A person who follows Christ does not live in sin. To become a noble person, it takes purging, cleansing self from behavior that is dishonorable and unrighteous.

(**Prov. 14:12**; **Isa. 55:8-11**; **Rom. 12:1-2**) As a man commits his total life for God's service, he separates himself from the world, the flesh and the devil. He does this by purging himself and renewing his mind from all behavior that is dishonorable, and from teaching that is false and cancerous. Thus, he prepares himself so that Christ may infuse his very being and to use him for every good work.

Work Out Your Salvation (Phil. 2:12-13)

Memory Verse(s):
>   **Eph. 4:22-24**

Devotion:
>   BSAF on **Eph. 5:1**; **2 Thess. 3:6**; **1 John 2:15-16**.

Put-Off/Put-On:
>   Examine your life in the light of **Col. 3:1-17**. Work out **Appendix A.10, "Change is a Two-Factored Process"**. List all your failures on left side of sheet, and correspondingly what God wants you to do in its place on the right side.

7.3. Turning from Evil

Perspective

(**Matt. 12:38-40**; **Rom. 1:4**; **Acts 10:39-45**) It is human reason that seeks after signs, works and proofs. God wants man to simply believe and love Him because of who He is and what He has done for man. The true religion of God is not a religion of works and signs, but of faith and love in Christ Jesus. God is finished with signs. He has given the ultimate in signs: He has given His Son by means of His death, of His burial, and of His resurrection.

Hope

(**Matt. 12:41**; **Acts 2:38**; **Acts 3:19**; **Isa. 55:7**) The worst sinners in history repented at the preaching of one man, the prophet Jonah. Now the Messiah Himself, God's own Son, has come. He has preached and announced, "The Kingdom of God" itself is at hand. Every person is now, beyond question, without excuse. Heavenly doors are now open to those who simply make a decision to repent of the old life in the flesh, and begin a new life in the spirit—a life in union with the trinity.

(**Deut. 4:29**; **Prov. 2:3-5**; **Luke 11:9-10**) The Queen of Sheba went to the farthest extremes humanly possible to seek the truth. No effort, struggle, energy, strain should be spared in seeking the truth. As you seek, you will find the truth: Jesus Christ, the Source of all good things, and the Holy Spirit, the very presence of God dwelling within our hearts and bodies.

(**Heb. 11:6**; **Prov. 8:17**) Though it can be put out of a life, and turned from, evil will always attack. As evil is a constant so is my trust in God who enables me to resist. What is needed is a supernatural power to turn from evil, and that power is in Christ. The love of Christ and His mission of redemption is to fill a man's heart and life. To keep out evil, a man must begin to do Christ's work of love and care: to meet the needs of others, of the world and community; to look after the orphan, the sick and hungry: be swamped with doing God's work. Then he will not have time to think and to do evil.

Change

(**Rom. 8:1-4**; **Gal. 2:19-20**; **Gal. 5:16-18**) Christ fulfilled and completed the Law. Christ is Spirit, He is life. It is His life that sets the standard and the rule for the believer. It is His Spirit and life that gives the believer the power to obey. A person's faith in Christ places him in Christ. Accordingly, we are to walk day by day in Christ, and believe that Christ takes care of the past sins, of our present welfare, and of our future destiny.

(**2 Cor. 5:17-21**) It is being 'in Christ' that makes a person a new creature, he no longer belongs to Satan. The believer is sinless and righteous because Christ is sinless and righteous. A spirit of repentance is to be cultivated, that is, to confess and repent each time we fail to walk in the light as He is in the light. Visualize the blood of Jesus cleansing us in order to maintain our godly fellowship on a continuous basis (**1 John 1:7-9**).

(**Gal. 5:22-23**; **Titus 2:12**; **Eph. 4:22-24**) No matter how corrupt or how low man has fallen, God longs to make a new creature out of him. All that is required is to believe in Christ, to realize and understand all that He has done. Thus, we are to act on this truth by establishing His kingdom on earth: of patience, of kindness, and of goodness.

Work Out Your Salvation (Phil. 2:12-13)

Memory Verse(s):
>   **Col. 1:12-14**

Devotion:
>   BSAF for **Col. 1:20**; **Heb. 2:17**; **Eph. 2:16**; **Heb. 10:19-20**.

Put-Off/Put-On:
>   Christ has defeated Satan and his evil spirits: all the forces, energies, powers and principalities of the universe. Man now has been delegated power and authority by the word of God to bind and loose: to bind the force of sin, and to loose the foul spirit so that God's will prevails in the situation (**Matt. 16:18-19**).

>   As this is so, list areas in your life where you feel defeated and condemned. Make a failure list of your sins and guilts. Replace this list by what God wants you to put in its place. Accordingly, to assist you to accomplish this, complete **Appendix A.10, "Change is a Two-Factored Process"**. In Christ practice the put-ons, knowing that you are more than a conqueror. Practice this until a new pattern of thought and actions are established. This takes time. God's word is more than sufficient to amend, to heal and to

deliver you from the evil one (**Ps. 91:1-3**). If problem persists, seek counsel from a mature disciple.

7.4. Physical Challenges

Perspective

(**Matt. 26:41**; **Eph. 5:18**; **1 Cor. 6:12-13**; **1 Cor. 6:19-20**; **2 Pet. 2:18-19**) Our physical condition may influence our response to spiritual needs. But regardless of our need, of our being under a heavy load, God can and will give peace and joy to those in need. Recognize, however, that God may not choose to heal the believer.

Hope

(**Deut. 32:39**; **Ps. 115:3**) God does whatever He pleases. He may allow the physical problem to remain to further and deepen maturity and for effective ministry.

(**Jer. 29:11**) Regardless of what has happened to you, keep your focus on the Lord. God will provide for your welfare, to give you a future and a hope. Thus, faith speaks of future events with as much certainty as though they were already passed. Thus, look for the spiritual growth and development of the inner man (**Rom. 4:17**; **2 Cor. 4:17-18**).

(**Rom. 8:28-29**) My responsibility is to insure that I am thinking and living according to God's principles. My goal is not to seek my needs primarily but to accomplish God's purposes in my life. Regardless of the adversities or the consequences, being obedient to God's will in all things, I will overwhelmingly conquer through Jesus who loves me.

(**Matt. 5:3-12**) God's peace and joy are available to believers regardless of others, of possessions or the lack of them, or of the circumstances of life. The key is to develop the character of Christ, to think as He does, to act accordingly. Though the outer man may perish, it is the inner man that is developing and growing.

Change

(**Rom. 8:28-29**; **Matt. 6:7-8**) Whether I have been born with a physical defect or problem, through carelessness, negligence, or an accident caused by others, my focus is to be on the God, and to approach the situation His way. Regardless of any limitation, physical or mental, work out the situation to its fullest being empowered and energized by the Holy Spirit. Transcend any limitations by maximizing what you do have.

(**Isa. 46:9-11**; **Phil. 1:6**; **Phil. 2:13**) My job is turn any thoughts off myself and obey God's commands for the moment that lies just ahead. Allow God to be His fullest through me at the present moment bringing to past His purposes. By obeying, God works in me to complete and to mature me in the image of His Son.

(**2 Cor. 6:3-10**; **2 Cor. 12:7-10**; **Job 42:1-6**) Maintain the integrity of God's word and promises in your life, that despite afflictions, hardships, distresses, beatings, hunger and pain, rely on His presence within. In the midst of sorrows, of dishonor, of evil reports, His Presence within, His strength will fill you with rejoicing: For in Him you are an overwhelming conqueror.

Work Out Your Salvation (Phil. 2:12-13)

Memory Verse(s):
> **2 Cor. 12:9**

Devotion:
> BSAF on **2 Cor. 6:3,4,10,16**.

Put-Off/Put-On:
> Meditate on the principles stated herein. Consider your particular situation, develop a contingency plan (**Appendix A.9, "Contingency Plan"** or **Appendix A.10, "Change is a Two-Factored Process"**) to counteract self-focus.

7.5. Commitment is Doing the Word

Perspective

(**James 1:22-25**; **Rev. 22:14**) Christian life is one of commitment to God and His Word. It is not to be part-time, of casualness, of indifference or of neglect. It is one of doing, of practicing, of exercising in the pursuit of excellence, in the spirit of integrity, working through failures time and time again. An effective christian life thus uses failures as opportunities to grow into a mature christian in the image of Christ. It is not enough to listen, to hear, to know. The word must be practiced, exercised, and applied until the person is set free from the bondages of sin and death.

Hope

(**James 1:19-21**; **Matt. 13:23**) Be quick to hear the word of God, not hanging on to one's own ideas, but be willing to listen to God's word instead of insisting upon what one thinks and likes. Respond rather than react to life by being slow to speak and slow to wrath, developing a gentle spirit as a child. Listen to God's words and allow God's words to be born within one's heart and life. This is the core of healing and growth, of patience, kindness, and goodness.

(**Col. 1:9**; **2 Cor. 10:5**; **Ps. 143:10**) Nothing is to flow through us nor out of us that is not of God's will. God's will involves all of life, everything we do, every moment of the day. Through His word God tells us how to live.

Knowing God's will involves both wisdom and understanding. Wisdom means a person knows the first principles of life. Understanding means the person has the ability to apply the basic principles to everyday life.

(**Prov. 2:1-2**; **Acts 20:32**; **Acts 27:7-16**; **Eph. 1:17**; **James 1:5**) We secure the wisdom and understanding by studying God's word and by prayer. Praying is the process by which we are being filled with the knowledge of God's will, and by which we find union with Jesus. This union is marked by a loving exchange of friendship between God and the soul.

Change

(**Rom. 12:1-2**; **Col. 1:10**) It is not enough to know God's will, to possess wisdom and understanding, it all must be put into practice. We are to live out the will of God. Christ is the pattern, and our conduct and behavior is to be upon Christ. To face life, death, disease, accidents, we need God's power. We secure this power through prayer.

(**James 3:17-18**; **Matt. 5:8**; **Heb. 12:14**) Source of true wisdom is God. To be pure is to be free from fault and defilement, from moral impurity, from iniquity and, thus, separated unto God. We must be peaceable and gentle, forbearing with people, being in a state of reconciliation with self and with others, weave with self, with God and with others. The last thing to do is to criticize, condemn, neglect and ignore people. We must be ready to listen to reason and to appeal—being willing to change when one is wrong. We are to have feelings of compassion, affection and kindness, eager to help others, and not show partiality or favoritism, being without hypocrisy, insincerity. The fruit of righteousness is brought about by making peace, being at ease with each other and with God.

Work Out Your Salvation (Phil. 2:12-13)

Memory Verse(s):
> **Col. 1:10**

Devotion:
> BSAF on **James 4:1-5**.

Put-Off/Put-On:
> Study **James 3:17**. List personal failures in each of the categories
> listed in **James 3:17-18**. Then prepare a plan of action on how to
> deal with each item biblically. Use **Appendix A.4, "Victory over**
> **Sin Worksheet"** or **Appendix A.9, "Contingency Plan"** as
> appropriate. In each encounter in life, your basic plan of action is
> to call upon the name of the Lord by quoting, "Thy will be done."
> This unites your will with His will which initiates and prompts a
> biblical response. This is a lifetime endeavor.

7.6. Lifestyle Change is Evidence of New Birth

Perspective

(**Eccl. 12:13-14**; **John 3:3-8**; **John 10:10**) It is necessary to be born-again, a spiritual birth in order to recognize, to admit, and to solve your problems in a biblical manner. Only God's solutions, grace, empowering, and wisdom are completely adequate for abundant living.

Hope

(**Eph. 2:8-9**; **Rom. 3:27**; **Rom. 4:2**; **Rom. 5:1**) Salvation is received by faith, all man has to do is to stretch out his hand and receive God's free gift of salvation. Man must believe just what God says and accept His word, accept His free offer of salvation. All man can do is accept the fact that God says He will save him, and to accept as true the free offer of salvation.

(**Rom. 3:23**; **Rom. 6:23**; **Rom. 10:9-10**) Realize there is no salvation in or within one's self or in the world. Salvation is by the word of God, as we confess it and verbally state God's word and believe. Then faith grows and increases effecting a reconciliation within one's self, with others, and with God. To 'reconcile' means to change, to change thoroughly, to exchange, to change from enmity to friendship, to bring together, to restore, to be related and united with God.

(**John 1:12**; **Acts 17:30-31**; **2 Cor. 5:17**) God the Father becomes Father of your spirit, and moving you from darkness to light. Satan is no longer your stepfather. By the resurrection of Jesus from the dead, you become a child of God, a citizen of the kingdom of heaven. You begin a new existence, and operate now from heaven whence you receive spiritual blessings, power, wisdom and knowledge in order to live a victorious life here on earth.

Change

(**Rom. 12:1-2**; **1 John 5:4-5**; **Titus 3:3-7**) Christ now lives in your heart by faith. Your spirit has been regenerated, you are empowered to live the victorious life. It all begins by the renewing of your mind, thinking God's thoughts after Him, removing the garbage of your past life, and developing biblical attitudes and motives to please the Lord.

(**Eph. 5:3-6**) Being led astray by immoral and seductive persons, by false teachings, and false systems of religion, these habits, practices and associations are to be changed. God has taken our unloving nature and made new people out of us:

but we must turn from living a selfish and worldly life and turn to Christ and begin a new lifestyle. Thus, we are to guard what we see, what we hear, and what we speak.

(**1 John 2:3-6**) The change process begins with the mind, and the mind is changed, fashioned and molded by the word of God. As the mind changes so does the thoughts, attitudes and motives. What you comprehend, you will be conformed to, and this is what will be communicated.

Work Out Your Salvation (Phil. 2:12-13)

Memory Verse(s):
  Eph. 2:8-9

Devotion:
  BSAF for **Acts 17:30-31**; **Eph. 2:8-9**; **John 1:12**; **Rom. 10:9-10**.

Put-Off/Put-On:
  Review the book of **1 John**. Note the references and vivid contrast to loving, to fellowship, to light and the dark, to backsliding, to false teachings: to that which distinguishes a child of God from the devil's children. Assurance that you are a child of God rests upon abiding in Christ and upon the pursuit of righteousness as He is righteous.

  It all begins in loving God and the proof that you are loving God rests upon your relationship with others, and your dis-involvement with the world, the flesh and the devil.

  Begin a process of change by noting when and where you are harboring grudges, resentments, bitterness. Make plans by using **Appendix A.4, "Victory over Sin Worksheet"**, **Appendix A.9, "Contingency Plan"**, and other worksheets as appropriate, to respond to these situations in patience, kindness and goodness.

7.7. Worried, Confused, Troubled

Perspective

(**John 14:1-3**; **John 3:15**; **John 5:24**; **John 11:25**; **Rom. 10:9-10**) Whenever troubled, disturbed, agitated, perplexed, worried, tossed about, confused, disheartened, continue to believe while in the midst of troubles. This will carry you through to believing that God and His Son will deliver your troubled heart. Thus, through belief and hope for God's house and its mansions, through Jesus' work, through Jesus' return and through an eternal habitation with Jesus, these things will deliver you from a troubled heart.

Hope

(**1 Pet. 1:3-4**; **Titus 2:12-13**) Earth is only a temporary place, we have a permanent one in a real world in another dimension of being. Jesus knew His Father's house, the truth and the reality of it. Thus, the one thing essential to inherit these mansions is belief in Christ.

In relation to God, the more a soul hopes and believes, the more it will attain. The more hope it has, the greater will be its union with God. Thus, we are to empty ourselves of all that is not of God. In this way we can purely hope for God Himself. Every possession that is not of God is against hope. In the measure the memory becomes dispossessed of worldly influences: its delights, its honors, its pressures, its oppressions, its fears, its materialism—any semblance of earthly properties... to this extent, one will exercise divine wisdom to reach beyond the earthly to the divine, and from the divine to the earthly (**Col. 1:27**; **Heb. 12:1-3**).

Therefore, perfect dispossession of all that is not of God opens up the human faculties to be filled with and under the absolute presence and direction of the Holy Spirit resulting in perfect possession with God in union (**Matt. 5:48**; **Matt. 6:10**; **Luke 14:26,33**).

(**Eph. 1:7**; **1 Pet. 1:18-19**; **2 Cor. 13:4**; **Rom. 5:2**) It is through Jesus' work that our deliverance comes about. Jesus went to the cross to prepare redemption for us by His death, His resurrection and His exaltation. Being raised from the dead, He prepared the conquest of death and a new life and power for us. He ascended into heaven to prepare our access into the presence of God and an eternal home for us.

(**John 5:25**; **John 17:24**; **1 Thess. 4:16-17**; **2 Cor. 5:8**; **Titus 2:12-13**; **2 Tim. 4:18**; **Phil. 3:20-21**) Believers are to be glorified with the Father and Jesus. In an instant, we will pass from this world into the next world, into heaven itself. In comparison, our present afflictions are but slight. Meditate on this and grasp the truth of this statement which will carry your troubled soul through any trial even martyrdom. The Lord will deliver you from any evil work—physical and spiritual.

Change

(**John 14:4-7**; **John 8:19**; **Acts 28:27**; **John 3:3-5**; **1 Cor. 2:14**; **Rom. 8:15-17**; **Gal. 4:4-7**) As with the disciples, our eyes are to be taken off of earthly things, of worldly position and power, of wealth and possessions, of pomp and ceremony. We are to think on Jesus' words that all roads lead to God Himself. We dwell on the words of Jesus, and we look through the things of the world and see the way to God is Jesus Himself and the destination of life is God Himself. Accordingly, do not think like the natural man and be caught up into the earthly atmosphere. Our perpetual residence is one of a heavenly atmosphere, having an eternal quality, beyond the senses, realizing that we will be in the Presence of God the Father forever.

(**John 14:8-14**; **John 12:45**; **John 16:15**; **Col. 2:9**; **Heb. 1:3**; **John 10:37-38**; **John 14:20**; **John 17:21-22**; **Acts 1:8**) As with the disciples, the same today, Jesus wants us to walk by faith. We will see the Father in Jesus in the Gospels. Jesus revealed Himself as the full embodiment of God—the very nature, character, substance and perfection of God. As we believe the word as Jesus did, then, we too will walk by the light of the word—in the midst of troubles, pressures, and persecutions as with Jesus—manifesting the Presence of God in our being and deeds. We are to believe Jesus as a Person, as the Son of God Himself, believe His claim, that His testimony and witness to Himself is absolutely true. As we believe and live in Him, we can go through any trial and come out victoriously.

Work Out Your Salvation (Phil. 2:12-13)

Memory Verse(s):
> **Matt. 28:18-20**

Devotion:
> BSAF for **Acts 4:33**; **Eph. 3:20**.

Put-Off/Put-On:
> Meditate on the following verses and make note on what the Holy Spirit is saying to you, and what should your attitude be in your

present situation: **Col. 1:12-14**; **1 Thess. 5:18**; **2 Cor. 3:18**; **Heb. 13:15**; **1 Pet. 2:9**; **Ps. 29:2**; **Ps. 100:4**.

7.8. The Pure Self Activated

Perspective

(**Heb. 4:16**; **James 1:5-8**; **2 Cor. 3:4-5**; **Phil. 4:13**) To appropriate God's gracious wisdom in facing and dealing with your problems, you must ask in faith, that is, to live according to God's word, and to depend solely on His power.

"'You shall receive power when the Holy Spirit has come upon you...' (**Acts 1:8**)—not power as a gift from the Holy Spirit, something that He gives us—the power is the Holy Spirit. The life that was in Jesus becomes ours because of His Cross, once we make the decision to be identified with Him. If it is difficult to get right with God, it is because we refuse to make this moral decision about sin. But once we do decide, the full life of God comes in immediately. Jesus came to give us an endless supply of life—'...that you may be filled with all the fulness of God' (**Eph. 3:19**). Eternal life has nothing to do with time. It is the life which Jesus lived when He was down here, and the only Source of life is the Lord Jesus Christ." (Reference: [Chambers2], April 12.)

Hope

(**John 16:7-13**; **1 Cor. 2:11-13**) Our human spirit is now in union with the Holy Spirit. Having the mind of Christ, all that Christ is, His fulness is within to be conveyed to our spirit—the wisdom, strength, and ability of God. From our spirit, His grace moves to our mind, and from there to our body to manifest Christ in any and all situations, replacing evil with righteousness. Through us the Gospel of the Risen and Exalted Lord is proclaimed and able to give eternal life to every person who calls upon Him.

"Eternal life is the life which Jesus Christ exhibited on the human level. And it is this same life, not simply a copy of it, which is made evident in our mortal flesh when we are born again. Eternal life is not a gift from God, eternal life is the gift of God. The energy and the power which was so very evident in Jesus will be exhibited in us by an act of the absolute sovereign grace of God, once we have made that complete and effective decision about sin." (Reference: [Chambers2], April 12.)

(**John 15:16**) We are to bear the fruit of our salvation and witness to others of what Jesus has done. Our job is to be a witness, by our lifestyle, as represented by a solid demeanor of confidence and boldness, flavored by patience, kindness, goodness.

However, it is the function and responsibility of the Holy Spirit to convict and convince the world (and each and every individual) of sin, righteousness and judgment. He is the one who persuades and convicts.

(**2 Tim. 3:16-17**; **2 Pet. 1:3-4**; **2 Cor. 3:18**) By the word of God, we live, move and have our being. The life which Jesus gives is a life of energy, force and power. By His word we become conscious of God's Presence, that we live just as God would live and walk on the earth. We receive life and godliness by the knowledge of Christ and His word conforms us to His image. Seed of corruption is sin, and this is replaced by the Holy Spirit indwelling the heart of the believer. We actually partake of the divine nature of Christ, escaping the corruption principle, and are enabled to live a life of righteousness. We move from glory to glory, and grace to grace, the very energy and presence of the indwelling God.

Change

(**1 Thess. 5:17**; **Heb. 4:15-16**; **James 1:5**; **Matt. 18:18**; **2 Cor. 9:8**) God sits upon a Throne, the seat of authority and power, honor and glory. By His grace, we can approach God and He will receive us in Christ Jesus. From His Throne, we receive Grace; and in prayer, we receive help to work through our trials, and to receive His strength to undergo any and all situations. In prayer, we bind the sin and loose the foul spirit by God's directions, replacing evil with righteousness.

(**James 1:5-8**; **James 1:22-25**; **2 Cor. 3:4-5**; **Phil. 4:13**) To appropriate God's gracious wisdom in facing and dealing with our problems, we must ask in faith, live according to God's word, and depend solely on His power.

(**Matt. 26:39**) "The agony in Gethsemane was the agony of the Son of God in fulfilling His destiny as the Savior of the world. The veil is pulled back here to reveal all that it costs Him to make it possible for us to become sons of God. His agony was the basis for the simplicity of our salvation. The Cross of Christ was a triumph for the Son of Man. It was not only a sign that our Lord had triumphed, but that He had triumphed to save the human race. Because of what the Son of Man went through, every human being has been provided with a way of access into the very presence of God." (Reference: [Chambers2], April 11.)

It is time to be increasingly separated from the world, the flesh, and the devil. Accordingly, place your will in the center of God's will and maintain what Christ obtained for us: to be His disciples, to be His intercessors, to be His ambassadors, to establish His kingdom and His will on earth.

Work Out Your Salvation (Phil. 2:12-13)

Memory Verse(s):
1 Cor. 2:12; **2 Tim. 4:18**; **Heb. 13:6**

Devotion:
BSAF for **Phil. 4:13,19**.

Put-Off/Put-On:
Realize who and what you are in Christ Jesus by fulfilling His prayer in **Matt. 28:18-20**. Be an example, be a teacher, be an intercessor by binding and loosing. Pray for others to become disciples so that they, in turn, will do likewise. It is about time that God's Kingdom principles prevail on earth.

Praying for others, you may wish to use **Eph. 1:17-19**; **Eph. 3:19-20**; **2 Cor. 4:4**; **Col. 1:10**; **Matt. 18:18**. To intervene and release those in bondage, you may be disposed to pray the following:

1. Lord, sprinkle their hearts clean from consciences oppressed with sin (**Heb. 10:22**).

2. Lord, we bind the sin over them, and loose the foul spirit that hovers (**Matt. 16:19**).

3. Remove the blindfolds over their eyes that they may see the truth (**2 Cor. 4:4**)

4. Holy Spirit brood over them until the life of Christ penetrates into their very souls (**Gen. 1:2**).

7.9. Holding Self Accountable

Perspective

(**Gen. 1:26**; **Matt. 7:1-5**) Since God created us and we are His own invention, He is our means of life and existence, our only resource. Accordingly, we are accountable to Him and from Him, and we receive whatever we need from Him in order to fulfill His purposes through us on this earth. On the basis of God's word, we are to judge ourselves by and through our actions especially in the area of critically judging and condemning others. The criticizer is inconsistent, self-righteous, self-deceived, a hypocrite, lacks love and abuses the Gospel by which our lives are to be changed. We are to be an example to the world by expressing the love of God to others (**Phil. 2:14-15**).

To judge yourself correctly, examine self in the areas of repentance, of renunciation, and of detachment. Life's effects are deposited in our memories. Our memories are connected to our emotions. Those areas that have not been dealt with biblically, Satan stimulates to bring forth guilt, shame, anger, bitterness, despair, and the like. Thus, keep your memory clean and fresh by being in a constant state of repentance (confess and repent immediately upon conviction), by renouncing all those things that hold you in bondage (vain thoughts, images), and separating oneself from the temptations and the false allure of the world's enticements (**Matt. 12:30**; **James 2:15-17**). Now you can be a fit vessel of the Lord to accomplish His purposes on this earth (**2 Cor. 6:16-18**).

Hope

(**Ezek. 18:20**; **Jer. 17:10**) I cannot blame my background, my parentage, the circumstances of life to justify sinful actions nor am I controlled by them. God's grace is available to me from heaven to enable me to live righteously regardless of what others have done. Being free of horizontal controls, God's grace will break the hold of the past, and He will guide me and lead me to an abundant life.

(**Ezek. 18:2-3**; **Eph. 5:18**) I am not responsible for other's sins, nor do the actions of others have to unsettle me. Being free of the past, of blame shifting and defensiveness, this allows for the Presence of the Holy Spirit. The believer is to be filled continuously to be conscious of His Presence, of His leadership, and of His guidance. The Spirit's filling is the personal manifestation of Christ to the believer who walks obediently day by day. He is filled only as he walks in obedience to the word of God.

(**John 14:21-22**; **Ps. 119:11**; **Acts 2:1-4**) To be filled requires that we walk obediently to Christ, as we walk through terrible trials and severe crisis, God will manifest His Presence to provide a deep sense of His love and care: lifting and strengthening us to conform to His Son. Thus, the meaning of life is to allow God to be His fullest in our lives at every moment of the day and night. This consciousness is the believer's privilege in being aware of His presence, and of His leadership.

Change

(**Rom. 12:9-10**; **2 Pet. 1:5-7**) To begin to love sincerely, the believer is to hate all forms of evil because evil destroys lives. A godly love desires the very best for people. He is to cleave to the good and to work for everyone to know and experience the good. He loves others in Christ by being kind and affectionate. He takes the lead in esteeming and expressing respect for others.

(**Rom. 5:3-5**) By faith, the power and provision to live a virtuous existence resides within the believer in the person of the Holy Spirit. But this faith must be worked out and demonstrated and experienced by one's responses to life. The believer is to add moral excellence, goodness of character, moral strength, and moral courage. He is to add practical knowledge and insight in knowing what to do and say in trials and temptations of life. He is to master and control the body or the flesh with all of its lusts.

(**1 Cor. 1:10**; **1 Pet. 3:10**; **Prov. 13:3**; **Luke 11:17**) To reach any situation, one must refrain the tongue in stirring dissension, division, but to bring peace, love, and brotherhood. We are to be restored within ourselves and with others. Union in mind and judgments involves thoughts, reasonings, emotions, motives and intentions. Judgments involve conclusions, purposes, goals and objectives. Restorations begin in and around conclusions that bring unity within ourselves and with others.

(**Phil. 2:2-4**; **Prov. 17:19**; **Isa. 14:13-14**; **1 John 2:16**) If we don't get our way or what we want, we are inclined to strive, to cause arguments and divisions. We are inclined to want attention, praise and honor. We are to deny these inclinations for the sake of Christ that we may help others. God works in us to offer ourselves in a spirit of submissiveness and lowliness, not to be high-minded, proud, haughty, arrogant, or assertive.

Humility must be developed which is learning of Christ—His disposition and His virtues—who placed everyone ahead of Himself. Humility reaches its height when we lose our lives in the cause of Christ to the benefit and welfare of others. This requires an honest evaluation of oneself because we are always at the center of all that we do. Self-centeredness weakens and limits relationships and achievements.

Work Out Your Salvation (Phil. 2:12-13)

Memory Verse(s):
> **Ezek. 18:20**

Devotion:
> BSAF for **Luke 9:23-24**; **Rom. 12:16**; **Prov. 21:4**; **Prov. 26:12**.

Put-Off/Put-On:
> Read **Phil. 2:3-11**, then work out **Appendix A.2, "Think and Do List"**. Evaluate yourself to the extent you seek your own interest, using the following characteristics we habitually think about that keep us self-centered:
>
> - ambition, desires
> - position
> - wants
> - being by-passed
> - being ignored
> - being neglected
> - being overlooked
> - not being recognized
> - not being honored
> - not given a promotion or not selected
>
> For each item replace by what God wants you to think and to do, considering the needs of others before your own, such as: visiting, consoling, ministering, helping, sharing, feeding, clothing, transporting, listening, advising, counseling, teaching, etc..

71

Review **Appendix A.5, "Dying to Self"** for additional insights.

7.10. Only God Can Change Us and Others

Perspective

(**Ezek. 36:26-27**; **Phil. 1:6**; **Phil. 2:13**) Only God can change people, so you are not and cannot be responsible for changing others. You are accountable to God solely for your own deeds, and to do your part in living at peace with others. Your job is to intercede in prayer, to be a godly influence and set an example to provide an opportunity for God to work in the hearts of others. For God is the one who arouses, stirs and energizes the heart of believer to do His will.

Hope

(**Phil. 1:6**; **Jude 24-25**) The believer has absolute confidence in the work of salvation or redemption which God has begun in his life. He has confidence through the Presence of God's Spirit who dwells within him and enables him to fulfill his role and function. For it is God who frees us from blemishes; it is God who delivers us daily when we confess; it is He who makes us blameless and keeps us from falling. All we need to do is to draw near to Him and stay in touch with Him by daily bible study and prayer, and by walking righteously (**Ps. 91:1-3**).

(**Phil. 2:13**; **1 John 2:27**) God arouses, stirs and energizes the heart of the believer to do God's will. God is working within us—energizing us, giving us both the will and power to do what pleases Him. God does not leave us alone to work out our salvation and deliverance.

(**Rom. 5:3-5**; **2 Cor. 4:7-18**; **Luke 22:23**) Do not be surprised at trials, even if they seem fiery; instead, rejoice in them because God uses them to develop Christlike maturity in our lives. If you should endure suffering for the sake of righteousness, you are blessed by the Lord. Trials and sufferings work good for us. Oppressions and afflictions stirs patience, which is the development of endurance, fortitude, steadfastness, and constancy. Through these experiences we develop character, integrity, strength. When one endures trials, he becomes stronger as he begins to sense the increasing presence of God. He draws close to God and the closer he draws to God, the more he hopes for the glory of God. All of this leads to the continuous experience of God's love through the presence of the Holy Spirit.

Change

(**John 7:24**; **Rom. 14:1-13**) Do not judge others by your own standards, perspective, or experience. You will be judged in the very same way you judge them. We are to form a just judgment by checking our own spirit and place ourselves in the position to help restore others, if need be, who are at fault (**Gal. 6:1**).

(**Ps. 19:7-11**; **Prov. 30:5-6**; **Heb. 4:12**) God's word is to be your only authority for faith and conduct and is to be the only legitimate standard by which you are to be evaluated. You are to rely on no other source, since God's word provides hope and gives direction for change in all areas of life (thoughts, words, actions). But you must labor to enter God's rest, that is, to study God's word and to learn to walk righteously. As you do your part God will do His.

(**2 Pet. 1:3-4**; **Matt. 5:1-20**) Nature of well being comes about by setting aside anger, contempt, lust, manipulation, revenge and payback, forsaking dependence upon human reputation, wealth, possessions. Our memories are to be possessed by God, not by the past, people or things. Thus, by faith, by repentance, we are to add to our faith the virtues of prudence, justice, fortitude, and temperance. As such, we will grow into the image of Christ as ordained from the beginning.

Work Out Your Salvation (Phil. 2:12-13)

Memory Verse(s):
>Ps. 128:1-4

Devotion:
>BSAF for **Titus 2:11-12**; **Ps. 31:19**; **John 6:63**.

Put-Off/Put-On:
>The fear of God will be the soil out of which your positive influence will grow and the basic reason your family and others will arise and call you blessed. Meditate on the following Scriptures and read what the Bible says will happen to you as a God-fearing person. In 50 words or so, describe what you have learned from these verses: **Ps. 25:12-13**; **Ps. 112:3**; **Ps. 31:19**; **Ps. 103:11-18**; **Ps. 112:1-9**; **Ps. 145:19**; **Prov. 1:7**; **Prov. 8:13**; **Prov. 9:10**; **Prov. 14:26**; **Prov. 15:33**; **Prov. 19:23**; **Acts 9:31**; **Job 2:3**; **Malachi 3:16**; **Ps. 147:11**; **Ps. 128:3**; **2 Cor. 7:1**; **Rev. 14:7** and **Eccl. 12:13**.

7.11. Judging Yourself

Perspective

(**Matt. 7:5**; **James 3:1-2**) To judge means to criticize, condemn, censor—a habit of censorious and carping criticism. To criticize others is to boost one's own image, at the expense of another. This makes us feel that our lives are better than the person who failed. We justify our decisions and acts by pointing out the failures of others, and this shows that we are stronger than they are. Criticism is really an outlet for our own hurts and desire for revenge. The criticizer will be judged for the very same thing he criticized: it is that for which he shall be condemned, and that by God himself (**Rom. 2:1-4**).

Hope

(**Ps. 19:7-11**; **Prov. 30:5-6**; **2 Pet. 1:2-4**) By judging and examining ourselves correctly, we open up and allow God's grace and peace to flow within to provide a fit place for the divine nature to inhabit. This nature is the power of Christ, the power to save us from death and to give us life and godliness. Just using God's word itself provides this hope and gives direction for change in deeds (thoughts, speech and action) consistent with God's nature. The Word is adequate to equip you for very good work, and to develop a Christ-like attitude of servanthood within.

(**Jer. 17:9**; **Heb. 4:12**; **Matt. 15:18-20**) You cannot fully understand your own heart but God's word is the measure and instrument by which the heart level of your problem is discerned. "'Let not your heart be troubled...' (**John 14:1,27**). Am I then hurting Jesus by allowing my heart to be troubled? If I believe in Jesus and His attributes, am I living up to my belief? Am I allowing anything to disturb my heart, or am I allowing any question to come in which are unsound or unbalanced? I have to get to the point of the absolute and unquestionable relationship that takes everything exactly as it comes from Him. God never guides us at some time in the future, but always here and now. Realize that the Lord is here now, and the freedom you receive is immediate." (Reference: [Chambers2], April 21.)

(**Eph. 5:14-18**) How the believer walks day to day is crucial to the cause of Christ and to the welfare of society. The wise person knows God personally and he knows that he is on earth to live a righteous and godly life. He walks throughout life exact, strict, disciplined and controlled. As such, people, circumstances or things in life do not cause his problems but only reveal the condition of his heart—the spirit within. By being under control and influence of the Holy Spirit, the believer can assess his heart and biblically respond regardless of the situation, and become a blessing under the prompting of the Holy Spirit.

Change

(**1 Cor. 11:28-31**; **Heb. 12:1**) Practicing God's word begins with judging yourself and removing sinful obstructions from your own life. Then, you will have the privilege and responsibility of restoring others to victorious living. We have no righteousness of our own. We can only be counted worthy when we examine ourselves to assure that we are walking in constant fellowship with Him. And constant fellowship means actively thinking upon and talking with Him through confession, repentance, praise and request.

(**Prov. 28:13**; **2 Cor. 7:9-10**; **Rom. 6:12-13**) Once you have identified sins in your life, you must repent of them, confess them and immediately put them aside. Repentance moves us from the old creation to the new creation, from the flesh to the spirit, from the natural to the supernatural realm.

(**Titus 2:11-12**; **Gal. 5:16**; **Eph. 3:16-21**; **Eph. 5:18**; **1 John 5:3**) The believer needs to be strengthened with power in the 'inner man', in his heart and in his spirit—in the spirit that God has renewed. This is the only way he can overcome the flesh with all its weakness. The source of this strength is the Holy Spirit who provides the energy and the force to live the overcoming life. Thus, the believer is to prepare himself through repentance, through renunciation, and through detachment of all that is of the flesh to allow the Holy Spirit to move one to stretch forward: "for the prize of the upward call of God in Christ Jesus."

Work Out Your Salvation (Phil. 2:12-13)

Memory Verse(s):
>   **Ps. 139:23-24**

Devotion:
>   BSAF on verses from above (at least choose 3 verses).

Put-Off/Put-On:
>   The four anchor posts in **Appendix A.12, "Anchor Posts"** provide a method and the means to examine and evaluate yourself in a structured and disciplined manner to insure a firm and godly spiritual foundation (**Phil. 2:14-16**). List the people of whom you

feel bitter, envious, jealous, and of whom you indulge in negative and critical thoughts. List the circumstances of life in which you murmur and complain. On the basis of your findings, process **Appendix A.4, "Victory over Sin Worksheet"**.

7.12. True Dying

Perspective

(**Matt. 10:38-39; Prov. 16:3-7**) To carry the cross means to practice the Presence of Jesus, and to allow His love to flow through us to others. It means that we are to carry the life of Christ to other people and say to them, "The Kingdom of God has come to you," that is, God's approval and peace, as well as the joy the Holy Spirit gives. The work of the Holy Spirit in us and among us is to understand the positive character of what it means to carry one's cross: He comes into us and empowers us at the point we obey.

Hope

(**2 Cor. 4:17; 1 Pet. 4:13; Isa. 63:9**) Christian suffering we undergo in carrying of our cross is when we allow Christ to live in and through us. It is His light in us which collides with the darkness of the world: the ignorance, lies, hatred, all the delusions of a darkened fallen world. Our suffering is redemptive when we carry His love and forgiveness into the lives of others affected by the world. We should rejoice when we take part in Christ's suffering because Christ is suffering with us.

(**1 Pet. 3:9-15; 1 Pet. 4:12-15**) When we suffer due to the sins of others or to the corporate sins of others, we can ask God to transform these sufferings into healing power. We forgive those who have sinned against us, and we accept the circumstances of our lives. Then we go on to make prayers of confession and intercession for ourselves and others. As we pray, that which is redemptive is accomplished. Accordingly, righteous actions follow, healing our own souls in the process.

Change

(**Rom. 6:3-8**) Our identity is with Christ and not on our past, the past is in the grave. The abuses of life as a child or adulthood: the depression, intense inner suffering of life as a child or adult, life in a dysfunctional family due to alcoholism, sexual addictions, mental illness, overt or subtle evil on the part of parents or others, and similar experiences: all of these violations are afflictions. But it is not the cross we are to bear. We are to take this cross of pain and suffering to Christ's Cross, and there acknowledge that Christ died to take into Himself this very pain and suffering.

(**Rom. 8:2-11**) We are not to deny or suppress our past and associated pain and suffering: accept them, then offer the pain to Christ, let the pain flow into Him. We die with Him to these sins, we die to these diseased feelings by allowing Him to take them into Himself. By this means, we get in touch with heretofore repressed grief, fear, anger, and shame. To dwell on the past is death, give death to Christ who kills it. Doing this we practice the Presence of Christ rather than practicing the presence of the corrupted self.

(**Col. 2:11-14; Matt. 6:14-15; 1 John 1:1**) We are to stand in Christ, identify with His suffering for us, and grieve at the grieves, and yield up our angers, naming them and forgiving others at the same time. Christ's suffering consists in the fact that He became the way of life. He channeled (by dying) His life to us. Our suffering consists in the fact that we become a channel of His life, His life and Light in us overcomes the evil and pain in the souls of men. This is where the battle lies, and this is where we experience suffering for Christ's sake: We share in life's sufferings, we rise above self and the circumstances of life in order to provide aid and comfort to others.

Work Out Your Salvation (Phil. 2:12-13)

Memory Verse(s):
> **Luke 9:23-24**

Devotion:
> BSAF on **Rom. 6:12-16**.

Put-Off/Put-On:
> Review and study **Appendix A.5, "Dying to Self"** and **Section 5.2, "Sin, Self, Suffering"**. List in priority areas that need addressing. Prepare **Appendix A.4, "Victory over Sin Worksheet"** or **Appendix A.6, "Problem Solving Worksheet"**.

7.13. True Patience

(**Luke 21:19**) Few virtues provide witness that our lives are based no longer on one's own nature but on Christ—Patience is one of them.

False Virtues

Indolence reflects a lazy spirit, and stoic actions reflect an artificial indifference in regard to all things. Only thing that matters to this person is his own imperturbability which implies a loss of response to values. In either case, these conditions lack an ardent zeal for the victory of our God.

Likewise, the Buddhist mentality sees all reality as mere appearance, or is to be detached and to dispense of all obligations of duty and accomplishment. One becomes merely a spectator looking unfavorably to all activity and tension. This makes it impossible for one to encounter reality and work through it to develop Christlike character.

The stoic develops an attitude to things insofar as they affect the mind. The Buddhist modifies one's basic relation to the world of reality and negates one's responsibility to do one's part within its framework.

Traits of Patience

The ups and downs of life challenge the pursuit of constancy and perseverance in the face of stark reality. Petulance, fickleness and quarrelsome aspects come about whenever an action seems to require a long period of time which is a common test.

Impatience is a form of self-indulgence. When we expect something and don't get it, we get upset. This involves an element of time. Three varieties of evil related to time may account for impatience: delay in securing of a coveted good; any kind of lasting unpleasantness (boring people); and the boredom inherent in pure waiting.

These tendencies show that one has not yet succeeded in establishing that distance between one's responsible self and one's unredeemed nature with the desires and impulses it harbors. This is a test of sovereignty—yours or God's. Impatience, therefore, is rooted in an illegitimate sovereignty of self.

Roots of Impatience

1. Self-indulgence—no pain, no waiting, no delays.

2. Sovereignty of self-egocentric attitude—disregard of others needs but my own. This severs our fundamental link with God which defines our creatureness. Accordingly, this attitude presents a negation and non-recognition of one's human creatureness; a substitution of a supra-human position of mastery; failure to note one's limitations and finiteness.

The reality imposed by God is that there is a space of time that exists between our will and decision and the fulfillment of our purpose. The impatient man ignores this reality. We become harsh, petulant, unkind which implies a lack of depth. We are to keep in mind that fulfillment of any aim of man is a gift of God. It is a question of the higher good in contrast to trivial goals. What irritates an impatient person above all is too sluggish effect of his order, his attempt to influence man's behavior, and the development of a situation.

Virtues of Patience (Hierarchy of Goods and Things)

The patient man preserves the right order on the scale of his interest. The requirement of the moment no matter how imperious, can never displace or overshadow his attention to higher values. This is due to the 'art of waiting'. He refrains from letting himself go. He checks his nature and its stirrings, and no matter the provocation, bears the cross that he may respond biblically.

He is always aware regardless of the experiences of the moment. He knows he cannot remain in communion with God except his soul is in a state of composure and self-possession (**Ps. 30:16**). Thus, he never pretends a false position of supremacy over the universe.

(**Eccl. 3:1**) God is the Lord of Time, that He has assigned to the course of events its temporal extension. Thus, it is up to us to realize the interval of time between a decision and the realization of its intended aim as a reality willed by God.

Patience is a life centered in Christ, an absolute dependence on Him, as well as an acceptance of our creature finiteness. He who has patience abides by the Truth. The impatient man submits to the bondage of the moment.

Holy patience is the realization that it is not we but God alone who determines the proper day and the hour for our fruitful performances of certain actions and, even more, exclusively, the ripening of our seed and the harvest.

Fulness of Time

To grow in inner and personal holiness requires a passage of time. Need to wait on God's timing not ours. As Noah in the ark performed his functions, he focused his attention on God, and waited, as God developed and matured the situation. Then Noah was told to depart. Paul spent a number of years in the desert as did John the Baptist before they started their work.

(**2 Tim. 4:2**) Christ wants us to fight with Him in our endeavors and ministries, but not to conquer with Him. We are to renounce any pretensions in determining the time of the harvest—"not as I will but as Thou wilt" (**Matt. 26:39**).

(**Luke 21:19**) Holy patience embodies an ultimate act of our surrender to God, a status of consummate self-possession. Only in the measure that we have surrendered our inmost being to God, do we possess ourselves.

Fruits of Patience

Within the attitude of patience, we let God act and allow all things to unfold from above. Accordingly, the fruits of patience are faith, hope and love.

- **Faith: (Rev. 13:10)** Faith teaches us that God the Universal Lord is also the Lord of time. He appoints the proper hour to everything. Thus, we place the success of all endeavors in His hands.

- **Hope: (Rom. 4:17-22)** Hope keeps us from getting discouraged in spite of all the failures and all the delays in achieving success. With God nothing is impossible.

- **Love: (1 Cor. 13:7)** We are to love His will above everything. Patience is an offspring of love in respect to constancy and perseverance.

(**Matt. 24:13**) Patience acknowledges man's creaturely status. We are finite and subject to persevere in the space/time continuum in the midst of obstacles and sufferings. Thus, we give proof of the constancy demanded of God as we hold on to Him to get us through this terrestrial life into the eternal.

(**Rom. 6:3-6**) Thus, only the patient man who lives by and in Christ can persevere to the end. "In your patience, you shall possess your souls" (**Luke 21:19**).

Reference: [Hildebrand1]

7.14. Mind Control

Perspective

(**1 Pet. 1:13**; **Col. 3:1-3**) Gird your mind is to control, guard, select what you are to put into it. Thus, be selective about what you read, hear and think about. All your thoughts are to please God, not self. Consciously thinking to please God allows the Spirit of God to be revealed in your spirit. We precondition ourselves by what we think, by what we believe, and by what we confess (**Prov. 4:20-23**; **Matt. 12:33-36**).

Hope

(**Eph. 4:23**; **Phil. 2:12-13**) The spirit of the mind refers to the 'will' of the mind. By an act of my will, I will my mind to think thoughts pleasing to God, to disregard feelings, but to think on God's word only, an attitude change. Ask God to make you willing to will to do the will of God, to be strengthened by His presence.

(**1 Pet. 4:1**; **Luke 9:23-24**) By suffering, I learn to die to self-pity, self-defensiveness, self-concern and self-interests. From that point on I am in the spirit responding to life from God's perspective, putting on the cross and allowing Jesus to live through me, looking for opportunities to be a blessing to others. Arm self is to arm the mind, to set it do what God wants regardless of the pain: then healing comes—the Presence of God in the situation.

(**Heb. 7:26**; **Heb. 9:14-15**; **Heb. 10:19-23**) Once and forever our sins are paid for. No need to try to pay for our sins by self-pity, by promising to do better, going to church more often, giving more time and money: Jesus paid the penalty. We are free now to allow Christ to live through us, and in Him to do those things that are pleasing in His sight: because our conscience is cleansed from guilt by His blood.

Change

(**2 Cor. 10:4-5**) All things begin with a thought. A thought becomes an idea, an idea becomes an action, an action becomes a habit, and a habit becomes a character trait—good or evil. All thoughts develop into imaginations, these lead to strongholds—godly or ungodly.

(**Phil. 4:6**) When anxious moments come, let them come, just fix your mind on Jesus, replace negative thoughts with godly thoughts. Then, in time, confusion ceases, peace comes. What you sow, you will reap.

The key word is **FIX**:

- FIX mind on what you put into your head.
- FIX mind on your will to think right.
- FIX mind to purpose, to determine, not to be moved by anything.

As Jesus set His mind to go to Jerusalem, to die on the Cross, do likewise—die to the old self thoughts, so that the new self in Christ can now live in your mind.

Work Out Your Salvation (Phil. 2:12-13)

Memory Verse(s):
> **2 Cor. 10:3-5**. Devotions on **Constancy**:
> Firmness, steadfastness, determination, perseverance, resolution, faithfulness.

Put-Off/Put-On:
> Takes time and repeated effort to succeed. When you fall, get-up, and start all over again, regardless of the number of failures. Key is getting up and doing it all over again. God promises victory to those who patiently and through longsuffering keep on, keeping-on. Rest will come, then peace (**James 1:2-4**). Inconstancy is a habit as well. One tries 2 or 3 times and gives up which becomes a pattern. Keep on, keeping-on until you are dominant and have control over your mind.
>
> Example of a think-list: (See **Section 5.4, "Transforming the Natural Self".**)

- Each time a negative thought comes, immediately think upon the blood of Jesus washing my sins away, forgiving me, and delivering me from the power of sin, making me white as snow, forgiving me, and delivering me from the power of sin. At the same time, pray for God's favor and grace also to be upon those who offended, who failed you or hurt you in any way (**Luke 6:27-28**).

- This opens the way for the Holy Spirit to be present within me to restore, to cure, and to heal my mind, my memories, my emotions, and my body (**Col. 3:10-14**).

- Continuously practicing being freed from the curse of the law. Place self in the position to fulfill your role as a disciple of Christ by serving and meeting the needs of others (**Matt. 28:18-20**).

- God promises success and prosperity to those who read and keep His word. As I meditate on these promises, daily I am being conformed to His image, and daily I am rising above self and life's circumstances (**Joshua 1:8**).

7.15. Purpose vs. Need

Perspective

(**Rom. 8:28**; **Eph. 1:11**) Needs will dominate your vision and motivation and become the reason why you pray, believe, work, and serve. Purpose motivation, however, is reaching out to the why am I here and what am I to do for Him: then things work together for good, and God will meet my needs according to His riches in glory.

Hope

(**Matt. 6:7-8,33**) Your needs are driving your prayer life, and most people are motivated by a historical created need; therefore, they move out to their future with yesterday's created demand. When you are need-dominated, you will always look for something to meet that need: Your hope is in things, not on God from whom all things come. As you change the focus to accomplish God's purposes (in Him you own all things), He will fulfill your needs as a by-product.

(**Matt. 6:24-26**) We are either trusting God, or in the supplier of our need which is a creation of our own desires. Whole world is dominated by its need, which causes man to trust in externals. Externals become gods. To recognize this and seek God's purposes starts the healing and salvation processes. Emotional and intellectual needs are part of need-domination. We put this need on others and expect them to perform to fulfill this demand. Thus, we are to take 'no thought' for life, but seek God's purposes in order to please Him.

(**Phil. 4:6**; **1 Pet. 5:7**) Take no thought for life, we are to let God be God for God is intimately involved in my well-being. We let God be God by having every thought centered on and directed by His word.

Change

(**Ps. 23:1-6**) Lord's leadership is a deliverance and is my security. His leadership sets me free from wants. Step into His shoes and see life from His perspective, His purposes, not by my wants. Be connected to His purposes and **Eph. 3:19-20** will be a reality. Don't trust in mammom or people to fulfill your needs. Our greatest troubles allows Christ's leadership to be manifested and this without stress and strain: no longer need-dominated but purpose-motivated.

(**Eph. 1:11**; **Rom. 8:28**; **1 Kings 17**) His purpose in anything is the release of provision in everything. We no longer depend on people, things or circumstances to change to meet my needs for the Lord is my Shepherd, I shall not want. No longer looking for things or people I could trust in to meet my need: but now I rather recklessly abandon my life to my Shepherd.

Work Out Your Salvation (Phil. 2:12-13)

Memory Verse(s):
> **Ps. 25:1-2**

Devotion:
> BSAF on **Ps. 23**.

Put-Off/Put-On:
> Make up a list of all your needs, desires, and problem areas, then fill out **Appendix A.8, "Freedom from Anxiety"**. Read and review this worksheet for input data. Allow God to speak to and in your spirit.

Part II.b. Basic Study:

Orientation to Biblical Counseling

Table of Contents

Chapter 8. Orientation to Biblical Counseling Mini Series

Table of Contents

8.1. God's Way vs Man's Way

Dynamics of Problem Solving

(**Heb. 3:13**) Being ignorant of sin desensitizes and causes hardening.

(**Rom. 1:20-32**) After awhile you become your own god by establishing standards to justify self-centered pursuits. People perish because of ignorance; therefore, it is a question of becoming knowledgeable, of becoming sensitive, of recognizing that living in this dangerous world cannot be taken for granted (**Hosea 4:6**).

The Ways of Man and the Ways of God

More than two hundred psychological schools of thought are practiced in the world dealing with the study of man's behavior, and the varied methods and means proposed for man to deal with life's issues. These schools are reduced to five common characteristics.

1. **Man is good**: Humanism—independence from God: Man has everything necessary within to solve own problems—mind merely blocked by negative thinking or influences—develop positive thinking and draw from one's own resources—see self as worthwhile and esteemed. What does God say? **Ps. 62:9**; **Rom. 3:10-18,23**; **Rom. 7:18**.

2. **Man is a superior animal**: Basic view of man is that his behavior is wrongly conditioned or programmed by environment and circumstances. He needs to be reconditioned or reprogrammed by manipulation of behavior through use of positive and negative stimuli... He is artificially maneuvered

to respond to reward and punishment in order to improve self. What does God say? **John 15:4-5**; **Rom. 1:18-32**; **James 4:10**.

3. **Man can change himself**: Although being wounded by circumstances of life, man can change bad behavior. This is a combination of the above positions: that through education, logic and reason, man can overcome self. What does God say? **Jer. 13:23**; **Ezek. 18:20**; **Ezek. 36:26-27**.

4. **Man, a victim of conscience**: Man driven by instincts, thwarted by family, by society, by upbringing, and by others, who are responsible for his problems. Deep analysis necessary, along with hypnosis, resocialization, catharsis, self-actualization, free association, etc.. What does God say? **Ezek. 18:20**; **Phil. 2:3-4**; **1 Tim. 4:1-2**.

5. **Man, a bargainer**: When the above doesn't work, the world uses "trade-offs". You do this, and I will do this, a 50/50 arrangement. Imbalances are inevitable, the self nature always wants more than its share. What does God say? God commands us to love without expectation of return, to return good for evil. **Rom. 12:21**; **Phil. 2:3-4**.

Man's way is always self-oriented. He is his own god, as evidenced by...

1. no biblical confrontation.
2. no conversion experience expected or even considered.
3. no repentance.
4. no work of the Holy Spirit.
5. and no sanctification process in bearing the image of God.

This typifies and characterizes man's attempt to save himself without God. Preferences (feelings) prevail and principles (absolutes) are disrgarded or ignored. Human reason and secular logic replaces the Ten Commandments.

God's Way of Handling Problems

(**Phil. 3:13**) God is the God of the 'I AM', He is not in the past, nor in the future, He is always in the present. We start from the present and each day thereafter—one day at a time.

- (**Luke 9:62**) Looking back into the past will make you unfit for the present.
- (**Heb. 11:15**) Thinking of the past makes one vulnerable, and weak.

- (**Rom. 8:28**) Past events in our lives are irreversible. Why waste time and effort there.

Our reactions to those events can be changed as we allow God to intervene in the present, to reach into our experiences, to redeem us, to free us to love and worship God. Eventually we become lovers of God in our spirits instead of lovers of self by dwelling on the past.

(**1 Tim. 4:7**; **Eph. 4:22-24**) Thus, it is through discipline we become godly: by commitment to live God's way in the present through the simple process of putting-off and putting-on, by the authority of God's word, and by the power of the Holy Spirit.

Accordingly, we change our coping mechanisms from reacting to life to responding to life on the basis of God's word.

God's Resources

- Holy Spirit—**John 16:7-8,13**; **1 Cor. 2:11-15**.
- Bible—**2 Tim. 3:16-17**; **Heb. 4:12**.
- Teachers/Advisors/Counselors—**Gal. 6:1-2**; **Rom. 15:14**; **Prov. 15:22**.
- Start up the spiral by tackling the immediate problem first (**James 1:2-4**). Act on known solutions, postpone acting when solutions are unknown (**James 1:5-8**; **John 7:17**; **Rom. 14:23**). Continue up the spiral (**Heb. 5:14**).

Work Out Your Salvation (Phil. 2:12-13)

Memory Verse(s):
> **2 Tim. 3:16,17**

Devotion:
> BSAF on **John 16:7,8,13**; **Heb. 4:12**; **Gal. 6:1**. Do one a day.

Put-Off/Put-On:
> Study **Eph. 4:22-32**. Make a list of your failures to respond biblically.

Reference: [Adams2]

8.2. Prerequisites to Biblical Change

Four Stages of Spiritual Development

I. Born-Again Stage is the new birth, new life—eternal life from above.

- (**John 1:12**) Child of God, God is now the Father of our spirits.

- (**Phil. 2:12-13**) Salvation is not just a destination change. It is the beginning stage of the development of a new life. We were the slaves of Satan, but now we are children of God, joint-heirs with Jesus. Accordingly, we are to resist the residual evil tendencies of the old life by submitting the natural life to the spiritual life on a continuous basis until we "become like little children" (**Matt. 18:3**). Takes a moment to be born-again from above, but a lifetime to work out being conformed to the image of Our Lord.

- (**1 John 2:3-6; John 14:21**) To obey is to really hear, to really listen, to see, and to understand what I listened to, and to act upon what I heard. If we are obeying, we will walk as Jesus walked.

- (**1 Cor. 3:16**) Obedience builds the temple. Doing the word are the bricks of the temple making it suitable for God to dwell in it.

II. Spiritual Stage is knowing the fulness of the Holy Spirit, being fully empowered to live the christian life.

- (**Luke 11:13**) Simply ask and receive.

- (**Luke 24:48-49**) Receive power from on high.

- (**Acts 1:8**) When the Holy Spirit comes upon you, you will receive power to be His witnesses.

- (**1 Cor. 6:17**) One spirit with Him. You are a co-worker.

- (**Rom. 5:5**) Love is poured out into our hearts when acted upon by faith. Love is ready to flow out as a river of living waters. From obedience faith, hope and love flows.

III. Pathway of the Cross Stage is a daily exercise of getting down into the death of Christ, to allow Christ to live out His life through us.

- **(Rom. 6:3-6)** Old nature buried, no longer slaves of sin. As we put-off daily sins, we arise immediately in the newness of life in Christ and able to respond biblically to all of life's encounters.

- **(Eph. 4:22-24)** We must do the doing: putting-off corruptions— renewing ourselves in the spirit of our minds—and putting-on truth in all areas of living. Daily, we have our calvary, our resurrection, and our ascension.

- **(Luke 9:23-24)** No longer defend or protect self, but practice death to private aims, selfish passions and prejudices, to worldly reputation and honor.

- **(Phil. 2:3-5)** As with Jesus, now I am to seek the interests and betterment of others. I am no longer central but to use self to be a blessing to others.

IV. Ascension/Overcomer/Spiritual Warfare Stage is where the believer realizes and knows he is in union with Christ.

- **(Eph. 1:17-23)** We are seated with Him "far above all authority..."

- **(Luke 10:19)** Given all authority over the power of the enemy.

- **(Rom. 8:29; 1 John 3:8)** God created us to be conformed to the image of His Son, and as such, to do as He did: to destroy the works of the devil.

- **(Col. 2:13-15)** Our problem is not with Satan, he has been defeated. The issue is our relationship with God, knowing who and what we are in Christ Jesus. Therefore, we are to keep the enemy from having any footholds in our lives by being free in the following areas: **(James 4:6-8)**

- o **Genealogy**: (**Gal. 3:13-14**) Realize and know that the Blood of Jesus has freed us from all generation curses (**Exodus 18:20**).

- o **Circumstances of life**: (**Matt. 16:24-25**; **Col. 1:10-11**) No longer react to or controlled by the externals of life, by personal attacks, by pressures of the world, by trials and tribulations, but respond by and according to the promptings and power of the Holy Spirit (**James 1:2-4**).

- o **Environment**: (**1 John 2:15**; **2 Pet. 1:4**) Partaker of the divine life and nature, and have escaped from the world's system of lusts. The devil has nothing on us. We are now in the position to overcome him in all areas of life in the name of Jesus Christ. To the extent we grow in virtues, to that extent Christ inhabits our lives.

The Characteristics of an Overcomer

- • (**Eph. 3:9-10**) Proclaims God's wisdom to the enemy: for this is a battle of wisdom.
- • (**Phil. 1:11**) Do all to the honor and praise of God that His glory may be both manifested and recognized.
- • (**Prov. 24:10**) Nothing can ever limit or defeat us in Christ. We proceed until victory prevails.
- • (**Prov. 21:22**) No compromises: we ascend, we assault, and cast down all opposition.
- • (**Luke 11:20-23**; **1 John 4:4**; **Isa. 9:6**) We move from strength to strength for there is no end to God's kingdom. We are commissioned to establish His Kingdom of peace and joy on earth.

Being an overcomer we accomplish God's purposes for our lives by being conformed to the image of His Son. We do as He did, walk as He did: do all to destroy the works of the devil in ourselves and in others.

Work Out Your Salvation (Phil. 2:12-13)

Memory Verse(s):

1 Cor. 10:13

Devotion:

BSAF on **Rom. 12:1-2**; **Gal. 5:16-17**.

Put-Off/Put-On:

Review sample list (below) and **Eph. 4:22-32**. Note problems you are experiencing that God wants you to work on during this course. Work out one problem at a time by using **Appendix A.4, "Victory over Sin Worksheet"**.

Sample list of problems to help you decide problem areas: adultery, anger, anorexia, bulimia, evil talk, depression, lack of discipline, fear, fornication, greed, guilt, homosexuality, impatience, laziness, gluttony, loneliness, lust, lying, marriage problems, pride, procrastination, rebellion, self-pity, substance abuse, worry, bitterness, frustration, stealing, child discipline problems, jealousy, envy, frustration, stealing, interpersonal conflicts and disputes.

95

8.3. Why There is Hope

Your Hope in the Midst of Trials

1. **Those in Christ are freed from the power and penalty of sin (Rom. 6:3-7,14,18,23).** The past is dealt with once and forever. To listen to the past is to listen to demons, and to dishonor the Blood of Christ (**Heb.l0:10,14-22**). We are to give our time and effort to the present.

2. **God will not allow believers to be tested or tempted beyond what they can bear.** He gives His grace and strength to endure every test and resist every temptation so that you never have to sin (**Rom. 8:35-39; 1 Cor. 10:13; 2 Cor. 4:7-10; 2 Cor. 12:9-10; Phil. 4:13; Heb. 4:15-16; 2 Pet. 2:4-9**).

3. **Our Lord Jesus Christ will grant mercy and provide grace to help in every need.** He constantly intercedes as an advocate for you to God the Father and fully understands your weaknesses (**Heb. 2:18; Heb. 4:15-16; Heb. 7:25; Rom. 5:10; John 20:23**). Don't defend self when treated unfairly, or suffering injustices. As your advocate, let Jesus handle evil done to you on earth. Our job is to love our enemies, do good to those who persecute you, to express goodwill to them: put them in the hands of God; pray that they may receive spiritual blessings in Christ (**Rom. 12:19**).

4. **Trials and testings will develop and mature you in Christ** if you respond to them in God's way (**Rom. 5:3-5; James 1:2-4**). He never devises evil or harm for you, rather His plans for you are for good (**Gen. 50:20; Deut. 8:2,5,16; Ps. 145:17; Jer. 29:ll-13; Rom. 8:28-29; Prov. 24:10; Prov. 21:22**).

5. **God's peace and joy are available to believers** regardless of others, possessions or circumstances (**Luke 6:35-38; Matt. 6:33; Rom. 5:3-12; John 14:27; John 15:11; John 17:13; Rom. 14:17; Phil. 4:4-7; 1 Pet. 1:6-9**). Follow God's will, His word which is His righteousness and the Kingdom of God is yours to proclaim. We reign in life through righteousness.

6. **Only God can change people (Ezek. 36:26-27; Phil. 1:6; Phil. 2:13).** You cannot and are not responsible for changing others. You are accountable to God solely for your own deeds (**Jer. 17:10; Ezek. 18:1-20;** especially verse

20; **Matt. 16:27**; **Rom. 2:5-10**; **Col. 3:23-25**; **1 Pet. 1:17**), and are to do your part in living at peace with others (**Matt. 5:23-24**; **Mark 11:25**; **Rom. 12:9-21**; **Rom. 14:19**; **1 Pet. 3:8-9**; **1 Pet. 4:8**).

7. **When you confess your sins, God forgives and cleanses you (1 John 1:7-9; Rom. 5:10; Heb. 7:22-25; Heb. 10:22-23**). Our job is to honor the Blood of Jesus by acting and proclaiming ourselves forgiven by His great sacrifice for us. To act guilty, condemned or self-pitying is to make the cross ineffective. Self-pity is negative pride.

As we follow God's way, walking in His word, living by His truths as so stated, we enter into His promises of an abundant life now, here on earth, as well as in eternity (**1 Cor. 6:17**; **John 5:24**; **John 4:24**; **John 10:10**).

Work Out Your Salvation (Phil. 2:12-13)

Memory Verse(s):

John 16:33: Meditate on this verse, read and listen to it carefully, mull it over until you really understand. We are 'overcomers' in Christ. It is about time, we begin to replace evil with righteousness.

Note: During the meditating process, seek others interpretation of the verse, ask Holy Spirit to reveal deeper meaning, etc.. For example, on the memory verse, Jesus on the Cross exclaimed: "It is Finished!" To me this verse means that Satan is defeated, I am no longer in union with Satan, my sins are forgiven, I am set free from the world, the flesh and the devil, I am complete in Christ, I am an overcomer in Christ, now in Christ I can work through all the trials, tests and temptations of life and overcome them because Jesus overcame the world so can I in Him. When I do sin, I confess and I am immediately cleansed and I begin to praise Him for His great sacrifice (**1 John 1:9**).

Devotion:

BSAF on **Heb. 6:19-20**.

Put-Off/Put-On:

Continue working on 'problem areas' via **Appendix A.4, "Victory over Sin Worksheet"**.

97

Reference: See page 99, [BCF1] for further readings.

8.4. Effecting Biblical Change

Approach to Problems

Feelings

(**Matt. 12:33-37**) We are the sum of what we encountered in life and our reactions to these events. Being conditioned by life's experiences, we are prone to react to life impulsively and instinctively rather than to respond on the basis of considered judgment. Man's words and manner of speech reveal his inner life, his focus, and who and what determines his peace and joy (**1 John 2:3-6**; **Matt. 5:44**; **Gal. 5:19-21**; **Col. 3:5-9**).

"Separated from God, fallen man became a flesh person, living from the created flesh as the source and center of life. In the realm of creature flesh, man searched for the meaning of life within his brains, intellects, memories, emotions, feelings and passions, which all exists in the organs of his body." [Smith4] He looked to himself—self-interest, self-protection, self defensiveness—for the means to survive which became the meaning and purpose of his life: traits that characterizes fallen man.

Man thus becomes vulnerable to what others have done or failed to do to make him secure—it is the fault of others. This state of apprehension opens the door to self-pity, fear, worry, anger, bitterness, jealousy, despair, depression and the like... All these reactions are 'feelings', and 'feelings' are fertile areas in which Satan operates and upon which he feeds (**Gen. 4:7**).

Doing

(**John 14:21**; **James 1:22-25**) Residuals of the fallen life exist in our members: the self-defensive, self-interest, self-protective life mechanisms. We are responsible to deal with these areas in which feelings initiate reactions rather than being prompted by the word of God. Regardless of feelings, we are to do what God's word says to do: practicing loving our enemies, being kind to those who hate you, blessing those who curse you, and praying for those who insult you. By God's grace, you will eventually change maliciousness and retaliation to compassion and benevolence. Anything done without faith, without reference to God's word is sin (**James 4:17**; **Eph. 4:29**; **Rom. 2:6-9**; **John 3:21**; **1 John 2:3-6**; **Prov. 1:22-31**; **Rom. 8:13**; **Luke 6:27-31**).

Root

(**2 Cor. 5:17**) Our responses or reactions to life reflect our true roots—the source of our being. The essence or substance of a man are his thoughts, his speech and his actions. Here we can identify the sin patterns and strongholds developed over the years that characterize the lifestyle and personality of the individual. Be aware of the 'body'. It is not an entity unto itself, but the body is God's vehicle to establish His Kingdom on earth. Accordingly, through our body, our thoughts, our speech, our actions are to reflect the taproot—the character of Christ Himself.

Category of root problems are many: hypocrisy, manipulation, lying, cheating, stealing, boasting, blame shifting, self-centeredness, self-protection, self-interest, anger, impatience, self-pity, lust, immorality, greed, malice, deceit, and the like—a life characterized by self being on the throne of life.

- **Key:** We establish godly roots by changing 'I' to 'We', you in union with Christ. This begins with the new birth, followed by daily renewal of the mind as we begin to confront life on the basis of God's word (**2 Cor. 10:3-5**; **Gal. 5:22-23**; **2 Pet. 1:3-8**; **Eph. 4:22-24**; **Col. 3:10**).

Approach to Solutions

1. Perspective

(**Isa. 55:8-9**; **Prov. 14:12**) We are to look at life from God's perspective, His view, not from our way, experiences, ideas, opinions, what others say, the world's philosophy or its psychology. The basic problem and the supreme challenge you will face in making Christ-honoring changes is dying to self. The biblical perspective concerning 'self' is exactly opposite to what the wisdom of this world proclaims (**Luke 9:23-24**). Accordingly, to live biblically is to respond to life's challenges in a manner that pleases and honors God—no longer pleasing and gratifying self (**1 Cor. 3:19-20**; **1 John 2:15-17**; **1 Cor. 2:12-13**; **1 John 2:20,27**).

2. Hope

(**Heb. 6:18-20**) Hope is an anchor of the soul because it affects our mind and emotions. Christ within me, the Anointed One, breaks the yoke of life's pressures on me. My job is to develop this inner image of Christ within me, that in Him, I am more than a conqueror, never under but always over circumstances, no matter what I face in life. To really believe this in the inner core of my being that all God's promises are mine depends upon my living in and by the living word of God (**John 16:33**; **James 1:2-4**).

(**Ezek. 36:26-27**) God gave me a heart of flesh, put His Spirit within me. He gives me power to carry out His commands.

(**1 Cor. 2:12-13**) Being a child of God, I receive revelation knowledge by the word of God in and through my human spirit.

(**Rom. 8:28-29**) No matter what happens to me in life when I call upon God He will intervene in my life. He will reach into my experiences, redeem my past, and cause things to work out for my benefit.

(**1 Cor. 10:13**) God is the One who is faithful. As I put my faith in Him, He will bring me out successfully.

(**Heb. 4:15-16**; **Heb. 7:25**) All I have to do is ask boldly, and God's grace is available to me. The blood of Jesus Christ intercedes always, washing and cleansing from all sense of guilt and shame whether real or imaginary.

(**Rom. 6:3-6**) My old human nature and all my past has been buried with Christ when I was baptized into His death. At the burial I was also raised with Him into the newness of life, freed from the power of sin, and free now to do acts of righteousness.

3. Change

(**Gen. 4:7**; **Eph. 5:14-16**) We must choose to change. We cannot take living for granted, being careless or casual about our thinking, speaking and acting. God put us on this earth to actively replace evil with righteousness.

(**Matt. 7:1-5**; **1 Cor. 11:28-31**) Critical that I judge myself daily, that I am walking in the Spirit, responding to life God's way: Then I will be in the position to help restore others.

(**Rom. 12:1-2**) My total being belongs to the Lord for His use. This requires a total overhaul of my person, separating myself from my past, the world's system and influences in order to be conformed to the ways of the Lord.

(**Eph. 4:25-32**; **Col. 3:5-17**; **Rom. 12:9-21**; **1 Pet. 2**; **1 Pet. 3**) Listed in these references are the basic put-offs and put-ons to guide and lead one to live a biblical lifestyle.

(**Rom. 8:29**; **1 John 3:8**) Examine self daily to see if I am living by God's standards for that day, being a blessing and destroying the works of the devil.

4. Homework—Working Out Your Salvation

(**Ps. 1:1**; **John 15:5**) The enemy never stops working, which compels us to be completely dependent upon the Lord 24 hours a day. We are to be always conscious of His Presence—to be actively involved in the pursuit of establishing His righteousness in all of life's endeavors.

(**James 1:21-25**) Through the meditation process, we change our inner man, the root. From the godly root, God prompts our thoughts, our speech, and our actions. This continues until we experience the fulness of God and express His Presence wherever we go.

(**Eph. 4:22-24**; **1 John 2:3-5**) We are to identify areas that need changing, being specific to identify put-offs and appropriate put-ons.

Work Out Your Salvation (Phil. 2:12-13)

Memory Verse(s):
>   **Josh. 1:8**

Devotion:
>   BSAF on **Eph. 4:25-32**.

Put-Off/Put-On:
>   Continue working on failures and complete columns 1 through 4
>   on **Appendix A.4, "Victory over Sin Worksheet"**. Review the
>   change verses above especially **Eph. 4:25-32**; **Rom. 12:9-21**; **1**
>   **Pet. 2** and **1 Pet. 3**. Preview **Appendix A.2, "Think and Do**
>   **List"**.

8.5. Dealing with Self

Marriage Concept

(**Gen. 2:7**; **Phil. 3:8**) God formed man out of the dust of the ground. By God's breath, man received consciousness, a capacity to think, and an awareness of his environment and surroundings. Man's very being depends solely upon God. Man without God is nothing.

(**Gen. 1:26-28**) God created mankind, Adam and Eve, as one entity. Mankind is mated to God and through the imaging process to be the revelators of God's love to the world. God blessed them, and endued them with power to be prosperous in all areas of living. All that was required was for man to voluntarily stay mated and submitted to God's authority—His word.

(**Eph. 5:21**) Both husband and wife, as separate entities, are subject to the Lord first, then to one another. By this act of obedience, recognizing God as Creator and Sustainer, they would merge into one flesh. The concept of marriage applies to the Body of Christ as His bride being merged into one by obedience—individually and collectively.

Loss of Image

(**Gen. 3:1-6**) Man tested to choose to be dependent upon God or to be independent—to become their own gods. The desire that was put into them to please God, now turned to lust to please themselves. Becoming gods they looked to themselves for resources to handle life, to find within themselves wisdom, strength, and ability to understand and control life in all its manifestations. By this choice, as they changed from self-loving-others to self-loving-self, fear became their constant companion.

Self Promotion

(**Gen. 3:7-10**) Reverential fear and awe of God and His magnificence changed to fear of punishment and a concern for the survival of the self. All man had to do was look to God, obey His word, and God would take care of everything else. Separated from God man has to look to himself for security, God no longer there to provide. Man now looks horizontally to find acceptance and approval by performing and impressing others how great he is, by controlling others, by seeking power over others, by wealth, by position. Man is always seeking to find the meaning of life within himself: when the meaning of life can only be found by manifesting the glory of God in his behavior.

Remarriage

(**Luke 9:23-24**) By and through the Cross of Christ, we are enabled to resume the original relationship with God before the fall. By the cross, we are freed from the self-loving-self and become the self-loving-others, expressing the glory of God in our behavior to others.

(**Eph. 4:22-24**) We are all conditioned by life's experiences. We are the sum of all that we encountered in life. Our culture, our environs, our circumstances in life have impacted our lives and has affected our reactions. Thus, our coping mechanisms are sensitized to cover and protect the self in competition with others. The answer to this worldly, fleshly self is to study our union with Jesus Christ, and this by the daily putting-off of the corrupted self and the putting-on of the new self by the renewing of the mind.

Battleground

(**Gal. 5:16-26**; **Prov. 28:13**; **Jer. 17:9**; **Rom. 6:12-13**) You will face constant temptations to self centeredness that leads to thoughts, speech, and actions that are devastating to the Body of Christ and your own walk with the Lord. Those sins that characterized your life apart from Christ must be confessed and repented of if you are to mature as a child of God.

(**Eph. 1:3-14**; **Matt. 7:12**) Man's problem is that he pays too much attention to himself, not too little. We already know how we want others to treat us. Thus, we are commanded to treat others the same way with the focus on the other and not on self. God has given to us all we need or want. There is nothing we should seek for ourselves but to exercise who and what we are in Christ Jesus.

Intimacy

(**Rom. 8:14-17**; **1 Cor. 1:26-31**; **Matt. 5:16**) A proper view of self comes from an understanding of who you are in Christ: that God is actively involved in your life, that He has chosen you to be a testimony of His power to the world, and that He gives you a purpose for living by conforming you to the image of His Son.

(**Gen. 4:7**; **John 14:21**; **John 15:10-11**; **2 Cor. 4:7-10**; **2 Cor. 4:16-17**; **Matt. 6:33**) Your contentment in all circumstances of life is dependent on your obedient responses to God in your thoughts, speech, and actions. By obeying the Lord in your daily walk, this demonstrates the Lordship of God over your life. The sense of value, of worthiness, of self-esteem comes by first seeking His Kingdom and His righteousness.

(**Rom. 6:3-4**; **Rom 6:13-14**; **Col. 3:5-11**; **1 Pet. 2:11-12**) Envy, jealousy, covetousness, and greed reveal a self-focus that questions God's work and provision in your life. These sins must be put-off out of your commitment to live for Jesus Christ.

(**2 Tim. 3:2-7**; **2 Pet. 2:1-3**) In latter days, we will be lovers of self, led on by various impulses, always learning and never able to come to the knowledge of the truth. Being a hearer only, you will be deluded.

Bearing His Image

(**Col. 1:10**; **1 John 3:8**; **Phil. 2:12-13**) Daily walking in Christ, committing our will to please God, being fruitful, increasing in the knowledge of God, strengthened in His power, these changes in lifestyle give evidence that we are a child of God. As such, the potential of Christ resides within you always ready to be a blessing, destroying the works of the devil, and to reign in life through righteousness.

Work Out Your Salvation (Phil. 2:12-13)

Memory Verse(s):
> **Luke 9:23-24,** meditate on this verse.

Devotion:
> BSAF on **Eph. 4:26-27,29**.

Put-Off/Put-On:
> Review **Gal. 5:19-21**; **Col. 3:5-13**. Check out sinful thinking patterns. Work through **Appendix A.2, "Think and Do List"** to change these patterns and establish right thinking, and right doing.

Reference: Chapter 9 of [BCF1]; and [Smith1].

Attachment: Continual Self-Evaluation

(**Matt. 7:5**; **Eph. 4:29**; **Matt. 5:16**) In biblically evaluating your thoughts, words, or actions in any situation, answer the following questions. You should memorize both the questions and the references verses.

1. Is this profitable? In other words, does this contribute toward the development of godly traits or help to accomplish biblical responsibilities in my life or in the lives of others? (**1 Cor. 6:12**; **1 Cor. 10:23**)

2. Does this bring me under its power or am I controlled by it in any way? (**1 Cor. 6:12**)

3. Is this an area of spiritual weakness (a stumbling block) in my life? (**Matt. 5:29-30**; **Matt. 18:8-9**)

4. Could this lead another brother in Christ to stumble? (**Rom. 14:13**; **1 Cor. 8:9-13**)

5. Does this edify (build up) others? Is this the biblically loving thing to do? (**Rom. 14:19**; **1 Cor. 10:23-24**)

6. Does this glorify God? (**Matt. 5:16**; **1 Cor. 10:31**)

Reference: Page 130, [BCF1].

8.6. Anger and Bitterness

We are the sum of what we experienced in life and our reactions to these experiences. To the extent we are offended, become angry and irritated, we are limited to that extent in our spiritual walk.

- (**Rom. 12:10-11; Gal. 6:1**) Our job is to restore, not to condemn or criticize, so that we can establish God's Kingdom of peace on earth by walking free of irritations, of criticism, of faultfinding, of blame shifting. This is accomplished by purity of heart, love and prayers for each other, consciousness of being in the spirit by faith (**Gal. 5:22-23**).

- (**Eph. 4:31-32; Gal. 6:14**) By an act of our will, we put-off sin, and by an act of the will we put-on being a blessing. No longer controlled by life's irritations, but we use these irritations as opportunities to reveal Christ within and to touch the other person(s).

- (**Matt. 12:34-35**) No one person or thing is the cause of your anger. The offense reveals the spirit that is in you. Sinful anger reveals that you are living to please self.

- (**Eph. 2:1-6**) Desires of the flesh and mind are inhabited by envy, jealousy, greed, and pride: the sources of anger. The enemy's job is to keep you occupied and earthbound by these selfish feelings. This will keep you from realizing the fulness of who and what you are in Christ Jesus.

- (**Rom. 5:3-5**) Anger and bitterness are two noticeable signs of being self-focused, and not trusting God's sovereignty in your life. Don't need to protect your 'rights', the defense of self. The very things that upset you, God will use to perfect and to motivate you to work through these tribulations, becoming a blessing instead of a curse.

- (**2 Pet. 1:4**) Being a partaker of the divine nature, working through the experiences of life God's way, we begin to realize that we are growing in Christ, and truly being freed from the corruption of this world.

- **(Matt. 5:16; Eph. 4:1-3)** Anger and bitterness are formidable obstacles to biblical love, harmonious relationships, and maturity in Christ. Failing to put off anger grieves the Holy Spirit and gives Satan a place in your life obscuring your witness to others, and disrupting unity in the Body of Christ. Dealing biblically with anger and bitterness requires wholehearted obedience to God's word in every circumstance and with every person, even if your feelings dictate otherwise.

- **(1 Pet. 1:13-16; Eph. 2:10; Phil. 3:13-14)** Anger and bitterness have no place in thought. We are to think dispassionately. The world lives by experiences, by reason, by feelings: but we are to live by faith. We are to live above experiences and reason. In order to think with security, we must think about thinking. A thinking person realizes who and what he is in Christ. He is above feelings and lives by his will based on the word of God. He fights a good fight of faith, not feelings, and he pursues excellencies being daily conformed to the image of Christ.

- **(Gen. 4:7; Prov. 24:10; Prov. 21:22)** You are responsible for controlling your spirit. Since God's word commands you to put away anger and bitterness, then it is possible to do so.

- **(Luke 9:23; Gal. 5:16-17)** Because of the ever-present temptation to live for self rather than to live for God, you must obey God's word, pray habitually, constantly depend on God's Spirit.

- **(Col. 1:10)** You are not to allow anger to get the upper hand and gain control of your mind or conduct, since Satan uses these opportunities to affect your life. You must live in a manner to please the Lord no matter how you feel.

- **(James 1:19-20)** Quick to listen means to be quick to ask questions, to get facts, to give time for the Holy Spirit to influence you: then you can act in a biblical manner.

Think Biblically

(**Phil. 4:8**; **Ps. 23:1-6**) We are to think biblically that God has promised to care for us in any situation, no matter how unsettling it may seem. Discipline your mind to honor and glorify God, to please Him in all situations. 'Think' kind and tender thoughts toward the very person with whom you are or have been irritated. Focus your thoughts on solving the current problem (**James 1:5**; **James 3:13-18**).

Speak Biblically

(**Ps. 51:1-4**; **James 5:16**; **1 John 1:9**; **Phil. 3:13-14**) We are to speak biblically, confess sins to the Lord and to those whom you have failed to love in a biblical manner. Don't talk about your past accomplishments, sorrows or defeats, hurts and pains but talk about the goodness of God in your life. Do not slander, gossip or use words that do not edify (**Prov. 10:18**; **Eph. 4:29**).

Act Biblically

(**Col. 3:13**; **James 1:21**) Forgive others readily as God has forgiven you. Meditate on Scriptures related to overcoming anger and bitterness to remove the root of the foul spirit within.

(**Ps. 1:1**) Identify all danger signals, such as situations, places and personal contacts that bring temptation.

(**Matt. 5:23-24**) Make amends for wrongdoing and seek reconciliation.

(**1 Pet. 3:8-9**) We are called to be a blessing especially to those who revile us.

Work Out Your Salvation (Phil. 2:12-13)

Memory Verse(s):
> **Eph. 4:26-27,29**

Devotion:
> BSAF on **Luke 6:27-31**.

Put-Off/Put-On:
> (**Phil. 4:5**) Gentleness means forbearing, large-hearted, courteous, generous, lenient, moderate. These are qualities which are opposite to irritability, rudeness, abrasiveness. To put on gentleness, ask self:
>
> 1. "What or whom are you most likely to be irritable? What is it about your surroundings that irritate you? About

yourself? About friends, associates, family? When are you most likely to be irritated? How do you express irritability?" (Homework Manual for Biblical Counseling, Wayne Mack.)

2. Make plans to deal with these situations in your thinking, speaking and acting patterns as described in the respective headings in the above paragraphs. See **Eph. 4:22-32** for communication guidelines on how to biblically respond.

3. **Note:** Do not suppress feelings of anger. Turn all offenses over to God the Father, let Him deal with the situation. Ask Him for grace to respond biblically (**1 Pet. 2:23**).

8.7. Depression

Perspective

- There are some organic malfunctions that may trigger feelings of depression. Most symptoms and maladies defined as depression are the consequences of unbiblical habits and/or sinful reactions to circumstances and other people. Depression may be experienced by anyone and must be dealt with from God's perspective and not from your own perspective or any other person's point of view.

(**Gen. 4:3-7**) God commands us by His word not to live by our feelings, but to decide by our will to respond in a manner which is pleasing in His sight. To react to please self is to be mastered by the reactions.

(**John 15:8-12**; **James 1:22-25**) Depression is not to be used as an excuse for you to live in an unbiblical manner. Even if you feel depressed, you are still to live biblically. Your thoughts, words, and actions are always to edify others and bring glory to God instead of just obeying God's word when you "feel like it."

(**Ps. 32:3-5**; **Ps. 38:1-10**; **Col. 3:25**) Symptoms defined as 'depression' are sometimes precipitated by sin which means you are living to please yourself instead of living to please the Lord. If you do not repent, confess your self-centeredness and return to living in a biblical manner, you will experience even further difficulties.

(**1 Pet. 3:10-12**; **Rom. 8:11-14**; **Heb. 4:15-16**) To love life and see good days, you must turn from doing evil and be obedient to God's word. In spite of 'feeling' depressed, you can live biblically because of divine resources that God graciously provides for you. By faith, be in the spirit, see self in the Throne room looking at life from God's perspective (**Gal. 5:16**; **Rom. 8:2**). Pursue peace and harmony, run after it, flee from fear, agitating passions, and immorality (**Ps. 23:1,6**).

(**Rom. 14:17-18**; **1 John 4:18-21**; **Phil. 4:6-7**) The way you feel and the way you view yourself, your relationships, and your circumstances are often indications of whether you are living to please yourself or living to please the God. It is not the world or things of the world that should occupy our thoughts and time: but are you approaching life from God's perspective, living and thinking God's word. Fear, darkness, depression reveal an absence of loving God and your neighbor. It is our thinking which refuses to be taught by Christ or anyone else. This spirit exalts itself against God—the spirit of antichrist.

Hope

(**John 16:33**; **Rom. 5:3-5**; **1 Cor. 10:13**) No matter how difficult any situation appears, the Lord Jesus Christ has overcome it. God will not allow anything into your life that is beyond His control or beyond your ability to handle it without sinning. Trials are for your good, they will bring out the power of God in your life when you respond biblically.

(**1 Pet. 1:6-7**; **2 Cor. 4:7-10**) All the terrible things that are happening to you are but 'light afflictions'. Look beyond the circumstances and see God in control, perfecting and maturing you for an eternal destiny.

Change

(**1 Tim. 4:7-11**; **Rom. 6:11,13,19**) All that I am, my talents, my time belong to the Lord. A good steward is one who starts with God and from God. He puts off disobedience to God's word, and puts on living a disciplined and obedient life out of a consistent desire to please the Lord instead of self. Persistency is the key, it takes sweat and tears to break lifelong habit patterns.

(**Matt. 7:1-5**; **2 Cor. 10:3-5**; **Col. 3:2,5-9**) In order to put off sinful habits, you must first identify them by examining your life in light of God's word. Once you have identified sins, repent, confess, and immediately put these sins aside.

(**Gal. 5:16**; **Eph. 3:16-21**; **1 Pet. 4:11**) As you put on righteous deeds in the power of the Holy Spirit, you glorify God and demonstrate your love for Him. We are to do regardless of how we feel. Be conscious of and practice the Presence of Christ within at all times.

Practice

(**Eph. 5:14-18**; **James 4:17**; **Col. 3:17,23-24**) Establish a biblical schedule for fulfilling your God given responsibilities, keeping the schedule regardless of feelings of depression you may experience. Do all your work heartily as unto the Lord for His glory.

(**2 Cor. 4:10-12**; **Matt. 20:26-28**; **Phil. 2:3-7**) Stop living to please self by following God's commandments. Regard others as more important than yourself, be a servant to God and others.

(**2 Cor. 12:7-10**; **Eph. 5:20**; **Heb. 12:1-2**; **Rev. 12:11**) Do not be bitter about your conditions. Thank God for your circumstances or physical condition that you cannot correct. But correct all deficiencies in your life that hinder you from serving God and others. Share your sufferings with the Lord and deepen your faith.

(**1 Cor. 11:31**; **Eph. 4:29**; **Col. 4:6**; **2 Cor. 10:5**; **James 1:25**) Biblical self-evaluation is necessary in every area of your life which includes your actions, your relationships with others, your words and your thought life. As you obey God's word in all areas of your life, you will receive the Lord's blessings.

Work Out Your Salvation (Phil. 2:12-13)

Memory Verse(s):

> **Gen. 4:7**

Devotion:

> BSAF on **Phil. 4:4**.

Put-Off/Put-On:

> Complete **Appendix A.11, "Scheduling Worksheet"**, and begin to re-evaluate your use of time and talents to do what God wants you to do. Ask God to help you do what you should do regardless of how you feel, and plan a schedule which gives you time to do all that you must do. Then get busy fulfilling your responsibilities. Make a "think and do" list of profitable things (**Appendix A.2, "Think and Do List"**) you can think about and do when you are tempted to be despondent. Compare **Phil. 4:8-9**.

> List your abilities and gifts, see **Rom. 12**. Prepare a list of specific ways in which you can serve God and other people.

> Study the following verses and list things that could be circumstantial causes for depression: **Ps. 32:3-4**; **Ps. 73:1-14**; **Gen. 4:6-7**; **Ps. 55:2-8**; **Luke 24:17-21**; **2 Sam. 18:33**; **1 Sam. 1:7-8**; **Habakkuk 1:1-4**.

Reference: Page 319, [BCF1].

8.8. Fear and Worry

- **Fear** invades and underlies the whole of life's activities such as: fear of failure, of change, of success, of rejection, of being abandoned, of loneliness, of the future, of the unknown and the endless list of phobias.

(**Gen. 3:9-10; 1 John 4:18**) Fear is the first emotion expressed by man, and the first emotion dealt with by the Cross of Christ. Fear is replaced by love, faith works by love, love action destroys the feelings of fear.

(**Heb. 3:12-13**) Main causes of fear are self-concerns, self-interest and self-protection. Fear is really unbelief that Christ is not living within you.

- Fear, worry, anxiety along with anger, bitterness, resentment, guilt, envy, and other sins are just feelings. How do we overcome them? It is by faith—acting on God's word by one's will, an act of love, that supersedes feelings.

(**Gen. 4:7; Gen. 15:1**) When God commands us to "Fear Not!", He is addressing our will and our mind, not our emotions. You work through fear by an act of your will because God is with you, willing you to love. Love casts out all fear (**1 John 4:18**).

(**Gen. 1:26-28**) God commands us to replenish and to subdue. Fear is a necessary part of our design. Fear tells me something or someone who appears bigger than I am is approaching and affecting my mind and my emotions. Fear is a red light that tells us danger is about—to signal us to call upon God and in Him to face the fear—swallow it up and go on to the next thing. We are to replace the fear with a deliberate trust and rest in God who lives in us, drawing upon Him for wisdom, strength and ability. Thus, fear triggers one more way in which God is manifested and revealed in our behavior.

(**Rom. 12:1-2**) Most of us have a belief bank full of junk. We are to renew the mind, get the junk out, and replace it with thoughts of God's Presence. He is my Light, my Salvation, whom shall I fear: for He will give me all I need as I seek His righteousness.

(**Ps. 42:1-11**) Talk to self, tell self who God is, rehearse this reality and fear will properly disappear. For God can now be revealed in the situation.

(**Ps. 23**; **Ps. 24**; **Ps. 27**; **Ps. 91**; **Deut. 28**) Feelings only obey what I think. If despair, then despair comes, if fearful then more of the same, etc.. Truth in God must be learned, that I know within that He is my strength, my adequacy, my wisdom, that His angels are all about me! We control fear by believing the truth in God.

(**Heb. 13:20-21**) God is with me at all times, He will never leave nor forsake me. God loves me, accepts me and approves of me regardless of what others say or think.

(**Matt. 5:43-44**; **1 John 2:9-10**) Regardless of what others do or not do, be always in a state of forgiving offenses, develop a permanent state of reconciliation. Choose to love, develop this disposition to love. It takes time for this idea to grow and develop into the image of Christ because it is what Jesus did. Our blueprint states that we were made to love, otherwise life does not work.

(**1 John 3:17**) Love is an action, activated by compassion. We don't have to pray about it, just do it! Don't have to ask for God's help, Holy Spirit is already in us. It is our choice to respond God's way allowing His love to be manifested.

(**Phil. 4:13**; **2 Cor. 12:7-9**) Fear is part of living. We will always fear changes, new situations, and a sense of inadequacy will surround all situations. All this does is reveal the creatureness of my being and to remind me that I can't handle anything in my own strength and wisdom. Rejoice that you can't handle it because in each and every circumstance that you call upon the Lord who is your strength, the more and more you grow into Him.

(**1 Cor. 1:30**) By faith and not by feelings, call upon the Lord and ask Him that His thoughts become your thoughts, His strengths your strengths, His adequacy your adequacy. This is what is called a normal christian life.

(**Prov. 24:10**; **Prov. 21:22**) With diligence and perseverance you can be victorious in all new situations and changes that life offers. The enemy will challenge your growth. Use the barriers he sets up as opportunities to strengthen your faith until you become perfect and complete, lacking in nothing.

(**John 14:21**; **John 16:33**) He will guide us into the unknown, new territories, new ideas, new situations, and new revelations. Look forward to great opportunities to reveal your potential in Christ. Areas that frighten, God has already given them to us in Christ. As with Moses with just a staff in hand, go with whatever you have in hand, and see miracles.

(**1 John 1:9**; **1 Cor. 13:4-8a**; **Col. 3:12-14**; **2 Cor. 5:14-15**; **Phil. 4:6-9**; **1 John 4:18**) In order to deal biblically with fear, you must confess your self-centered fear to God and fulfill your responsibilities in Christlike love regardless of your feelings.

(**Matt. 6:33**; **Matt. 25:26**; **Prov. 16:9**; **Eph. 5:15-17**; **Col. 3:23-24**) Worry is wickedness and laziness, reveals a lack of trust in God. To overcome worry, make a plan to accomplish today's task and do each task heartily as unto the Lord.

Work Out Your Salvation (Phil. 2:12-13)

Memory Verse(s):
> **1 John 4:18**

Devotion:
> BSAF on **1 John 4:18**; **John 16:33**; **John 15:5**.

Put-Off/Put-On:
> Review **Appendix A.8, "Freedom from Anxiety"**, follow the instructions to deal biblically with any problem you may have. Expect and look for miracles.

Reference: [Smith2]

Part II.c. Basic Study: Strengthening Your Marriage

Table of Contents

Chapter 9. Strengthening Your Marriage Series

Table of Contents

9.1. Marriage—God's Plan to Establish His Kingdom on Earth

Reference: "Life in the Spirit", by D. Martin Lloyd-Jones; **Eph. 5:18-6:9**.

> Doctrine/Principles: **Eph. 1:1-4:21**
> Application/Practice: **Eph. 4:22-32**
> Text: **Eph. 5:22-33**

God's Objectives

(**Hosea 4:6-7**; **Matt. 6:9-13**) Ignorance allows Satan to control our lives, to control our families, and to establish his kingdom of evil on this earth through us. Whereas, God has given us His authority to establish His kingdom and His will on earth.

(**2 Tim. 3:16-17**; **Heb. 5:14-16**; **James 1:2-4**) Through skillful use of God's word, by faith in His word, we become overcomers. No longer controlled by our genealogy, environment, nor by the circumstances of life, but we become complete, influenced by the Spirit, lacking in nothing.

(**Prov. 1:7-9**) Accordingly, parents are to apply God's principles, to be examples, to multiply righteousness and to exercise dominion over this earth system. This experience qualifies us to rule and reign in eternity.

(**Gen. 1:28**; **Gen. 2:24**; **Gal. 6:1,4-5**) Family is the basic training unit, an excellent classroom for teaching, a birthplace for creativity, a formation center for human relationships, a shelter in a storm, and a perpetual relay unit of truth passed on from one generation to the next. To establish God's truths as demonstrated in family living is the prime role of husband and wife.

(**Malachi 4:5-6**; **Eph. 6:11-13**) For congregations, for the Body of Christ, to increase their abilities to stand, holy and strong, families must be restored according to God's principles.

Perspectives for Biblical Change in Family Dynamics

The following principles are foundational to our christian walk, and are to underline all our thoughts and reasonings, especially in dealing with marital and family situations.

(**John 14:21**; **Matt. 21:28-31**) We worship and demonstrate our love for God by obeying His word.

(**John 3:21**; **Matt. 7:24**) By deeds, not by feelings, we reveal our love. Remember, the old self gets its life from feelings (a fertile area in which Satan receives his food). Give him no ground.

(**John 14:27**; **John 15:11**; **John 16:22-24**) Our peace and joy are not dependent upon others, on things, on possessions or on circumstances of life but only on doing what God says to do.

(**Ezek. 18:20**) Not dependent upon or controlled by what others do or not do, God is to be the Lord and director of our lives.

(**Matt. 7:1-5**) The only authority I have to judge is to judge and to change myself first: then, I can help and influence others.

(**Rom. 8:28**) Whatever happens in life, if I biblically respond, God will turn the situation to my advantage.

(**2 Tim. 2:23-26**; **Deut. 8:2**) Irritation is a signal that I must change. The situation or the other person does not create my spirit, but only reveals what is in my heart.

Work Out Your Salvation (Phil. 2:12-13)

Memory Verse(s):
> **Matt. 7:5**

Counseling Exercises

Becoming a doer of the Word requires:

- **Devotions:** Daily contact with God the Father for spiritual life and sustenance (**Matt. 4:4**; **John 15:5**). See **Appendix A.12, "Anchor Posts"**.

- **Changes:** Daily examining one's walk and talk to insure a biblical response to life's confrontations (**Eph. 4:22-24**; **1 Cor. 11:26-32**)

- **Actions:** Separate self from the world and pursue the Lord's plan for your life in losing self by meeting needs of others, beginning with your family, and then the widow, the orphan, etc. (**1 John 2:15-17**; **Heb. 10:25**; **James 1:26-27**).

- **Recommended Reading:** Unit 1 of Strengthening Your Marriage [Mack1].

120

9.2. Principle of Authority

(**Gen. 2:16-17**) **Tree of Life:** Eternal life depends upon being subjected and being submitted to live according to God's word, His authority, and His ethical and moral principles—the supernatural life.

(**John 6:35**) **Tree of Knowledge Of Good and Evil:** Independent of God, who is life, not submitting to His authority, but relying on one's own conscious and deliberate capability to distinguish good from evil—the natural life.

Choice: Man given power and ability to choose, to submit to authority or not. The act of choosing is what makes man truly human. In **Gen. 3:6**, God's chain of authority was violated. The act of submitting voluntarily in the Trinity, Adam to God, Eve to Adam is all necessary in order to complete man in God's image. Being God's representative on earth, man in union with his wife, are to establish God's kingdom and will on earth—the supernatural life of faith, hope and love.

Redemption Plan to Establish the Church

(**Gen. 3:15-16,20**) God's mercy and grace given to Eve to become the means of the redemptive process, "the mother of all living." Here, again, Eve is told to submit to Adam and Adam to exercise his authority.

(**Gen. 2:7,18**; **Gen. 2:22-24**) Man was made from earthly elements, woman was made from the substance of man—the ribs over man's heart.

Woman is of substance, mother of life, giver of life. Thus, she has greater spiritual dimensions and the depth necessary in order to make up the 'deficiencies' in man. Man is incomplete and needs woman to complete him in order to bring forth the church.

(**Eph. 5:22-25**; **1 Pet. 3:7**) Adam is the protector of life, given dominion. Man is to exercise control and authority to protect his wife from any harm whatsoever: because his very spiritual effectiveness depends on her.

(**2 Cor. 4:10-12**) Both husband and wife are to act in the redemptive process: daily dying to reactions of the flesh, meeting the other's needs, helping to remove the dross from one another, becoming one flesh in mind and spirit (See **Section 9.13, "What Makes a Man a Man"**).

(**Heb. 5:8-9**) Through suffering, we learn obedience, becoming perfect as Jesus (See **Section 5.2, "Sin, Self, Suffering"**).

Perspectives

(**Eph. 5:16-21**) Evil remains unless we replace it with righteous actions. Being drunk is being filled with the world's ideas, its philosophies (TV, movies, magazines, etc.), living by feelings, by worldly wisdom, reacting in the flesh instead of responding biblically in the power of the Holy Spirit.

(**Rom. 12:1-2; Eph. 4:22-24**) Commitment is critical, and it all begins in the mind. Push out and cast away the garbage of self, the world's ideas, and dwell and act on God's truths.

(**Phil. 2:3-4**) A christian is a person who is governed by thought, by understanding, by meditation and by developing a spirit of consideration for the honor and glory of God: and this by seeking the interest and welfare of others.

(**Eph. 1:17-23**) In the depths of our being, we are to know intimately who we are, what we are, and what we can do in Christ. He is our wisdom, our strength, and our ability. Dwelling on Christ, we begin to live by divine grace.

- In ourselves, we are thoughtless, selfish, self-centered, individualistic, self-assertive, opinionated, resentful of criticism, impatient of others' points of view, and tend to be dictatorial, hyper-sensitive and usually 'walk out' when things are not going our way.

- There is nothing in ourselves to boast of; we are all damned, all lost, all sinners. Thus, we are in a good condition to forego all personal rights and seek the development and enhancement of the whole and of every other part (See **Section 5.4, "Transforming the Natural Self"**).

(**John 13:12; John 14:21; Matt. 20-28**) Controlling principle is that Christ is the Lord of our lives. This is what rules and governs us: His life is our example. We are to be servants to one another because Jesus taught us to be. He gave His life, and in gratitude we keep His commandments that His name might be recognized and glorified by our behavior.

(**1 Cor. 3:11-13; Phil. 2:12-13**) Works and reasons outside of God's word are always based on fear. The human standard is the sense-ruled mind which results in fear, sickness, worry, bitterness, etc.. Cultivate the fear of offending God until every thought, every image, and every action is initiated by God Himself.

(**1 Pet. 2:21-24**) We are to live this life not because it is the thing to do or because others are doing it, but because Jesus did it as an example for us to follow. As with Our Lord, we turn over all negatives: anger, bitterness, offenses, and the like to God. Now we are free in spirit to deal biblically with life's challenges.

(**Phil. 2:5-8**) Jesus' ultimate obedience, submission to the Father, even unto death, gives us the power and authority to do likewise as we submit one to the other, sacrificing our own needs to meet the needs of others.

(**Heb. 13:20-21**) A mind dominated by God's thoughts, nature and ways is a Word-ruled mind which is never prepared to fail because it is supernatural in content.

Work Out Your Salvation (Phil. 2:12-13)

Memory Verse(s):
> **Phil. 2:3-4** and meditate on this verse.

Put-Off/Put-On:
> Read **Appendix A.4, "Victory over Sin Worksheet"** and Unit 2 of Strengthening Your Marriage [Mack1], and make a list of failures noted in your readings.

9.3. Submission—Act of Bringing Forth Wholeness

Biblical Submission

To voluntarily place oneself under the Lordship of Jesus Christ so that He may live out His life in and through us, we use our endowed gifts and talents to be a blessing to others in order to establish His purposes on earth.

Thus, all of life, every person's actions, is to be characterized by a spirit of submission. We did not make ourselves. God made us to fulfill His purposes. Thus, God is the very source of our ability to even think, to speak, to act—our every breath comes from Him.

Therefore, by the power and provision of the Cross, as with the 1st Adam, we have the choice to partake of the Tree of Life—a taste of supernatural grace—which enables us to sacrifice our own interests in order to fulfill the needs of others: an act of self-donation.

Or we can choose to partake of the Tree of Knowledge of Good and Evil, to exercise natural grace, will-power and natural wisdom to find the meaning of life: being a god without God and His supernatural grace—a death process.

Since we all begin life with a fallen nature, we are to move from an independent spirit to a dependent one, one in submission to God and His word. And begin a life of submission as Our Lord who knew nothing and did nothing until He heard from His Father. We are to do likewise: "he who humbles himself shall be exalted" (See **Section 5.4, "Transforming the Natural Self"**).

Order and Harmony

(**Eph. 5:21-23**) It is the duty of all to submit one to another, but it is a special duty of the wife to submit to her husband. Not as a slave to him, but as a slave to Christ, submitting as an expression of her submission to the Lord—not for man's sake, but for the Lord's.

(**Gen. 1:26-28**; **Gen. 2:15-18**) Man was created first, made a lord of creation, put into position of leadership, authority and power to make decisions and rulings.

(**1 Pet. 3:7**) Because of his role, man was made physically stronger to equip him to guard, protect, honor and respect his wife. As head of the wife, and the head of the family, God endowed man with faculties and powers to fulfill his responsibilities.

(**Gen. 2:23-24**) God made woman to 'complement' man, to make up a 'deficiency' in man. Man is not only responsible for himself, but for his wife, for his family, and in all ultimate matters. Therefore, man needs help. His wife is to support him, to aid him in everything, to encourage, to exhort, and to console him, thus enabling him to function effectively as the lord of creation. God placed man into this position, this is not man's idea.

(**1 Tim. 2:11-15**; **Gen. 3:16**) Authority usurped, self placed as a god into leadership. After the fall, woman's subordination to man increased.

(**1 Cor. 11:3**) We are dealing with God's order of creation, not equality of man and woman. Order of creation is God's plan, not man's. Father, Son and Holy Spirit are co-eternal. But for the purpose of salvation, the Son subordinated Himself to the Father and the Holy Spirit to the Son and to the Father. Likewise, we are to be of the same spirit, fulfilling our roles in order to be the church, to bring forth salvation. Therefore, a woman voluntarily subordinates herself in order to complete man: to comfort, to strengthen, to encourage, to bring forth purposes of salvation. Man is to forsake his own interests in order to meet the needs of his wife.

Issue of Authority

ERA, unisex, feminism, the aggressiveness of woman challenges God's plan of creation. Today, there is the problem of authority and honor. People are losing respect. Loss of respect really starts in the home, in the marriage relationship. The family is the center of life and of society in order to perpetuate God's plan (restoring the principles of authority and submission) to bring about salvation for mankind.

Order of Creation

God ordered and ordained wives to submit to husbands who is the head of the wife as Jesus is the head of the church. Sin started with Satan challenging God's authority. Thus, original sin is being independent of God and being one's own god, which is rebellion; rebellion is as the sin of witchcraft.

- (**Eph. 1:19**) The greatness of His power is in us to bring about an organic and vital union and intimate relationship in the church body.
- (**Eph. 4:16**) One aspect of this union is the role of the wife depending upon and supporting the husband, causing growth of

the body, the union, building up itself in love. This is the true nature of the christian marriage—each building the other in love. It is one life, the same way as the life of the church in her relationship to the head which is Christ. Therefore, via dependence and submission, life is flowing. Dependence is related to submission necessitating a spirit of humility—each meeting the needs of the other. An independent spirit stops the life flow. Just as Christ nourishes and cherishes the church, so does the husband nourish and cherish his wife. Thus, as the wife submits, she gives life to her husband which enables him to keep, preserve, guard and shield his wife. To do otherwise is self-defeating.

- (**Gen. 2:22-24**) Woman was taken out of man, to be a helpmeet, to complement, to make up the wholeness and completeness of the head.

- (**1 Cor. 12:25**; **Rom. 12:14-17**) The wife is to husband what the body is to the head, what the church is to Christ. It is an organic, vital unity. Husband and wife are not two kingdoms related by a treaty, in a state of tension, subject to quarrels. The wife is never to be guilty of action independent of the husband, else chaos and confusion will result. The wife must not act before the husband. The initiative and leadership are ultimately the husband's, but the actions must always be coordinated. Coordinated action brings about 'one flesh' wholeness and completeness which is to be demonstrated to the world.

- (**1 Cor. 12:25-27**) As the church does in respect to the Lord, wife does to the husband, manifesting the essential spirit of christianity, building up one another in love. Each family is a unit, learning and training to build selves up in love, serving as examples to others, and helping other families.

Perspectives

(**Ezek. 18:20**; **John 16:8**) As the church is to Christ, so the wife is to her husband, that nobody should act against his or her conscience. Each is accountable for his or her own moral actions and each is subject to the Holy Spirit. Scripture exhorts us to obey conscience in all circumstances, but that is not the same thing as holding on to one's own opinion. It is easy to confuse one with the other. The husband is not to force his opinions, which opinions need not be accepted by the wife. The wife is not to submit to her husband to the extent that this interferes with her relationship to God and Jesus.

(1 Pet. 3:1-5) The wife can give her opinion, but if the husband is stubborn, she should abide by his ruling. To maintain peace and gentleness, the wife may go to the extreme: sacrificing self for Christ's sake, short of violating God's principles.

Work Out Your Salvation (Phil. 2:12-13)

Memory Verse(s):
> **Eph. 4:22-24**

Devotion:
> Select your own verses from this sheet and do a BSAF on at least three verses.

Put-Off/Put-On:
> Read Unit 2 of Strengthening Your Marriage [Mack1]. Develop a log-list of failures with a view of working through **Appendix A.4, "Victory over Sin Worksheet"**.

9.4. The Husband's Role in Submitting

- **(Eph. 5:25-33)** The duty of the husband towards his wife in terms of the union between Christ and the church and husband and wife.

- **(Eph. 5:29-33)** Doctrine of the mystical union between Christ and the church.

- **(Eph. 4:21-25)** The controlling idea is the husband's love to and for his wife. Submission is part of wife, love is part of husband. To maintain harmony and peace and unity in the home, the wife has to keep her eye on the element of submission, while the husband has to keep his eye on love.

- **(2 Tim. 1:7)** The husband is the leader and authority figure. To keep him from becoming a tyrant, this power is to be tempered with love. The reign of the husband is to be a reign and rule of love requiring a mind that is sound, disciplined, and self-controlled.

The Nature of Love

- **Eros:** Essentially 'loving if loved' in return. The world exists by this kind of love.

- **Phileo:** Brotherly love, or being simply fond of one another.

- **Agape:** Unconditional love, not with terms or conditions, not feelings, not erotic, not merely being fond of one another, but having fruit that resembles God's love (**Gal. 5:22**).

Eros and phileo are natural and okay in their places; man and woman should physically and mutually be attracted. Eros, the sexual, is part of man's make-up. Phileo represents companionship. All three loves should be experienced by christians.

We do not get drunk with all kinds of feelings (**Eph. 5:18**), but filled with the Spirit. In this spirit, the husband is to respond to his wife as a matter of course. Agape is the highest of the loves and should be sought (**1 Cor. 13:13**).

Love Wife as Christ Loves The Church

Christ loved the church in spite of her deficiencies. Christ gave Himself for the church. Sacrifice is characteristic of this kind of love. Christ gave His life and His present concern is for her well-being and for her to be perfect. Likewise, the husband comes up against deficiencies, difficulties—things he feels he can criticize in his wife. The husband is to express the love that gives, not for what he can get out of it, but seeks primarily to benefit his wife, to shield, protect, and guard her (See **Section 9.13, "What Makes a Man a Man"**).

- (**John 14:21**) Love must be expressed in action, in the doing—not just the saying, but in what is done.

- (**Phil. 2:5**) The Lord did not consider Himself, He became a servant, He did not count the cost, the shame: but He came to make the church perfect. Likewise, the husband is to look beyond his wife's faults, and to give her what she needs, not what she may deserve.

- (**James 1:21**; **1 Pet. 1:23**) The Lord set the church apart for Himself; we are His special possession, His bride. We have a polluted nature, lusts of mind and flesh—an infection. Regeneration is the work of the Holy Spirit. We are cleansed by the Holy Spirit within who operates through the Word of God. Through the Word, we are progressively cleansed from pollution and being brought into a state in which we will be finally perfect—without spot or wrinkle.

- (**Phil. 2:12-16**) Christ is cleansing His church through the Holy Spirit whom He has sent and who uses His Word to accomplish the task. As we obey, this gives the Holy Spirit something to work on, conforming us to Our Lord. We are to work out what the Holy Spirit works within. God can only sanctify us as we respond biblically to life's challenges.

- (**Isa. 6:3**; **Col. 1:10-11**) Do not start with your needs, your problems. Start with God, His being, His nature, the character of God. Growing in the knowledge of God leads to holiness and sanctification. Daily devotional practices and prayer are the keys to spiritual growth (See **Appendix A.12, "Anchor Posts"**).

- **(Eph. 1:3-4; Eph. 5:27-28)** We are baptized into the Lord Jesus Christ. Thus, the process of sanctification begins in our union with Him which leads to His Second Coming. In the same way, husbands are to separate wives unto themselves in order to enhance her in the process of purification. The husband is to take the lead in separating the family from the corrupt influences of the world's system by establishing Kingdom principles in the family unit.

- **(Eph. 5:30-32)** The doctrine of the mystical union between Christ and the church helps us to understand the union between husband and wife. 'Mystery' means something that is inaccessible to the unaided human mind; spiritual truth that is only understood by a born-again person. The mystery concerns Christ and the church, not husband and wife; but it sheds light on the marriage between husband and wife.

- **(Eph. 1:18)** To understand these mysteries is the reason God gave to us the five-fold ministries to instruct us accordingly. The church is the 'body' of Christ; thus, husband and wife are not merely an external relationship, but an internal "edifying of itself in love." "Members of His body," of His flesh, of His bones—vital, organic unity is involved.

- **(Gen. 2:23)** While Adam was asleep, woman was taken out of man; so, the 'body', the church, was taken out of Jesus, the second Adam, at the cross—the mystery. The emphasis here is that we are part of Christ's very nature as Eve was part of man. When man pays attention to his 'body', Eve, he is paying attention to himself. He cannot divorce himself from himself; what he does for his 'body' he does for himself.

- **(2 Pet. 1:4)** "Partakers of the divine nature," We derive our lives, our very being from Him. We are truly a part of Him as we live by His Word which is His flesh.

One Flesh

(**Eph. 5:31-32**; **Gen. 2:24**) Woman taken out of the substance of man. In a sense, they are now two; in another sense, they were not two. Thus, two and one at the same time, this oneness, is the idea of 'one flesh.'

(**Eph. 1:23**) Adam was incomplete without Eve. Thus, she makes up the fulness of Adam. Likewise, the church makes up the fulness of Christ. As husband and wife fulfill their respective roles and functions according to Kingdom principles by completing one another, and by increasing in godly virtues, they separate themselves more and more from the world's system. And, thus, by increasing the Presence of their union with Christ, God's Kingdom and His will are being established on earth as it is in heaven.

Work Out Your Salvation (Phil. 2:12-13)

Memory Verse(s):
>   **Gal. 6:1-2**

Devotion:
>   Select your own verses from this sheet and do a BSAF on at least three verses.

Put-Off/Put-On:
>   Read Unit 3 of Strengthening Your Marriage [Mack1]. Review **Section 5.2, "Sin, Self, Suffering"**. Continue working on problem area via **Appendix A.4, "Victory over Sin Worksheet"**.

9.5. The Bride's Privilege

The ultimate explanation of the state of the world is the state of the church.

- **(Col. 3:4)** He is 'our life.' This means we are sharers of His life, members of His body... His flesh... His bones.

- **(2 Cor. 3:15-16)** We are new creations in the supernatural realm of the Spirit: sharing His life on earth.

- **(John 17:22)** The 'standing,' the dignity, the position that belongs to the bridegroom belongs to the bride also.

- **(2 Cor. 4:15-18)** "All things are ours." We are sharing in His possessions, His interest, His plans, His purposes. Likewise, the husband tells his wife everything, every desire, every ambition, every hope, every thought. His wife is one with him. Thus, we as His bride, we are His 'help-meet.' We share His burden and preach the Gospel in the same way that the wife is the 'help-meet' to her husband.

- **(Col. 3:4)** Finally, we share in His glory.

The Husband's Duties

There are three basic principles to be considered:

First Principle: We must realize in connection with marriage, as with all else in the christian life, the secret of success is "to think, to understand." Nothing happens automatically. If you don't think and understand, you will revert back to elemental forces which are governed by instincts and impulses such as anger, fear, sickness, greed, weakness, and the like. These factors hit you before you can think. Feelings will reign, human reasons prevail and God's truths will be forgotten.

Second Principle: Conception of marriage must be positive to be lifted up to the position of the relationship between the Lord and His church. Questions to ask yourself daily (**Matt. 5:48**):

- Does my married life correspond to, and is it governed by, God's ideal?

- Is my marriage conforming and attaining to the ideal increasingly?

Third Principle: The real cause of failure, ultimately, in marriage is 'self' and the various manifestations of self. This is the basic trouble in and of the world. As a christian, the denial of self is to be practiced daily until husband and wife are "one flesh."

One Flesh Concept

1. In marriage two are one; that is, two become one flesh. When two become two, problems result.

2. The wife is the body of the husband, even as the church is the body of Christ.

3. The husband is to be governed by this principle: that his wife is part of himself, not two but one. She is not just a partner, she (whole in herself) is the other half of man.

4. Therefore, "He that loveth his wife, loveth himself." Thus, in a sense, he is loving himself.

5. The whole of the husband's thinking must include his wife, never himself in isolation or in detachment. He must include her not only physically but intellectually and spiritually.

6. To do the contrary, man damages and hurts himself when he thinks and acts in isolation. This detachment breaks the marriage bond which allows fear and insecurity to enter.

Unity—The Central Principle of Marriage

Unity: The two shall be one flesh. One for all and all for one. Unity is the key (**Eph. 5:31-32**).

Divorce: Individuality is stressed here. Two people are asserting their rights. The results are clashes, discord and separation.

Leaving, Cleaving, Weaving:

- (**Eph. 5:33**) Both husband and wife were in deference and submission to their respective parents. Now the husband must assume headship and the wife must defer to the husband. This is the beginning of a new unit. The parents are no longer to control them, but God is to be God. The parents are not to be God.

- **(Col. 3:19)** The husband is inclined to dominate. He is cautioned not to be harsh. If he is not harsh with himself, he will not be harsh with his wife as well.

- **(Eph. 5:18)** Do not be drunk with your own ideas, but be filled with the Spirit. A good place to start application of God's wisdom is in the home. As head of the home, the husband is not to abuse or misuse authority by being harsh or unkind or unfair. To act in this manner reveals the absence of the Spirit.

Reverence of Wife: As the church is subject to Christ, so wives are subject to their husbands.

- **(1 Pet. 3:2)** She is to respect, defer, honor, esteem, admire, praise and be devoted to him. Above all, she is to encourage husband—never demean. Each is responsible to the Lord to change their respective lives to conform to godly principles regardless of the other's responses. By godly responses, we can influence, but only God has the authority and power to change the heart, the motives of another.

- **(1 Pet. 3:6)** Sarah recognized the biblical view of marriage—the husband as head of a new unit. As head, he conveys to his wife by thought and by deed that she is valued, that he cannot do without her. She in return views her husband with great honor and respect. Husband, above all else, is not to take his wife for granted. He is to convey to his wife, in spirit and in action, that she is 'needed'. Wife needs to know that she is needed in entirety, else sense of detachment and separation opens the door to fear.

- **(Psalm 45:10)** The wife formerly owed deference to her parents, now she owes it to her husband: but neither are to be controlled by their parents. The wife is never to be the head. However, decision making is to be coordinated. When Sarah called Abraham 'lord,' she recognized and honored the authority which is of God. It is this God-given authority that she honors, not just the man only.

She submits to him, to fulfill him, does not compete or strive with him.

Secularism Vs. Christianity

Secularism always talks about generalities. The individual is forgotten.

Christianity realized that the mass, the nation, is nothing but a collection of individuals. Thus, it is as individuals are put right that a nation is put right. It is not by attending disarmament or population conferences, earth summits, etc., but it is by the application of christian doctrine in practical living that will change a nation. One of the major means is the family unit, the marriage relationship.

(**Phil. 2:5**) Above all else, the supreme factor is for each to consider his/her personal relationship to Jesus Christ. And when they do, the husband's and the wife's relationship to each other will grow and abound in grace and fruitfulness. As each concentrates on Christ, two become one in mind and in judgment.

The Concept of Authority

Lucifer's pride challenged God's authority. He did not want to submit, which resulted in rebellion and chaos.

God reinstituted His chain of authority in the garden. With this chain is the strength and ability to live God's principles which begins by an act of submission. This requires a giving up of self, an act of humility which is necessary to swallow up the pride of Lucifer and sin in its entirety—the corruption of deceit and lust upon which the world subsists and operates.

As christians, we are no longer independent of God in our thoughts and actions, but everything we think and all that we do is dependent upon God and His Word. As we move from self-loving-self to self-loving-others, we exercise the very nature of God.

Therefore, in humility and dependence upon God we complete the plan God originally intended in the garden, that is, being conformed to the image of God's Son and in Him to destroy the works of the devil. By doing this, we are establishing God's kingdom, His righteousness, and His will on earth.

Work Out Your Salvation (Phil. 2:12-13)

Memory Verse(s):

Rom. 12:1-2

Devotion:

Work out a BASF on three verses.

Put-Off/Put-On:

Read Unit 4 and 5 of Strengthening Your Marriage [Mack1].
Review **Section 5.1, "Cleansing and Purifying the Soul"**.
Continue developing log lists of failures and working through
these failures.

9.6. One Flesh Marriage

(**Heb. 13:20-21**; **Rom. 5:5**) We don't pray for love, it is already living within us. As we die to selfish acts, Christ is allowed to work in us to do all that is pleasing in His sight. Love is an action, an act of the will, regardless of feelings to the contrary.

(**1 Cor. 13:4-8**) The authority to exercise love came by the blood of Jesus, the blood which forgave us and cleansed us from all sin. Therefore, the power to love is resident within the person of the Holy Spirit who empowers us to exhibit and demonstrate the fruit of the Spirit.

(**Matt. 7:1-5**; **John 14:27**) Your peace and joy and ultimate happiness are not dependent upon your spouse, on others, or anything else, but it comes by doing what God says to do regardless of the actions of others or the conditions of life.

(**Ezek. 18:20**; **Phil. 2:12-13**) I am not held responsible to change others or to bring about moral and ethical results except for myself. I am responsible to examine myself only to insure that I am biblically responding to life according to God's word.

(**Phil. 2:2-4**; **Rom. 12:9-21**; **Rom. 8:28-29**) Practicing dying to self, to fleshly instincts and impulses, requires that my focus be on God. Allow God through me to work out responses to life situations in a manner which brings glory to God and honors His reputation.

(**Eph. 4:15,25,29**; **1 Pet. 3:1,7,8-15**) A believing spouse has the responsibility to present God's truths to an unbelieving spouse in speech and actions that are Christ-honoring and biblically submissive.

(**Matt. 22:37-39**; **1 John 2:4-6**; **1 John 3:14**) To love is an act of the will, not of feelings. God will not ask us to do anything unless He first equips and empowers us to do so. But we must take the initiative. God will not do for us what we are expected to do: but when we take the first step to biblically respond, God will do the rest.

(**1 John 3:23**; **Luke 9:23-24**) To love your spouse as God commands requires that we daily die to our own selfish desires and live to please God by serving our spouse.

(**Col. 3:19**; **1 Pet. 3:7**) Husbands are inclined to be harsh and embittered towards wives, to abuse them, to neglect them or take them for granted.

(**Matt. 20:25-29**) As spiritual head of the home, husbands are to set the example by being a true servant, giving up their own desires to meet the needs and desires of the family.

(**Prov. 21:9; 1 Pet. 3:1-6**) Wives are inclined to be quarrelsome and contentious, usually challenging and contending for recognition. Instead, she is to put on love, submission and respect for her husband.

(**2 Cor. 4:10-12**) Both husband and wife are to act in the redemptive process, daily dying to reactions of the flesh, developing one mind and one spirit: a spirit of sacrifice.

Perspective

God's solution to problems in your marriage is for you to:

1. First, make a commitment to please the Lord in all things (**Col. 1:10**);

2. Examine and judge your own failures in a biblical manner, do not blame shift (**1 Cor. 11:28-31**);

3. Confess your sin to the Lord and confess your marital shortcomings as sin to your spouse (**1 John 1:9**);

4. Seek to edify your spouse biblically and do it heartily as unto the Lord (**Rom. 14:19; Rom. 15:1-2**);

5. Seek to resolve conflicts and live at peace with your spouse. If your spouse refuses to resolve problems biblically, continue to trust in Christ Jesus for your peace and joy.

Work Out Your Salvation (Phil. 2:12-13)

Memory Verse(s):
> **Phil. 2:3-4**

Devotion:
> Work out a BSAF on three or more verses as the Holy Spirit directs.

Put-Off/Put-On:
> Review Unit 6 of Strengthening Your Marriage [Mack1].

9.7. Parent/Child Relationships

(**Ezek. 18:20**) We can't blame others, not our past, not our present, nor the circumstances of life. God is sovereign over my life. If I cooperate with Him, He will use all of my experiences to conform me to the image of His Son.

(**Eph. 6:4**) Fathers are inclined to provoke a child. The parents' responsibility is to train a child in a godly manner and to make it easy for a child to receive and accept the training.

- Child may be untrainable, but the parent is to "keep-on, keeping on." Don't go beyond a child's will and force him to accept training. It is the responsibility of the Holy Spirit to change the heart of the child, not ours. Our job is to obey God's commandments, and not follow our feelings.

- Being led by the Holy Spirit, parents can't blameshift either, but are to do what God's word says to do.

(**Luke 9:23-24**; **Prov. 18:21**) Living is a 'life and death' situation. Life is really learning how to die to self, not defending self or protecting self: but getting rid of self in order to be a blessing to others. This is the theme of the New Testament.

Major Principles in Relationships

1. When someone bothers or irritates me, the other person needs help, not condemnation.

2. Always ask self, "What good can I do for that person who is acting in such an unbiblical manner?"

3. When I get my attitude right, God will give me the answer on how to respond in a nasty or trying situation.

(**1 Cor. 3:18-20**) Children belong to the Lord. We are to raise them according to His commands, not our feelings, impressions, or what others say: but according to what God says.

(**Deut. 4:9**; **Deut. 6:6-7**; **Deut. 6:20-25**) Scriptures are our guide, nothing else, day and night.

(**Prov. 22:6**) You are to raise your children according to the gifts and talents God has placed in your children, not what you want them to be. Parents can't change thoughts, motives, and attitudes in a child: this is God's sovereign work and responsibility.

(**2 Pet. 1:3**) God's principles and precepts are applicable to parents and children alike. Parents are to be of one mind as they teach Scriptures to their children: to develop the character of God in such areas as virtue, moral excellence, knowledge of God, self-control, perseverance, godliness, brotherly kindness, and love.

(**Eph. 6:1-2**; **James 1:2-4**) Disobedience warrants death which still applies in the spirit. Children have no option but to obey and honor parents.

- As with the parents, children are not to be led by their feelings, especially when parents are harsh, mean, untrained and selfish.

- As with adults, children, under God's grace, have great opportunities to grow in grace and patience when subject to unfair and unjust treatment.

(**Eccl. 12:13-14**; **Prov. 3:5-6**) As you study and follow God's word for your life and the training of your children and decisively put off any reliance on yourself, your background or your upbringing, you will gain the wisdom and direction that you need to be a godly parent. The **key** is: Get rid of the old self, so that God's light can shine through you.

(**Deut. 21:18-21**) Disobedience is very serious: for it is rebellion against God and siding with the enemy.

(**Eph. 6:2-3**; **Gal. 3:20**) Parents are to teach children to honor and to obey parents because the parents represent God's authority and His standards. As a child honors and obeys parents, he is honoring and obeying God. By honoring God this will guarantee the child's success in life: for it is God who will watch, guard and keep the child forever.

Work Out Your Salvation (Phil. 2:12-13)

Memory Verse(s):
        Eccl. 12:13-14

Devotion:

BSAF on three or more verses from this worksheet.

Put-Off/Put-On:
Review Unit 7 of Strengthening Your Marriage [Mack1].

9.8. Children Submitting to Parents

(**Eph. 5:18,21**) As in previous discussions, the key is being filled with the Spirit. Submitting to one another follows this infilling.

(**Rom. 1:18,30; 2 Tim. 3:2**) In the end days, times of apostasy, when you have ungodliness, you will always have unrighteousness. One of the most striking manifestations of this lawlessness is "disobedience to parents." Unrighteousness is always the result of ungodliness and the only hope is to have a revival of godliness.

(**Eph. 6:1**) As in the marriage relationship, submitting also applies to children. To obey parents is to listen, realizing one is under authority, to listen 'under' their authority. To honor parents is to respect and reverence them in the spirit of the law: to rejoice in it, and to regard it as a great privilege. "For it is right", this is essentially right and good in itself.

(**Gen. 2:24; Rom. 13:1-2**) The principle of "order of nature", as with husband and wife, so it is with children. Without order, life would be chaotic and would eventually destroy itself.

(**Eph. 6:2**) This is the commandment with a promise. The first four commandments deal with our relationship to God; and the fifth begins our relationship with one another. God gives a promise in order that it may be reinforced to encourage us.

When neglected, these laws lead to the collapse of society. God's order of nature has been violated from Genesis onward. When the family idea, family unit, family life is broken up there is no allegiance to anything and chaos is the result.

(**Acts 17:28; Eph. 3:14-15**) Relationship between parents and child is a replica, a picture of the christian relationship with God the Father. God, Himself, is the Father and all of us are His children.

(**Eph. 6:1**) "In the Lord," obeying parents is required in the "order of nature" (Genesis), "in the law" (Ten Commandments), and today (in Grace). Obey, honor and respect parents because it is part of our obedience to our Lord. He asks us to do it: It is His commandment.

(**Rom. 8:4; Eph. 3:10**) Obedience is proof that we are like Him. To obey is to do what Jesus did when He was on earth. To obey is to say 'Yes' to God's truth and to say 'No' to the alternative. To assent to God's way implies a commitment to exercise, to apply, to practice the biblical response until it becomes habitual.

Discipline Involves the Whole of Life

(**Eph. 6:4**) The father has the authority and the position to exercise discipline. To the extent the parent disciplines and controls himself, to that extent will he influence the child. It is up to the parent to judge himself to insure a biblical response to counteract a spirit of harshness (**James 1:2-4**).

The breakdown of society involves the whole problem of discipline. In fact, the whole future of civilization, it appears, rests upon this! The Bible deals with right, truth, justice, and righteousness. Discipline may be defined as imposed or self imposed standards and restraints to keep one from following the natural inclinations of the flesh in order to follow the life style of self-control and self-donation. This is characterized by not giving or taking offense; by humility in considering other's needs and interest before one's own; and by being teachable in not excusing one's failures or defending one's weaknesses.

(**Prov. 13:24**; **Eph. 6:4**) The problem of discipline lies between these two verses: going from one extreme to another; e.g., Victorian age of austere discipline to "no spanking" philosophy currently in vogue. Rebellion ensues in either case. The opposite of wrong discipline is not the absence of it, but the right discipline.

Balanced Discipline

(**Eph. 6:4**; **1 Cor. 9:21**; **Rom. 1:18-32**) Discipline a child in the nurture and the admonition of the Lord. We are under the law, the discipline of it, to Christ. A christian is to be more disciplined because he sees the deeper meaning of it. God punishes sin by abandoning the world to its own evil because the world refuses to submit to Him.

Biblical teaching recognizes man is in a state of sin which requires that laws be enforced in order that man can see and know God: then man can be brought into the grace of God to get to know the higher law of God, and delight in pleasing God by doing His commandments.

(**Eph. 6:1-2**) Don't exasperate your child. Repeated attacks on the child provoke a child to become resentful. We are incapable of exercising true discipline unless we are first able to exercise self-control, controlling our own tempers.

Negative Influence

An unpredictable and moody parent is a real chore for a child for he doesn't know from one day to the next what is expected of him. Parents can be harsh on some minor offense and casual on a major offense another day.

Parents must develop a listening ear and never be unreasonable or unwilling to hear a child's case. Parents are to punish for correction's sake not to inflict harm and not to humiliate in front of others.

Possessive or domineering parents impose their personality on a child which crushes his own identity. Parents expect and demand everything from the child. The child's whole life is to be lived for the parents' sake; whereas, they are only custodians and guardians to insure God's life flows through the child.

Positive Influence

Recognize growth and development in your children and treat them accordingly. Don't treat them as small children all of their lives. Allow them to develop a conscience of their own.

Don't impose your will over the child. Allow for him and the grace of God to operate through him to allow him to make mistakes and hold himself accountable in order to develop a conscience and self-discipline.

"Nurture." A general term which includes the whole process in the cultivation of the mind and spirit, morals, and moral behavior: the whole personality of the child dealing with conduct and behavior.

"Admonition." This puts greater emphasis on speech, things addressed to the child, words of exhortation, encouragement, reproof, etc..

"Of the Lord." Not simply good manners, but brought up in the knowledge of the Lord as Savior and Lord, that the child may come to know Jesus personally.

Work Out Your Salvation (Phil. 2:12-13)

Memory Verse(s):
> **Eph. 6:1-2; Matt. 7:1-5**

Devotion:
> BSAF on three or more verses from this worksheet.

Put-Off/Put-On:
> Review Unit 7 of Strengthening Your Marriage [Mack1].

9.9. God's Standard

Perspective

(**Eccl. 12:13-14**) The secret for success in life is one word: obedience. Through obedience, we develop a consciousness of God in our thoughts, in our thinking, in our words, in our speech, and in our actions.

(**Isa. 40:8**; **1 Pet. 1:25**; **Gen. 2:8**; **Gen. 1:28**; **Gen. 2:16-17**) God's word abides forever and never changes. God planted the garden, we are to work it by His Word, not by our own ideas, opinions or suggestions. Be in agreement with God's word, which allows His wisdom, strength and ability to flow in order to establish God's Kingdom on earth.

(**Matt. 18:18-20**; **Matt. 16:16-19**) When husband and wife agree on the basis of God's word, this counteracts the spirit of independence of Adam and Eve in the garden. Hearing from God, we have the power to bind the sin and loose the spirit just as Adam had before the fall. Now, we can exercise this power to work God's garden. Christ who is the Word becomes the center of our lives.

(**Matt. 6:33**; **Prov. 3:5-8**) The key to fruitfulness is to have reverence for God and to consistently keep His commandments in every aspect of living. We are to move from the natural to the supernatural by separation and detachment from the world, the flesh and the devil (being influenced and conditioned by the world's system). What possesses us in our minds, our memories, our imaginations, controls us. We are to be possessed wholly by His Presence in our soul: for christianity is God in the soul of man (**Luke 14:33**; **1 John 2:15-17**).

Hope

(**2 Cor. 3:18**) This is a process, we move from one stage to another until we reach maturity.

(**Matt. 11:28-30**; **James 4:6-7**) Turn our burdens over to the Lord; in turn, He will give us His thoughts and ability to work the burdens and to be perfected by them.

(**1 Cor. 11:31-32**) If we judge ourselves, we will not be judged: Let this be a natural process in every encounter.

(**Phil. 2:12-13**; **Matt. 6:9-13**) God works through us, but we do the doing. We are to work out our salvation. Salvation is not just a change in destination, from hell to heaven, but a daily change in relationships and responsibilities. God is now my

Father—Satan is no longer. Now my responsibility is to be conformed to the image of Christ (**Rom. 8:29**), to establish righteousness on earth, and to destroy the works of the devil (**1 John 3:8**).

(**2 Pet. 1:10**; **Rom. 13:12-14**) Working out God's plan is evidence that we are children of God. The decision is ours to make: It is our choice to put off works of darkness, and to put on light.

(**Rom. 5:3-5**; **2 Cor. 4:10-12**) Tests and trials are great opportunities that God uses to perfect us. All we need to do is to cooperate, to choose God's way. The world is evil, but the power of resurrection enables us to swallow up evil with good. As Jesus lived, so do we.

(**1 Pet. 4:1-2**) Patiently suffer rather than fail to please God. Thus, we learn to stop pleasing ourselves and the world in order to please God. Thus, we move from the natural to the spiritual realm, and begin to look at life from God's perspective.

(**Gal. 5:22-23**) By faith, by choice of our will, we make the decision to die to self, getting down into the death of Jesus. And, by faith, we acknowledge that we are now in the Spirit, and thus we are to act accordingly: allowing the fruit of the Spirit and His glory to flow through us.

Change

(**2 Pet. 1:2-10**) Considering all that has been discussed, all that God has done on our behalf, all that God has given to us, our function now is to fulfill our responsibilities by the...

1. pursuit of excellence in a spirit of commitment, diligence and perseverance.
2. study of God's principles.
3. exercise of self-control.
4. increase of patience and endurance.
5. exercise of putting God's word first in our lives.

Thus, the love of God is demonstrated by our biblical responses to others. As we do, God will provide and meet all our needs as we seek to glorify Him.

Work Out Your Salvation (Phil. 2:12-13)

Memory Verse(s):
        1 John 3:8

Put-Off/Put-On:

Review Unit 8 of Strengthening Your Marriage [Mack1].

9.10. Upbringing Goals for Children (and Adults)

Love of God

(**Deut. 6:5-9**) The first goal of raising children is to cultivate the love of God in them, in the following three areas:

      a. Salvation (**1 John 2:15**);
      b. Heart devoted to God (**Matt. 22:37**);
      c. Mind of God—His thoughts and desires (**Phil. 2:5**).

Love of Neighbor

There are three areas that children have to learn in order to relate to others:

      a. Treat them as yourself (**Matt. 22:38-39**);
      b. Being an ambassador for Christ (**Gal. 6:1-2**);
      c. Use talents to be of service to others (**Rom. 15:2**).

Character

(**Matt. 16:24-25**) Equip children with these character traits:

      … Be rid of selfishness (**Eph. 4:22**);
      … Be contented (**Phil. 2:14**);
      … Be upright (**1 Tim. 4:16**);
      … Be disciplined (**2 Tim. 1:7**);
      … Redeem the time (**Eph. 5:16**).

Principles of Decision-Making

(**2 Tim. 3:16-17; Deut. 6:1-9**) Children are to be taught the Law. The Law is to be remembered, and not to be forgotten, in order for them to pass God's truth on to others. God's truth is to be taught at home. We are not to rely on school, church, etc..

- Scripture is the basis of life's activities (**John 8:30-31**).

- God's purposes are primary: seek to please God in all things (**Matt. 6:33-34**).

- Act on faith, living on and by God's wisdom, His word—not doubting (**Heb. 11:6**).

- Not being a manipulator, overcoming selfish motives (**Rom. 12:9**).

The primary responsibility of parents is to secure the child's welfare and the child's soul on the basis of eternal values and the teaching of Scriptures.

(**Matt. 6:33**) The child's career or popularity in the world are secondary factors. As the child learns to depend on God, to learn God's ways, His thoughts, His principles, to learn to honor, to please and to glorify God, then His heavenly Father will take care of the child's needs on this earth. As the child depends on God in everything, God will take care of everything else.

All of the above is the long-range plan; reduce it to the level of the child, which is the short-range goal. Code of conduct is essential; that is, a system of rewards and punishment are necessary in order to control behavior. The goal of the parents is to teach the child to gradually be independent of the parent in order to be completely dependent upon God.

Priorities for a Married Woman

(**Ps. 128:3**; **John 15:5-8**; **Gal. 5:22-23**)

Her relationship with God.
Her ministry to her family.
Her development of a godly character.
Her expression of godly conduct toward other people in and out of the home.

Priorities for a Married Man

1. To be in awe of God; to worship the beauty of the Lord (**Ps. 128:1-4**). The God-fearing man who reverently fears and worships God enables God's blessings to flow into the home (**Jer. 32:38-40**). We are not inclined to fear God, but God will inspire us as we ask and beseech Him (**Ps. 25:12**). To develop fellowship, partnership, communion with God in order to establish God's will and purposes on earth through his family and associations.

2. To be a man of prayer, as the spiritual head, he is to lead the way (**Eph. 1:17-19**; **Eph. 3:16-19**). To know God and His ways, that God's personality be expressed fully through the husband. Through prayer, this wholesome fear of God will be nurtured and increased and enable the man to build his family God's way.

3. To be a meditator (**Ps. 46:10**). "Be still and know that I am God." Meditating on God requires spending time learning Scripture, learning about the person and work of Jesus, developing a God-conscious and Christ-centered life.

The Established Heart

(**Rom. 8:31**) If God is with me, no one can successfully be my enemy (**1 Cor. 3:3**). The human standard is the sense-ruled mind which engenders fear, sickness, poverty, and weakness (**James 1:5-8**). A mind dominated by God's thoughts, nature and ways is a Scripture-ruled mind that is never prepared to fail.

(**1 Cor. 2:16**) We have the mind of Christ; therefore, we have the thoughts and purposes of His heart. We are either ruled by impulses or God's word. Being ruled by God's word, no matter what happens, we can stand unruffled and unaffected. And as we do this, we bring glory to the Father; we bring joy to Jesus; and we bring victory to our own hearts.

AMEN! (**Gen. 1:26**)

Work Out Your Salvation (Phil. 2:12-13)

Put-Off/Put-On:

> Review concluding chapter of Strengthening Your Marriage [Mack1].

9.11. Maintaining Good Marital Communications

Guidelines

1. When there are problems, each must be willing to admit that he/she is part of the problem (**Gen. 8:8-19**; **Prov. 20:6**).

2. Each person must be willing to change (**John 5:6**; **Matt. 5:23-26**).

3. Avoid the use of emotionally charged words. "You don't really love me."; "You always do........"; "You never do anything right."; " I don't care." ...

4. Be responsible for your own emotions, words, actions, and reactions. Don't blame them on the other person. You got angry, lashed out, became depressed, etc. (**Gal. 6:5**; **James 1:13-15**).

5. Refrain from having reruns on old arguments (**Eph. 4:26**).

6. Deal with one problem at a time. Solve one problem and then move on to the next (**Matt. 6:34**).

7. Deal in the present and not in the past. Hang a "no fishing" sign over the past unless it will help you to solve the present problem (**Phil. 3:12-14**; **Jer. 31:34**; **Isa. 43:25**).

8. Major on the positive instead of majoring on the negative (**Phil. 4:8**).

9. Learn to communicate in non-verbal ways (**Matt. 8:1-2**; **Rom. 8:14-15**; **Ps. 32:8**).

Change

Express your thoughts and concerns to each other. Relate your activities. Listen, understand, and respond to the meaning behind what a person is saying. When he flies off the handle at you, he may be saying, "I had a terrible day at the job. Nobody respects me." When she says, "You don't love me", she may be really saying, "I desperately need some affection. I'm starved for love." (Example of Jesus in **John 1:45-47**; **Mark 5:1-15**; **John 11:20-35**.)

Practice the golden rule—**Matt. 7:12**. What would you like your mate to do to you? Would you like your mate to: Tell the truth? Ask your opinion? Help in time of need? Be natural around you? Thank you for your help and services? Well, do the same for your mate.

Practice the principle laid down in **Luke 6:35**. "Do good—do that which will help others; and lend expecting and hoping for nothing in return."

Work Out Your Salvation (Phil. 2:12-13)

Memory Verse(s):
> **Phil. 2:3-4**

Put-Off/Put-On:
> **(1 Cor. 6:19-20**; **Rom. 12:1**; **Ps. 24:1)** Consciously recognize that as a christian, all you have and are, (rights to yourself) belong to God. Dedicate all that you have and are, including your 'rights', to God. Trust Him to take care of His property. Cease to think in terms of your 'rights', and concentrate on God's will and purpose and promises. Whenever you are tempted to become sinfully angry, write down:

> - What is happening?
> - What qualities may God be trying to develop in you through this situation?
> - What personal rights of yours do you think are being denied? (Your 'rights' belong to God)
> - What may you have done to promote the situation?
> - What does God want you to do, and how does He want you to act? (Search the Scriptures)
> - What is keeping you from doing the right thing when you are tempted to become sinfully angry?
> - Is it your ignorance? Lack of desire? Fear? ,etc.

> Or—simply ask youself three basic questions:

> 1. What happened?
> 2. What did I do to contribute to the problem?
> 3. What must I do now to fix the situation biblically?

Reference: [Mack1].

9.12. Maximum Husband and Father

Perspective

(**Prov. 22:17**; **Heb. 10:24**; **Ps. 128:1-4**) Psalm shows that to be God's kind of husband and father, you must be a man that fears God. Appropriate fear of God makes a man an unusual blessing to his wife and children. The fear of God will be the soil out of which the man's positive influence will grow and the basic reason a man's family will arise and call him blessed.

Hope

(**Rom. 5:9-10**; **Rom. 8:15**; **Rom. 8:17**) If you have trusted in Christ alone for salvation and forgiveness of sins, confessing Him as Lord, the Bible says that you have no cause to be in bondage to the negative fear of God. God now is the ultimate and compassionate Father who is the maximum Husband and Father, who will give us His grace to function to the fullest as husband and father.

(**Col. 2:20**) As with Moses and Abraham, a godly christian chooses to put God's will before everything else, including his own feelings and desires.

(**Jer. 33:38-40**; **2 Cor. 4:6**; **Eph. 1:17-19**) It is prayer that connects us to God, and through prayer God Himself inspires us to comprehend His majesty and glory. It is He who turns on the light in the darkness of our hearts. He provides illumination in our inner man. If we are to understand His splendor by which we fulfill our responsibilities on this earth, prayer is the key, the link, the channel by which God's wisdom, strength, and ability flow through us to our families.

Change

(**Ps. 46:10**; **Phil. 3:10**; **John 5:39**; **Ps. 19:7-9**; **Heb. 7:25**) "Be still and know" the Lord means taking time to reflect on who and what God is. Jesus is the Radiance of God's glory, reflect on Jesus what He did, see how He responded to the people. Go often to the cross on which He died for your sins, proceed to the empty tomb, see Him as He arose from the dead, contemplate the throne room, see Jesus in the Presence of His Father, see Him interceding for you now, praying for you to respond to life as He did, being a blessing to your family and to others.

(**2 Tim. 3:16-17**) Develop the attitude that God is speaking directly to you as you read the Scripture. The Bible is God's book, it reveals His attributes, His works, His concerns, His will, His intentions, His plans His desires for His people, and His design for the world that rejects Him. See everything in the Scripture as an invitation to enter into a deeper relationship with your majestic, infinite Father and Redeemer.

Work Out Your Salvation (Phil. 2:12-13)

Memory Verse(s):
> **Eph. 1:17-19**

Devotion:
> BSAF for **Ps. 46:1,10**

Put-Off/Put-On:
> As you look at the following passages, ask self what is God saying about my relationship with Him? How should what I see be applied to my life and family? How well am I doing in implementing the teachings of the passage?
>
> **2 Chron. 20:7; Isa. 41:8; Jer. 2:23; Gen. 12:1-8; Gen. 13:8-9; Gen. 14:14,24; Gen. 21:10-11; Gen. 22:11-12; Rom. 4:19-21.**
>
> What does the following teach about the excellencies of God, of fearing God, what our relationship with God should be like, what place God should have in our hearts, how to develop the fear of the Lord, and what happens to the person who fears God?.
>
> **Gen. 5:22; Exodus 15:11; Exodus 34:6-7; Deut. 6:10-13; 2 Chron. 20:6-19; Ps. 19:7-11; Ps. 34:7,11; Ps. 128:1; Ps. 130:4; Ps. 139:1-6,13-16,23-24; Ps. 147:11; Prov. 1:7; Prov. 8:13; Prov. 14:26-27; Prov. 19:2-3; Prov. 28:14; Isa. 40:10-31; Matt. 10:28; Rom. 8:26-39; Rom. 11:36; Rev. 4:8-11; Rev. 5:9-14; Rev. 15:3-4.**
>
> Reflect on what you have just studied and write out your response to this question: what difference should all this make in my own life and family relationship?

Reference: [Mack2]

9.13. What Makes a Man a Man

Perspective

(**Gen. 1:1-2**; **Gen. 1:26-28**; **Gen. 2:19-20**; **Gen. 3:1-6**) When God spoke, He spoke over that which was in disorder to create order and harmony. Created in God's image, man, likewise, is given authority to speak into creation, to rule and reign, to have dominion, to be fruitful, to multiply, to replenish, and to subdue. Therefore, when life is chaotic, man is to speak, to say something, to do something, to get involved. If man remains silent as Adam in the garden (**Gen. 3:6**), then he is sinning. Thus, to be a man is to be godly, by speaking and by doing, by getting emotionally involved in order to establish the Kingdom of God and His will on earth.

Hope

(**Matt. 22:36-40**; **Luke 9:23-24**; **Rom. 7:5**; **Eph. 5:25**; **Prov. 3:5-7**; **Prov. 4:20-25**) God's purpose for us is to love others, to build relationships, to move into other people's lives, and help them move towards God. As in marriage, relationships can be messy. Husband needs to move towards wife to build a relationship with her. In the process, she may fight, reject, resist, disappoint, not respond. This is where sacrifice comes in: to be willing to be hurt and rejected in the process of moving towards his wife. This is entering into chaos and the mystery of relationships.

Likewise with wife who is to complement, and encourage and build up husband to fulfill his role as leader of the home.

As Christ was rejected and crucified, we likewise, proceed to save that which is being lost. The immediate self that faces the externals of life, must die to the instinct of self preservation, to fear of failure, to withdrawal and remaining silent— waiting for certainty. At this point, he is to call upon the Lord, remain silent in His presence, and He will move and speak through man which brings His presence into the situation, and restoration begins.

(**Gen. 1:28**; **Gen. 18:19**; **Deut. 11:19-20**; **Deut. 13:4**; **Ps. 103:17-21**; **Matt. 6:24**; **Eph. 6:6-7**) Man is to move into that which is uncertain for that is his function and purpose in life, to create order and harmony. Man's mandate is to be fruitful, to multiply, to bring seed to maturity, to replenish, to rule and to have dominion. But man must initiate, to choose to move forward. At the point he moves, God will provide the wisdom, strength and ability to accomplish the task at hand.

Life is but one of mysteries and uncertainties, such as: who to marry, which job to take, which home to buy, how to deal with nasty or unpleasant people, how to discipline children, how to love spouse, etc.. Simply put, the answer lies in taking the first step forward, then to rely on God, and in the face of chaos, ask God what to do, do it, and trust God for the results.

Change

(Gen. 1:2; **Gen. 3:6**; **Matt. 22:36-39**; **Eph. 4:25-32**) God moved into chaos and darkness and created life and order by speaking. Man's natural tendency is to avoid darkness, to avoid messy situations by shutting down emotionally, by withdrawing and doing something else, placing the burden on others. God created us to enter into life and establish order and harmony: to love our neighbors, to build relationships, to move into other people's lives and move them towards God.

(Gen. 4:7; **Josh. 1:2-9**; **Prov. 3:5-6**; **Isa. 55:8-9**; **Matt. 20:25-28**; **James 4:6-8**) We hate chaos and uncertainties, we want certainty in life. To follow the Lord's teaching is to challenge and to run against the grain of the world system orchestrated by the enemy to destroy man.

We are inclined to avoid challenges by ignoring the problem, avoid the situation and devote our energies to things we can manage, put the responsibility on others, become dogmatic to cover our fears, or dull our sense of inadequacy by wine, drugs, pornography, etc..

(John 15:5-7) Realize and accept this tendency to avoid confrontation. You cannot handle life alone. Abide in God, and God in you and through you, to enable you to speak the word of truth: thus, creating order and harmony out of chaos and darkness.

Work Out Your Salvation (Phil. 2:12-13)

Put-Off/Put-On:

> As spiritual head of the home, man is responsible for his part in establishing the Kingdom of God and His will on earth. Review your areas of responsibility. Are you extending God's Kingdom as husband, as father, and as a leader in the workplace, community, church, social concerns, politics, etc.. To gain insight in areas that need addressing, list your failures. Review **Section 9.12, "Maximum Husband and Father"** and **Chapter 9, *Strengthening Your Marriage Series*.**

Note:

(Prov. 14:12) Do not pray your will or the problem to God, pray God's word dealing with the situation back to Him, wait till His will becomes your will. From this you will receive power to do (strength, ability, wisdom), and His provisions will follow. Thus, prayer, power, provisions are the means to establish God's kingdom and His will (righteousness and justice) on earth.

When the wife, the woman, exercises initiative in her respective role to create order and harmony out of chaos such as completing her husband or fulfilling a need that is not being met, she also employs inherent masculine attributes within the feminine mystique. As such woman shares equally in the creative process.

Reference: [Mack2]

158

9.14. Fulfilled and Fulfilling Wife and Mother

Perspective

(**Ps. 128:3**; **John 15:1,5**) Jesus described Himself as the vine because this vine symbolized life, refreshment and ministry. God underscores the woman and her strategic ministry in comparing her to a vine. In God's kind of family, a wife and mother must be more concerned about being than doing, more concerned about what she is than how she performs. Christian conduct is rooted in christian character. Without Christ within, we cannot do a thing.

Hope

(**Gen. 1:28**; **Gen. 2:18**; **Deut. 33:29**; **Ps. 25:9**; **Ps. 121:1-2**) God gave a command to both the man and woman: woman is a partner in being fruitful and ruling the earth. Because of what woman is by divine creation, she is the very helper man needs to fulfill his God-given responsibilities in the world and in the home.

(**John 15:8**; **Gal. 5:22-23**; **Prov. 31:30**; **2 Cor. 12:9**) A fruitful vine is a woman who fears the Lord. She is a God-centered person, and God is a powerful reality in her life. God is the motivating force, her strength, her hope, her counselor. The secret of her fruitfulness stems from her vital and deep relationship with God. Her sufficiency is from God: else she would burn out by doing and going, seeing motherhood as a duty rather than as a service and privilege to be used of God to accomplish His purposes in the family unit.

Change

(**Prov. 31**) Priorities are established here showing that a God-fearing wife and mother is a family-oriented person. She is utterly devoted to her family as her number one ministry. Her family is not neglected while she does other important things.

(**Prov. 31:11-12,23,28**; **Gen. 2:18**) She is also a husband-oriented person. She does not look to people or things for meaning rather than to God. She serves rather than being served, and ministers out of her fulness of her relationship with God rather than looking to be fulfilled.

(**Prov. 31:10,29-30**) A noble and excellent character is a consequence of a woman in commitment to and relationship with God, a woman who has established four priorities in her life:

1. Her relationship with God.
2. Her ministry to her family.
3. Her development of a godly character.
4. Her expression of godly conduct toward other people in and out of the home.

Work Out Your Salvation (Phil. 2:12-13)

Memory Verse(s):
> **John 15:4-5**

Devotion:
> BSAF for **Prov. 31:10**.

Put-Off/Put-On:
> Study the following verses about women, wives, mothers, fruit and fruitbearing. Write down how they apply to your life, and what do they suggest about the privileges, responsibilities, role and value of women:
>
> > **Gen. 1:26-28; Ex. 21:12; Josh. 16:3-6, 2 Kings 4:8-10;
> > Prov. 1:8-9; Prov. 6:20; Prov. 11:16; Prov. 12:4;
> > Prov. 14:1; Prov. 18:22; Prov. 19:14; Prov. 20:20;
> > Prov. 21:9,19; Prov. 23:22-25; Prov. 31:10;
> > Prov. 31:11-12; Prov. 31:26; Prov. 31:28-31;
> > Ezek. 24:16; Matt. 26:13,27; Matt. 26:55-56;
> > Luke 1:30-38; Luke 2:36-38; Luke 8:3; Luke 10:42;
> > John 15:1-16; John 20:11-18; Acts 1:14; Acts 2:17-18;
> > Acts 9:36-39; Acts 16:14-15; Acts 21:9; Rom. 16:1-2;
> > Rom. 16:3,6; Rom. 14-15; 1 Cor. 7:2-5; Eph. 5:22-24,33;
> > Phil. 4:3; 1 Tim. 5:1-2; 1 Tim. 5:9-14 2 Tim. 1:5;
> > 2 Tim. 3:15; Titus 3:2-5; 1 Pet. 3:1-6.**
>
> Reflect on all you have studied and record to the best of your ability the most important overall impression you have received about being a fulfilled and fulfilling woman.

160

9.15. Rugged Love

Perspective

There is no biblical reference to support being tough and staunch in order to change the behaviour of a child or an adult or anyone else. It is the power of God's word and the influence of the Holy Spirit, the power in the word which convicts and changes others, not the power of the human personality (**John 16:8-15**).

The world operates out of the emphasis of intellectual skills and abilities to reason out the problem, to eventually outwit the child. All this does is to teach the child to also outwit and manipulate the parent.

- **Power Struggle**

  What follows is the suggestion of 'will-power', one pitted against another, one trying to control another. This speaks of witchcraft which in reality is turning over one's will to another human being, the spirit of Jezebel. The only Person qualified to change another's will is the Holy Spirit (**2 Tim. 2:22-26**).

- **Holy Spirit**

  The only way to allow the Holy Spirit to act in the situation is for the parent(s) to act in the wisdom, and in the love and power of God's word.

- **Sin**

  Parent and child both are born in sin. All of us have a rebellious and independent spirit. Not a question of will-power but the question is one of obedience, the breaking of this disobedient, independent spirit of doing your own thing. This requires a 100% biblical approach whereas both the parent and the child are placed in the realm of the Holy Spirit. Both parties learn to depend on the Holy Spirit. The parents serve as an example to teach child to gradually be free of depending on parents and to be completely dependent on the Holy Spirit. Human reasoning, strength of personality, witty schemes, tricks, will not do it.

Principles

(**Prov. 22:15**) Folly is in the heart of a child, the rod of discipline drives it out. To reject counsel of the parent who is responsible to God for training the child, the child would be the greatest of fools (**Prov. 19:11**). A wise man restrains his anger. He applies patience, overlooks offenses, even for a child, that is, don't be a nit-picker by being on the back of the child all the time.

(**Prov. 16:23**) A wise man's heart guides his mouth, and his lips promote instructions.

(**Rom. 12:9-21**) These truths apply to the child as well as to your peers. As you follow **Rom. 12**, not only will the child be trained to be conformed to Christ but the parent as well.

Conclusion

Experience as a guide leads to reliance on one's own ability and intellect to discern problems which leads to manipulation—an arm of the flesh— trying to force a change in the behaviour of another. Only God can change the heart, the motives of another—this is the sovereign work of God. He is responsible for the results.

Our responsibility in challenging situations is to check our own spirit, to call upon the Lord for wisdom, and for grace to respond in an exhorting and edifying manner, and thus, to allow the Holy Spirit to do the rest (**Gal. 6:1-5; Eph. 4:29**). Review **Section 7.9, "Holding Self Accountable"; Appendix A.9, "Contingency Plan"**.

Our sole source, and all that we need, is the word of God for the Gospel is the power of God. This is the power that changes the hearts, the minds and the behaviour of man (**Gal. 5:22-26**).

9.16. Marriage Partnership

Perspective

(**1 Pet. 3:1-7**; **Rom. 8:15-17**) In God's eyes men and women are joint or equal heirs, husband not above wife nor wife above husband. Husbands are to know their wives by loving and tenderly taking care of them with warmth and tenderness, as joint heirs of the grace of life. Wife is to submit herself to her own husband's God given authority, influence and leadership. Wife stands in awe and reverence of God to help complete her husband: to provide support, encouragement, so that both husband and wife operate in order, in cooperation, in relationship and partnership. Thus, walking together, hand in hand throughout life.

Hope

(**Eph. 5:18-21**; **Col. 3:17**; **John 14:21**) In order to fulfill one's responsibilities and functions, to counteract the inclinations of the flesh, we are commanded to be filled with the Spirit, that is, being conscious of His Presence at all times. Accordingly, being filled with the Spirit rests on the shoulders of the believer, that is, he is filled only as he walks obediently to Christ, denying his own self and interest in order to be a blessing to others.

(**John 7:38-39**; **Heb. 13:17**) As the believers obey, Jesus' Presence is illuminated, manifested and quickened in them, within their hearts and lives. When a believer needs to fulfill his/her role and function, God's Presence gives a deep sense of His love and care, helping and giving confidence, forgiveness and assurance: giving wholeness the believer needs. This process begins at the point each dies to their own need and desires in order to complete and fulfill the other.

(**Rom. 5:5**) All the love we will ever need is already residing within us. All we have to do is exercise it by an action of our will as God commands. Love is not biblical love unless it involves an element of sacrifice: this is illustrated by responding kindly when treated harshly (**Matt. 5:43-48**; **1 Pet. 3:9**).

Change

(**Matt. 18:4**; **Matt. 11:28-30**; **1 Pet. 5:5**) A Spirit-filled person has a submissive and respectful spirit. He does not have a spirit of criticism, dissension, envy, divisiveness, or selfishness: but he goes out of his way to minister and to serve. Even upon the most dire situations when one is heavily laden, weary and burdened, exhausted and despairing, Christ will enable the believer to work through any struggle. Under His leadership, direction, guidance, and care, one can learn from Him how to live and labor in a spirit of rest in any challenging situation (**Heb. 4:1-13**).

(**Eph. 5:22-24**) To submit is God's will. We submit because we love God, we do it as to Him, to please Him. It is the God given authority and function in the person we honor, not necessarily the person or his actions. Christian wives do not obey the Lord out of resentment and reaction—they need to check this spirit. They focus their lives to please the Lord and then their husbands: their function is to encourage and develop a partnership and order in the family. Need of woman today is not to compete or long after man but to find herself in a recognized position, and a honored relationship. Thus she fulfills her role by being the number one encourager, to back up her man, to stand firm, to cover his weaknesses, to share in his leadership by providing godly wisdom and influence.

(**Eph. 5:25-33**) Husband is to love wife by a selfless and unselfish love, a giving and sacrificial love, a love of the mind and will as well as the heart. A love that works for the highest good of the person loved, to nourish and to cherish. He is to be a leader in developing relationships by being intimate with wife and children, and for disciplining children in the Spirit of Christ. He is to be the ultimate servant in the home. He is to establish value, order, harmony, and to exemplify traits of integrity, honor, justice, courage and self-denial. Accordingly, the christian home is to be lived in the very presence and atmosphere of the Lord—to be governed by the Lord. Decisions are to be made in the light of the Lord and His will. Thus, the christian home is not to have two partners, but three—husband, wife and Christ.

Work Out Your Salvation (Phil. 2:12-13)

Memory Verse(s):
> **Gal. 3:28-29**

Devotion:
> BSAF for **Titus 2:4**; **Prov. 31:27**; **1 Pet. 3:7**.

Put-Off/Put-On:
> The christian life is not one of doctrines only, but of relationships. Read **1 Cor. 13:4-8**. Review **Eph. 4:1-32** on how we should relate and communicate with one another: thinking, speaking and acting out the truth in love. Note how we should speak to one another in verses 25 through 32. Review **Section 9.13, "What Makes a Man**

a Man" and **Section 9.14, "Fulfilled and Fulfilling Wife and Mother"** as well as **Appendix A.3, "Love is an Action"**.

Part III.a. Life Study: Guilt and Shame

Table of Contents

Chapter 10. Self-Acceptance Series

10.1. Self Hatred

Perspective

(**John 14:21-23**) Through Jesus Christ our human spirit is in union with the Spirit of God. Jesus is the mediator between God and man. He reveals the Father, unites us with the Father, and comes with Father to make His home with us. Jesus' life radiates throughout our soul, through our memories, feelings, willings, the intuitive and imaginative faculties, even to our sensory and physical being. His Light encounters the dark places of unforgiveness and woundedness within us.

Hope

(**Rom. 8:1-2**) No longer living our lives from a guilt and shame ridden past in which we hated or were hated by others resulting in self pity, sense of inferiority, failure to accept self or others. We realize our true center is Christ, and we are to operate from the law of the Spirit of Life. We are to acknowledge this self full of hatred and begin to deal with it God's way. Confess and repent before Christ. This opens the heart to receive healing from the One who redeems.

(**2 Cor. 5:17,21**) Self hatred is usually hidden deep in the heart through repeated acts of being violated, and through our subjective focus on our own means to deal with the evil without reference to God. This is idolatry, trying to deal with sins through one's own feelings. But Christ took our sins on the cross: give it to Him. Now be free, in Christ you were made good with the goodness of God. Your self acceptance must be grounded in the awareness that God accepts you in Christ. Thus keep your eyes focused on the Source of your salvation, not on your 'diseased' habitual attitudes formed over the years.

(**Rom. 8:12-13**) No need to live from the lower self, obeying its drives. But by an act of your will acknowledge your need for emotional healing. Deal simply with inner insecurities and self hatred and gain a secure identity in Christ. You are justified in Jesus, learn to practice the Presence of Christ. Choosing to think this way, healing follows.

Change

(**Matt. 16:24-26**; **Gal. 5:18**; **Rom. 6:6**) We must differentiate between the self that works with the principle of evil and selfishness, and the self that abides in Christ and collaborates with Him. That is the true self, the justified new creation, the soul that is saved and lives eternally. Thus, practice Christ-awareness to counteract self-awareness.

(**Isa. 61:10**; **Gal. 5:18**) Only with the full acceptance of this new self can we find our true center: the place of quiet strength and solid being, that center from which we know and see ourselves to be white-robed in the very righteousness of Christ Himself.

(**Matt. 5:23-24**; **Matt. 6:14-15**) Failure to forgive others and/or to receive forgiveness for ourselves are great blocks of wholeness in Christ. This results in a judgmental spirit that is harsh and demanding on self and others. This strong perfectionist attitude demands the impossible from self and others, creates a fear of future events, and develops a sense of aloneness and abandonment in times of decision. All of this compounds preoccupation with one's own guilt, and a compulsion to compete for position and success. By forgiving and being and acting forgiven, these diseased attitudinal patterns will gradually heal.

Prayers for Restoring the Soul

- **Prayer of Thanksgiving**

  Holy Father, I thank You that I am reconciled to You through the death of Your Son, and that through faith in Him as my Saviour from sin, my heart is not only washed clean from my own sin, but it can be delivered from its grievous reactions to the sins and shortcomings of others around and against it. Because of Your

Son, Father, I can look straight up to You and dare to let all these feelings surface, and I do so now, knowing that Christ is ready to take them and give me in exchange His Life and Your perspective on myself and others. Accept my thanksgiving, O God our Father. I thank You for Christ who has redeemed me from sin and death and who is even now pouring His eternal life into me.

Lord Jesus Christ, Son of the Father, in whom I am to abide, to fully live, move and have my being (my true and new self), I direct my thanksgiving to You. I bow before You as Lord of my life, and I thank You, Precious Holy One, crucified for me, that Your blood justifies me, that in oneness with You, Your goodness is mine.

Holy Spirit, Thou who dost so constantly and faithfully mediate to us the love of both Father and Son, I thank You now for the grace to receive all that is mine as a child of God. Empower me now as I renounce the sin of self-hatred and as I move toward the goal of wholly accepting my true identity as a child of God the Father, Son, and Holy Spirit.

- **Prayer of Petition**

Well you know, O Lord, that I have been unable to appropriate Your holiness and righteousness as I wish; I have been unable to practice Your Presence because my feelings about myself are so diseased. I have looked to You, just now, as my dying Saviour, taking into Yourself my sin and darkness, my diseased feelings about You, others, and myself. I thank You that you have done this and that in time even my feeling self will reflect this. Heretofore, Lord, I have taken my eyes from You and from the objective truth and have descended into and lived out of my unhealed feeling self. This, with Your help, Lord, I will cease doing, and I will note the very moment I am 'living out of' that subjective, hurting place and will look straight up to You for the healing word You are always sending. I confess to You the sin of pride that is bound up in my self-hatred. I thank You for Your forgiveness and for the full release from it.

- **Prayer of Renunciation**

Now, Lord, in Your Name and with the grace You shower upon me, I renounce the sin of self-hatred.

Work Out Your Salvation (Phil. 2:12-13)

Memory Verse(s):
2 Pet. 1:4

Devotion:

Daily pray and meditate on the Prayer of Thanksgiving, the Prayer of Petition, and the Prayer of Renunciation. Review **Appendix A.12, "Anchor Posts"**.

Put-Off/Put-On:

Whenever diseased memories arise, see those thoughts flowing to the cross. Forgive the ones who offended—do not react by feelings—give it all to the Lord and ask Him how you should respond to all situations. Visualize **Rom. 6:3-6**, and see all offenses buried with Christ, and see yourself in the Resurrected Christ: free at last to begin living a life of victory.

Review **Section 5.2, "Sin, Self, Suffering"**.

Reference: [Payne1]

170

10.2. Self-Acceptance

Perspective

(**Rom. 7:18**; **Rom. 8:12-13**; **Luke 9:23-24**) Nothing good lives in our sinful nature. We are not to look to our past, to change or heal, or to reform past memories through self-realization or self-actualization. We are to put the diseased memories to death with Christ on the Cross. Look to Christ, forgive others or be forgiven: then we find healing for past memories.

We are not called to self-realization but to identification with Christ. Our true self at any stage of becoming is in Christ. All the wounds we suffered in the past, accept as a reality and see Jesus take these wounds on the cross. There He took upon and into Himself our darkness and depression and gives us in exchange His light and life.

Hope

(**Eph. 4:17-24**; **Eph. 3:16-19**) Failing to love ourselves aright, we will love ourselves amiss. Concern over our sins, our 'inferiority' or shortcomings are examples of the wrong form of self-love. Our reactions to the past must be identified, recognized and come to terms with. Our grievous and subjective reactions to the shortcomings and sins of others against us, must be accepted and not denied, and forgiveness extended. Once these are identified, we take them to God the Father and with Him we deal with the situation. His truths begin to flow into our being and into our souls and we become that which God says we are in His Son.

(**2 Cor. 13:5**; **2 Cor. 3:16-18**; **Gal. 4:19**; **Luke 10:19**) You have the nature of God—the great and mighty Holy Spirit—and you are the son of God. You have the authority that is in heaven, all you have to do is to go and practice it. Practice of who and what you are in Christ Jesus, not what you were or have done, or what was done to you in the past.

(**2 Cor. 5:21**; **James 4:10**) We cannot become good enough on our own. We can't heal ourselves by our reasons or feelings or self-effort. We must live from a new center: Jesus Christ. It is He who will lead and direct us and make our lives significant.

Change

171

(**Isa. 55:1-3; Isa. 61:1**) Self-hatred in a christian is a substitute for humility—it belongs to pride. We are to repent of this focus on self. Go to the Lord, listen to His words and grow into His image. We bring dysfunctional, sinful, prideful patterns in the thought life and imagination into submission to Christ. In listening prayer, every thought of the mind, every imagination of the heart, is brought captive to Christ.

(**Gal. 5:16-18**) To walk in the Spirit is to live in the present moment—always looking to Christ—always practicing His Presence—always moving in tandem with him.

(**Ps. 51**) No matter how deep the wounding and horrendous the sin, the following will release us from self-hatred and shame: the acknowledgement of ourselves as sinful from birth, the reception of Christ's forgiveness, and the extending of this forgiveness to others. We are to train our minds to think, to think through all the issues of our lives with God: Then, as we learn to hear God, we will receive from Him the true word, enabling us to replace our old diseased negatives with the positive word He is always sending.

Work Out Your Salvation (Phil. 2:12-13)

Memory Verse(s):
> **Ezek. 36:25,27**

Devotion:
> Read **Ps. 1:1-3.** Practice the Presence of the Lord.

Put-Off/Put-On:
> Review **Rom. 6.** Sit or kneel quietly before the Cross of Christ. Ask the Lord to reveal to you the repenting you need to do, and the changes you need to make in your life. Make notes and plan to accomplish these changes. Pray this: "Lord, I have hurt others, I have not loved You or others as I should; forgive me, O Lord, even as I forgive others, even as I forgive all the circumstances of life." Review **Section 5.4, "Transforming the Natural Self".**

10.3. Healing of Memories: Forgiveness of Sin

Perspective

(**Gal. 2:20**; **2 Cor. 3:16-18**) At the moment of the new birth, God's Spirit descends into the human spirit—a place where the Holy Spirit lives—from which He radiates up through the soul as well as the physical body. Thusly, believers are to Practice His Presence within which opens up channels for healing of man's soul: the basis for further becoming in Christ. The spirit is the inner depth of man's being—the higher aspect of his personality. The soul expresses man's own special and distinctive individuality. The spirit is man's nonmaterial matter looking Godward. The soul is that same nature of man looking earthward and touching things of sense.

Hope

(**Ps. 32:5**; **Luke 11:2-4**; **Isa. 61:1-4**) When we forgive others and receive God's forgiveness for our sins, God's Spirit can now radiate through this barrier of unforgiveness and proceed to heal our soul. Forgiveness of sin impacts the soul in its totality: emotional, feeling, intuitive, imaginative faculties. God's healing presence wonderfully heals man's deepest hurts and memories.

(**Rom. 8:11**; **1 Cor. 2:9-11**) Jesus is the living fountain rising up into the wells of our personality. Dwelling upon His presence begins the process of healings, of guilt, of experiences, of rejection, of diseased or unnatural feelings, and of desires and thoughts that are repressed: all the shameful past. The Holy Spirit is God's finger on sore memories. Each incident that comes to light, we are to forgive: Then we will receive from God illumination and healing, and the subsequent steps we are to take to maintain healing.

(**Col. 2:5**; **1 Cor. 5:3-5**) Time and space are creatures, they are created. Jesus, the Infinite One, is outside of time and space. All times are present to Him where nothing has yet passed away and nothing is still to come. All our times, together with all that we are, are eternally present to God. Thus, through prayer we overcome the obstacles of time and space. God, who is eternally present, is present to all our times—past, present and future. As we learn to collaborate with Him in prayer, He will heal all. Time alone does not heal or erase our sins. Only by our repentance and His blood is sin and guilt lifted from past and present.

Change

(**Matt. 6:14-15**; **Matt. 18:7**; **John 16:33**) Failure to forgive another is a most formidable barrier to wholeness. Always, at the bottom of everything that is amiss, we will find pride which needs to be confessed. Our failure to forgive the merely petty things of life—the everyday irritations and transgressions that gets to us—leads us easily to despise those who offend us in these ways.

(**1 Pet. 3:8-11**; **2 Cor. 5:15-17**) We are to see others as Christ sees them. Ask the Lord to enable you to see the other person through His eyes. We will see the other's strengths and be reminded of our own weaknesses, and Christ's patience with the petty within ourselves. When tempted to react, see your irritation, anger, resentment come up and flow unto Christ on the Cross, who, in our stead, takes and carries all our sin and darkness. Then ask Christ to fill all these spaces, where this pain, anger, resentment have been, with His healing love and light. To do the contrary, to hate another is to eventually hate and destroy oneself.

(**1 Pet. 2:23**; **Rom. 6:3-6**; **Dan. 9:4-19**; **Neh. 1:5-11**; **Matt. 18:18**) Being grievously wounded by someone, we are inclined to react in kind and place ourselves in gross sin as well. We must confess these sins before God that have deeply pierced the soul. With the confession, we extend forgiveness to the sinning one: Then the power of that sin to continue to wound and to shape the sufferer is broken. We do not forgive evil, Satan, demons and evil principalities, but we forgive 'persons' in the clutches of that evil.

Work Out Your Salvation (Phil. 2:12-13)

Memory Verse(s):
> **1 Pet. 3:9-11**

Devotion:
> BSAF on **Matt. 5:44**; **Eph. 4:25-32**.

Put-Off/Put-On:
> List in specific terms incidents and people who offended and wounded you. See that person objectively controlled and dominated by sin. Ask God to forgive you for reacting in kind to the offense, then ask God for grace to forgive the offender because he does not really know what he is doing. Ask the Lord for grace to separate your identity from the offender so that you can accept yourself. Now free to be identified with Christ, God's grace will

174

flow in to work forgiveness through you to the offender Review **Section 5.2, "Sin, Self, Suffering"**.

10.4. Bind, Loose, Cast-out

Perspective

(**Col. 1:12-14**; **Rom. 12:1-2**; **Deut. 30:19**) We have been translated from the kingdom of darkness into the Kingdom of Light. Since God redeemed us, forgiven us, Satan no longer has any authority over our lives. We are under God's authority as long as we walk in the Light as He is in the Light. God put us into His Kingdom, now it is up to us to keep ourselves there. We determine whether we are blessed or cursed while on this earth. Our problem is not with Satan, Jesus dealt with him on the cross 2000 years ago. Our problem and resolution of same is in our relationship with God. Obeying God's commands we are blessed, to do the contrary is to subject ourselves to the curse.

(**Col. 2:13-15**; **Gal. 4:4-5**) When Christ died, we died with Him. When He arose from the dead, we rose with Him. Thus, we never have to die for our sins. Christ has already paid the penalty for our sins. He bore the shame, the guilt, the judgment, the condemnation, the punishment for our sins. Being freed by His redemption, we are adopted as sons, heirs of God, joint-heirs with Jesus. Jesus made us kings and priests. Satan has been stripped of his power over our lives, we belong to God now and forever.

(**Isa. 53:4**; **Isa. 11:2-4**; **Matt. 9:6**; **2 Cor. 5:17-21**) Jesus took upon Himself all sins we committed, and the sins committed against us, we are freed from bondages and yokes. This fact is to be realized in the depths of our being through teachers/advisors/counselors, study of God's word, prayer and obedience. In time, His Presence within us becomes real in our inner man. Through these means, we bind and loose ourselves from sin as we appropriate what God has done for us, in us and as us.

(**Rom. 6:4-7**) In baptism, we are 'buried with Him' and are 'raised to life with Him'. Visualize this imagery of baptism, see the releasing of your soul from sin, and call forth the new self in the Risen Christ. The healing of the soul is never separated from this central doctrine of the forgiveness of sin. This is the area where we are mostly held in bondage and enslaved. Daily, visualize the imagery of baptism, see self free and loosed from slavery and catapulted into the realm and reign of righteousness: clothed by Jesus Himself.

(**Matt. 16:13**; **Heb. 4:12**; **Rom. 5:17**) God's word revealed to your spirit sets in motion the forces and power of deliverance resulting in the healing of the spirit, mind, memories, emotions and the will. Clothed in His garments of Righteousness, we rule and reign through righteousness on this earth.

Change

(**Matt. 6:14**; **John 20:21-23**; **Matt. 18:18**) We do not 'bind' or 'loose' demons, principalities and powers. In Christ's name, we command them to leave, knowing that Christ's death and resurrection has already bound them. However, as sin is unremitted in a life, the demons and other dark forces have power in that life. Therefore, it is the sins and the effects of these sins we are to bind and loose. It is by confession and repentance that one binds the sins, and looses himself from its control and power.

(**Gen. 4:6-7**; **Gal. 5:16-23**; **1 John 1:9**) Sin is an entity and ready to pounce on you when you fail to name and renounce your sin. Demons have authority in your life when you give them access by sinning. It is sin that is to be bound and the person loosed from it, not the casting out of demons. However, long standing sin patterns leave wounds in the soul, this needs healing which takes time in applying God's word to one's life. During this process, demons may reside in these wounds. These are easily expelled once they are discerned by God's leading.

(**Eph. 6:10-18**; **Mark 16:15-18**; **Matt. 12:36-37**; **Neh. 6:3-4**) Do not focus on Satan, demons or principalities or powers. Do not practice praying against Satan rather than to God. You choose the battleground, not Satan. Jesus already bound Satan at the cross. Thus, our emphasis is to be on God, to sing and to speak to God, to worship, to give thanksgiving and praise. Always be found practicing the Presence of God, and not Satan. While doing this, as demons, principalities and powers are discerned directly in our path, we speak directly to them and command them to leave. Our emphasis is to be on the cross. We are set free by what Jesus done. It is finished. We are not to waste time talking to Satan or his hordes. We are in a battle already won. Do not guess but be led by the Holy Spirit when confronting the enemy is required: The Holy Spirit will lead you to bind or loose or to cast out as appropriate.

Note: Long-standing sin patterns cause diseased attitudes and consequent aberrant and perverse behavior. These wounds through God's word take time to heal, and in consequence, perverse behavior will still be manifested until full healing is accomplished. This is not necessarily demons being manifested. Diseased attitudes cannot be cast out, they are still part of the human personality. They are to be dealt with by God's word, through praise and thanksgiving. Thus, the emphasis in any case is to be on God, on His word, on the practicing of the Presence of God in our human spirit. See **Rom. 8:1-16** describing the battle between our human spirit and the desires of the flesh. As our human spirit stands united with the Holy Spirit, the desires of our mortal body are dead. Realize, as sons of God, that God's Spirit within enables us to rule and reign in life in righteousness.

Work Out Your Salvation (Phil. 2:12-13)

Memory Verse(s):
> **Rom. 8:12-14**

Devotion:
> BSAF on **Rom. 6:8-14**.

Put-Off/Put-On:
> Roots of sin cause diseased attitudes, motives, intentions, perverse behavior patterns. These are addressed by the renewing of the mind and living according to what God says to think and to do in all of life's confrontations. Watch out for the disease of introspection, of over analyzing the past, of practicing the presence of the 'old man' through endless dialogue with past incidents. Draw self to God and not to co-dependent others. Bearing this in mind, work out **Appendix A.2, "Think and Do List"**. List sins, patterns of thinking and doing, and develop **Appendix A.4, "Victory over Sin Worksheet"** to deal with entrenched sin patterns. Through these devices, practice the Presence of the Lord, see and expect healing. Change takes time, it is a process. Review **Section 4.2, "Sins of the Flesh/Self of the Flesh"** and **Section 15.9, "Union with God"**.

178

10.5. Barriers to Wholeness—Failure to Receive Forgiveness

Perspective

(Eph. 2:4-5; 1 John 1:9; Heb. 10:22) It is purely an act of God alone, by His grace, that we have been forgiven of all our sins. We do nothing to earn it, either by fasting or praying. We simply receive it by acknowledging our sinfulness. Realize that Christ died for and freely gives redemption by the forgiveness of our sins. We are made whole and washed clean in our conscience and kept that way by the water of the word.

Hope

(Rom. 8:12; Rom. 10:4; Luke 21:36; Rev. 12:11) Some do not receive forgiveness because they are still trying to be 'good enough' on their own merit, striving to be perfect under the law. Instead we are to be in listening obedience to Christ and His word, trusting in His righteousness: the practice of His Presence rather than practice the presence of the 'old man'. It is by the blood of the Lamb and by our testimony to all that Jesus did on the cross and in His Resurrection, that our sins are forgiven: by His resurrection we live in righteousness. We are to act forgiven by what Jesus did, receiving this truth is our responsibility. God will not do this for us.

(Ps. 19:12-13; Ps. 139:23-24; Rom. 7:15-20; Eph. 4:22-24) Allow God to search your heart, kneel as sinners before Him, acknowledge and assume that you may have been trying to deal with sin by your efforts, condemning yourself for failing and judging yourself as not 'good enough'. Or believing that your sin was too gross for God to forgive. Let God deal with these subjective feelings. Change your focus to the objective fact that only Christ can deal with your sin: that your responsibility is to accept that you are a sinner, and that it is Christ's blood that makes you a saint when you confess and repent. By an act of faith, receive forgiveness by Christ and from that point on act forgiven. Guilt, shame and conviction is to bring us to the point of confession and repentance which brings forth a covering of righteousness. We are to walk in this Spirit, the Spirit of Righteousness: Christ Himself.

Change

(Gen. 6:5; Matt. 12:33-35; Jer. 17:9) We are not only to deal with specific acts of sin but with its roots. The structure of sin in the human personality originated when we turned from the truth in God to embrace a lie about Him. As we respond to life from our darkened heart and mind, sinful thoughts and deeds flowed forth as water from a polluted fountain. Our heart becomes a reservoir of unconscious disordered motivations and responses. We deal with this by no longer living by our feelings but by our will and our will based on the word of God which, in time, will change the root of our being.

(Eph. 4:17-18; **Hosea 4:6-7**; **Rom. 1:18-23**; **Eph. 4:22-32)** Ignorance will destroy you and your family. Indifference will harden your heart until you feel that you cannot forgive yourself anymore and give up entirely. Biblical change is a process. Realize you cannot handle or deal with sin: but realize you are completely dependent on the Lord Jesus Christ. Confess and repent daily, see Jesus take your sin into and upon Himself setting you free. Act forgiven, honor Christ by thinking and doing and being what the word says to think, to speak, and to act—daily growing into the image of Christ.

Work Out Your Salvation (Phil. 2:12-13)

Memory Verse(s):
>   **Rom. 12:1-2**

Devotion:
>   BSAF on **Rom. 6:3-6**; **James 1:19-21**.

Put-Off/Put-On:
>   Work out **Appendix A.2, "Think and Do List"** and begin to practice what God wants you to think and to do. Review **Section 5.1, "Cleansing and Purifying the Soul"**.

10.6. Healing Presence

Perspective

(**Eph. 4:22-24**; **Rom. 6:3-14**; **Heb. 4:12**) By being indifferent to what we think, we separate ourselves from His Presence: casualness is a default into self-consciousness, a fall from God-consciousness. Becoming persons, the fulness of being, evolves as we remain in Christ. God's word and love is truly something more stern and splendid than mere kindness. This love divides darkness from light, the old self from the new self.

Hope

(**Eph. 5:13**; **Gen. 2:18**; **John 17:21**) Our Lord is not defined in terms of individuality and independence, but in terms of personality: "The Father and I are one." The true self, of personality, man as fully human, is to speak of man's fellowship with God and with others. Because evil is separation from God, from self, and from others, to know ourselves in this respect is to begin being healed of the effects of the Fall.

(**Matt. 7:11-12**) Remedy is to forsake our horizontal posture, looking to the creature. Instead, straighten up in Christ, and seek to meet the needs of others rather than using others solely for our own needs. It is in the state of 'listening obedience' to His commands to bless others, denying self, where we find healing and wholeness: our true identity.

(**John 14:21,26**; **John 15:11**; **Deut. 30:7-14**) Spiritual and mental wholeness consists simply of obedience, of serving others, of learning to invoke the Presence of God. When God is centered in us and we in him, we have a home within: a true self or center out of which we live.

Change

(**James 5:19**; **Matt. 4:4**) Self-centeredness involves seeing yourself walking alongside of yourself, viewing self as the center of all things which produces self-pity, envy, covetousness, and pride. Jesus as the new Adam came practicing always the Presence of His Father. The worship of God is the ultimate denial of the old self in separation. If you do not practice the Presence of God, you will practice the presence of another.

(**Matt. 10:37-39**; **Phil. 2:12-13**) When we make our will one with God, we find the integration of personality begins to take place: an identity that God can only give.

Review your dependence or inordinate need of others, possessions or things. Ask God to give you understanding to get at the roots of this idolatry or dependence, of getting a sense of value or worth from created things rather than from God.

(**Ps. 90:17**; **Luke 4:1**; **Luke 5:17**; **Acts 1:2**) Allow God to give you favor and success, learn to bless in the power of the Spirit, and to collaborate with the Spirit to do the works of Christ. Soul saving is the most creative work in the world. A healed self in Christ is in the position to do the works of Christ, to be a witness as Christ commanded.

Work Out Your Salvation (Phil. 2:12-13)

Memory Verse(s):
> **Isa. 53:3-6**

Put-Off/Put-On:
> List sins of idolatry: being controlled by people or things: people you need to forgive, areas where you feel guilt and shame, envy and jealousy, people you offended and other similar bindings. Review **Appendix A.4, "Victory over Sin Worksheet"** and **Section 5.1, "Cleansing and Purifying the Soul"**.

Reference: See [Payne1]

10.7. Healing Presence (2)

Perspective

(**Ezek. 36:27**; **Eph. 3:16-17**) To experience this prayer fulfilled in our lives is to find our true center, the 'home within'. From this center, we 'abide' in Christ and He in us.

Hope

(**Matt. 6:14-15**; **Matt. 5:23-24**; **1 John 1:9**; **Heb. 10:22**) Barriers that keep us from realizing our 'true center' in Christ are our failures to forgive others as well as receiving forgiveness from God for our own sins. One major area is our guilt and shame, and the failure to acquire the virtue of self-acceptance in Christ. The blood of Christ completely wipes out our past, making us fully acceptable in Christ.

(**Phil. 3:13-14**) The extent a person lives out of his diseased and corrupted attitudes and feelings toward the self to that extent he will fail to find and live from his true center. We must die to misconceived attitudes and the illusory self, else we cannot abide in Christ.

(**John 14:20**; **Col. 1:27**) Christ descends to us and into us. He incarnates us. We are indwelt by God who is above us, before He is within us and beneath us.

(**James 4:8**; **Heb. 10:22**) We look up to God who is other than me, sovereign over all. Thank God that Christ's Spirit is within me, saving me, hallowing me, linking me to Him.

Change

(**Phil. 2:12-13**) Practice His Presence within: Man and God working together. God will not do what you can do, that is, to choose. At the point you choose, it is God who enables you to do the doing. Passivity is waiting for God to deal with sin when it has been taking care of at the cross. My job now is to unite my will with His and allow righteousness to flow, changing my state of being from the natural to the supernatural.

(**1 Cor. 12:7-11**) The gifts of the Spirit are the nature of the manifestations of God. By practicing the Presence of Christ, we lay the foundation for understanding and moving of the gifts of the Spirit.

(Matt. 5:23-24) Healing gifts of the Spirit may face two big barriers to wholeness: failure to forgive others, and failure to receive forgiveness. Faith, knowledge, love, moral conduct, courage, hope, prayer, all have to do with Christ in us. Forgive and be forgiven: Daily cleansing of all slights and resentments keeps our union with Christ intact, and allows the free flow of grace.

(Jer. 17:9-10) All kinds of hearts within us: broken, grieved, discouraged, proud, wicked, trembling, double, subtle, perverse, sorrowful, haughty, fretting, heavy, jealous, envious, evil, deceitful, hard, scheming, callous and so on. However, Christ in us radiates through us, making our two minds hallowed, as well as our feelings, wills, intellect, and faculties. He completes us and we become: willing, perfect, tender, soft, pure, upright, clean wise, merry, meek and lowly, honest and good, single, true, compassionate and thankful and so on.

Work Out Your Salvation (Phil. 2:12-13)

Memory Verse(s):
> **Col. 2:11-12**

Put-Off/Put-On:
> List areas in your life which must be dealt with: people, circumstances, situations and prepare a failure list. Process **Appendix A.4, "Victory over Sin Worksheet"**. To change is a question of creating new habits in place of the old. Substitute and practice the godly response and, in time, the natural will be translated into the supernatural **(Rom. 8:14-17)**.

184

10.8. Creative Thinking

Perspective

(**Phil. 4:8**) When great and good symbolic images of God—the cosmos, fatherhood, motherhood, masculine, feminine, and so on—are rejected or are simply absent from the mind, lesser images develop to take their places. If you do not delight in higher things, you will most certainly delight in lower things. This is true of a society, a nation, a world, as well as each and every individual. What you think, in time, you will become.

Hope

(**Rom. 6:3-6**) What was done on the Cross washes and cleanses us from our false or perverted former selves. Thus, a sense of being, of well-being, comes by dwelling on who and what we are in Christ Jesus. A diseased image in the mind substitutes not only for missing images and symbols of good relationships, but it can also fill in for the lack of an adequate sense of being. This could result in a sense of non-being which requires deep meditation and prayer in order to get back in touch with God to mold our lives henceforth: a sense of being.

(**2 Cor. 10:3-5**; **John 15:5-7**) Developing the proper image and the proper form of the symbolic mind requires baptism in the Holy Spirit, listening prayer, and reception of words and pictures that come from God. Also, learning to practice the Presence through exchanging every negative word coming from the world, the flesh and the devil. And replacing these words with words from God who is always speaking to us to love as He loves, to respond to life in His Spirit.

(**Rom. 12:1-2**) We are to give up the 'conscious', rational mind which is turned on trying to analyze the 'unconscious', the creative ideas of God revealed to our spirit. Instead, we are to use our rational powers to dwell upon God's principles and concentrate on putting them into action. We are not to intellectualize, the introspective process, which results in focus on the self and brings forth futility: a practice of the presence of the self.

Change

(**Eph. 4:22-32**; **Heb. 10:22**) In severe cases when one is bound to deep introspection, prayer for the healing of the mind is required. Anoint the forehead with oil, make sign of the cross, lay hands on head, ask Jesus to enter in, to heal and quiet the mind. Visualize with the heart that this is being done, quietly praying.

Then ask God for further directions and knowledge of what and how to pray. Ask for wisdom and knowledge through pictures and word. Have person confess his sins of introspection in order to receive the needed cleansing and forgiveness.

(**James 1:21**) Person is to dwell and meditate on appropriate Scriptures dealing with his diseased attitudinal patterns, to look up to God, not within himself: then present his own heart to the heart of the transcendent God.

(**1 Pet. 1:13; 1 Pet. 4:1**) Gird your mind is to control and guard and select good input that Jesus may be revealed in your spirit. Purpose in your mind to purpose as Jesus who purposed to do the Father's will regardless of suffering.

Key word here is **FIX**:

1. Fix mind on selective input.

2. Fix mind on the will, the will to think and to do God's way. See **Section 10.3, "Healing of Memories: Forgiveness of Sin"**.

3. Fix mind to purpose, determined to proceed God's way, not be moved by anything.

Work Out Your Salvation (Phil. 2:12-13)

Memory Verse(s):
> **James 1:21**

Devotion:
> BSAF on **Col. 3:1-3**.

Put-Off/Put-On:
> Ask yourself the following three questions as you study each of the following verses:
>
> 1. What does this verse say to me?
> 2. What am I doing wrong?
> 3. What must I change?
>
> **Gen. 6:5; Gen. 11:6; Exodus 1:12; Exodus 8:12;
> Ps. 1:2; Ps. 4:4; Ps. 19:14; Ps. 38:12; Ps. 48:9;
> Ps. 119:59; Prov. 4:27; Prov. 6:18; Prov. 12:5;
> Matt. 10:22; Luke 9:62; John 15:9;
> Rom. 1:21; Rom. 8:6; Rom. 12:3;**

186

**Gal. 5:1; Gal. 6:9; Phil. 1:27; Phil. 2:5;
1 Tim. 4:15; James 1:12; James 5:11;
1 Pet. 2:19; 1 Pet. 5:9; 2 Pet. 3:17; Rev. 3:12.**

Review **Section 7.14, "Mind Control".**

10.9. Mental Obsessions

Perspective

(**1 Chron. 28:9**; **Prov. 6:16**; **2 Cor. 10:3-5**; **Gal. 5:16**) To break any habit, it takes a quality decision, an act of the will, which process begins in the mind. The disease of introspection, the mind dwelling upon itself, feeds upon itself and eventually destroys itself. Our mind can be held captive not only by a demonic imagery but by a continuous mental obsession. Constantly analyzing oneself looking inward to find some personal truth or reality, and constantly analyzing whether the truth I found is true or not, one becomes full of doubt.

Hope

(**Col. 3:3,5,8-9**) We are inclined to dwell on some mental or emotional conflict in life, and, in time, we will develop a diseased and distorted mindset. Not accepting my conclusion of self, I become critical of self, and even hatred of self: I become my own god. Scripture tells us to look up to God, ask Him to come in and shine His light into my heart: Then I will receive an objective good: either forgiveness or illumination.

(**Col. 1:27**; **Col. 2:10**; **Luke 16:10**; **Phil. 2:12-13**) To fail to center on Christ within is to 'walk alongside ourselves', rather than being and becoming conformed to the image of Christ. The one whose center is the illusionary self (the one whose center is a complex of diseased feelings, attitudes, images and symbols) has nothing to do with the new substantive, outwardly-centered self in Christ.

(**Prov. 27:17**; **Acts 17:28**) To be is to experience life firsthand, to live in the present moment. The one who squanders his present by trying to figure out a more secure or less painful future, lives always in the painful past and uncertain future. To live in the present, of 'isness' of 'being' is to use oneself by knowing others. By allowing God to be His fullest through us in the present moment, we become sharpened by what 'is' and we begin to rejoice in the realities outside of ourselves.

Change

(**Matt. 22:37-39**; **John 6:63**) To lift our eyes from ourselves to others is a decision, we can and must make. It is a minute to minute kind of discipline. Man becomes as he obeys. We 'become' as we are obedient to the best we know at one level, to the words that come from God on the highest level: that word becomes life.

(**John 5:19**; **John 15:5**) The power to be has to do with the power of being at home 'within': the present moment of being centered, of living serenely and meditating from the true center. To love God is to be drawn up and out of ourselves and into Him. In loving Him, I become incarnate of Him. God descends into us and we are drawn into Him. With Christ, we can say "I love the Father, I do what I see Him do, He has crowned me with glory and honor." Loving all that 'is', we learn to die daily to the introspective, self-conscious life.

Work Out Your Salvation (Phil. 2:12-13)

Memory Verse(s):
> **Rom. 12:1-2**

Devotion:
> BSAF on **Col. 3:1-3**; **Phil. 2:3-4**.

Put-Off/Put-On:
> Make note of any excessive introspections, of being self absorbed. Allow **Prov. 3:5-7**; **Prov. 4:20-27** to guide you. Process **Appendix A.2, "Think and Do List"**.

10.10. Breaking Physical Habits

Perspective

(**Rom. 4:17**; **2 Cor. 4:17-18**) It does not matter if we don't feel as conquerors or overcomers: The Word says we are, the Word does not lie. The essence of faith is speaking of things not manifested as though they were already an accomplished fact. We are dealing with the invisible, the transcendent, which impacts upon the visible.

Hope

(**James 1:21**) Meditating on the Word saves our soul, and 'save' means deliverance, safety, preservation, healing, soundness and wholeness. The engrafted word received in bold confidence is able to deliver us from the bondages of our intellect, memory, and will. Instead of being prisoners of self-indulgence, we become prisoners of the thoughts of God.

(**Col. 3:1-3**) Breaking physical habits takes a quality decision, an act of the will that starts with the intellect. Thinking God's thoughts after Him, restructures the strongholds (scaffolding) of the mind, redirecting the coping mechanisms to respond to life's uncertain events in obedience to Christ (**2 Cor. 10:3-5**).

(**Prov. 8:13**; **Prov. 16:6**; **2 Cor. 7:11**) Teach yourself to hate evil, do not be indifferent to it. The fear of the Lord is to hate evil because it hurts God. Begin to hate those things that enslave you and offend God. Develop a vehement desire and revenge against evil (**Ps. 22:3**). Then practice being in awe, in the Presence of the Lord and His holiness. At the same time, begin to praise God. God inhabits the praises of His people. By praising, you establish Jesus' Presence and lordship over your life and habits.

Change

(**James 1:21**; **Jer. 1:12**; **Heb. 3:1**) Accept with confidence that God's word works and will change your habits without panic on your part. Graft the Word into your spirit by putting it first in your life, and to stand on it regardless of circumstances and experiences of others. God watches over His word to perform it; thus, allow it to quicken, grow and develop in your spirit.

(**Isa. 61:1**; **John 8:32**; **2 Cor. 3:17**; **Rom. 6:14**) Through Jesus I am set free from all evil habits, appetites and thoughts. Knowing His truth sets me free because where the Spirit is, there is liberty; therefore, sin shall have no dominion over me.

(**Rom. 8:2**; **Phil. 4:13**; **Rom. 8:37**; **Isa. 26:13-14**; **2 Cor. 2:14**) Christ infuses His strength into my spirit. This law of the Spirit sets me free from the law of sin and death. Thus, greater is He who is in me, than he who is in the world. No longer inhibited or condemned by my past, I am more than a conqueror. "Thanks be to God who always causes me to triumph in Christ Jesus."

Work Out Your Salvation (Phil. 2:12-13)

Memory Verse(s):
> **Rom. 12:1-2**

Devotion:
> BSAF on **Luke 9:23-24**.

Put-Off/Put-On:
> Process **Appendix A.6, "Problem Solving Worksheet"**. Using this sheet as your guide, complete the following questions:

- What happened? (describe the problem or situation)

- What I did? (describe your responses or thoughts)

- What should I have done? (study this worksheet for ideas)

- What I now must do (work out **Appendix A.9, "Contingency Plan"**, **Appendix A.4, "Victory over Sin Worksheet"** or **Appendix A.2, "Think and Do List"**) to restructure the situation (your thoughts, your speech, and your actions) that would be pleasing to God.

Chapter 11. Overcoming Lust Series

11.1. Assaults against the Soul

Perspective

(**Matt. 5:21-22**; **Matt. 5:27-28**) Assaults against the dignity and beauty of the soul come about through any form of abuse which involves either a desire to destroy and/or a desire to use. Core kinds of harm involved are murder, anger, adultery, and consuming lust.

Desire for More

(**Gen. 1:26**) We all have a driving desire for more. Initially, God designed us that we may be filled with His Presence, to do as He does: being a blessing, a state of 'being' in God and thus, 'doing' what God commands. Not following God's commands and desires ('doing' in order to 'be') leaves a void, a vacuum. We are inclined to fill the emptiness horizontally through things and people which creates a relationship of co-dependency either as abuser or perpetrator or as a victim of the aggressor.

Destructive Anger

(**James 4:2**) We desire, we pursue through our schemes and devices in order to get that which satisfies, that is, we 'do' in order to 'be'. We use created things, people or things to fulfill our needs. This opens the way to anger and a desire for

192

vengeance, to bring judgment down on those who have stood in our way to gain satisfaction. Adding to this intensity is that our longings and desires are almost always partially blocked and, thus, disappointment is an ongoing reality, and so is potential anger.

The soil of our fallen being is ripe to inflict emotional and physical abuse which involves the omission of involvement (neglecting or abandoning the other emotionally) or the destructive commission of shaming the other. The elements of emotional abuse (abandonment and shame) and physical abuse (cruelty, inconsistency and rage) are perpetrated to some degree by all those with whom we have a relationship. Anger attempts to destroy those who stand in our way.

Destructive Lust

Harm also comes from those whose lust to avoid emptiness and find satisfaction causes them to use other people as food for their empty souls: a desire to find satisfaction illegally, apart from God and His righteous path. A person who so lusts not only sucks life out of a host in order to dim the intensity of his loneliness, but also relishes mastery and power over someone or something.

Lust is the effort to possess another in order to steal enough passion to be lifted out of our current struggle into a world that feels (for an instant) like the Garden of Eden. If anger is the desire to make someone pay for blocking our return to the garden, then lust is our efforts to push our way back into the garden. Lust, in part, is a desire for union, that is, a desire to be absorbed into another. Nonsexual lust is 'co-dependency'. Like sexual lust, it is the desire to find a host who will provide a vital energy that appears to be missing in the co-dependent.

The excesses of this need to be fulfilled and satisfied leads to perversion which is a wedding of lust and rage: someone to pay for the pain of emptiness we are forced to experience.

(**2 Cor. 10:1-5**) We all live in this world of war: being a perpetrator or a victim of anger and rage and consuming lust to fill our emptiness and longing to be satisfied. We are to become warriors, warriors of love, who despise evil, and anything inconsistent with the beauty and love of God. This requires a radical change, a radical conformity to the image of Christ as God initially planned (**Gen. 1:26-27**) (See **Section 7.12, "True Dying"**).

11.2. Lusts, Desires—Inordinate

Perspective

(**Exodus 20:4-5,17**; **Matt. 5:28**) The 'flesh' desires many things. It wants power, pleasure, wealth, status, admiration, and the like. Nothing wrong with liking things. But lust is more than liking. It is the will to possess. Lust turns good things into objects of worship and this is closely linked to idolatry. We are to image God in our thoughts, our emotions, our memories and in our wills—not people or things.

Hope

(**Gal. 3:13-14**; **Gal. 5:16-18**) It is a question of desire: replacing desire with desire, desire to please God rather than to please self. As we choose to honor God in our thoughts daily, the desire of the inordinate flesh will fade away. This battle is a lifetime of spiritual warfare: a continuous engagement in replacing ungodly images with godly ones in order to raise ourselves above ourselves—a purification process of the soul (**Rom. 8:5-13**).

(**Luke 9:23-24**; **Matt. 22:37-39**; **Gen. 2:18**) Pornography, masturbation, and other misdeeds are substitutes for intimacy. By these acts a person is addicted to self-centeredness, committed to serving themselves, doing whatever they can to avoid dying to self. This is a spiritual problem, not primarily physical. It always involves the spirit of man either in concert with the will of God, communing with the Holy Spirit; or in rebellion against that will, trying to push the Holy Spirit out of the way.

Change

(**Rom. 12:1-2**; **Col. 3:1-5**) Concentrate on setting your heart and mind on things above: then after you do this, put to death whatever belongs to your earthly nature by the entire renewal of your mind, especially memories, the past: it all begins here.

(**Matt. 5:29**; **Matt. 6:9-10**) Just because you can't help lusting does not make it acceptable. Jesus is dedicated to bringing in another kingdom. To be His disciple, you must put lust to death. You must learn to want what He wants for you, and to put away everything else. Accordingly, actively hate by thought, by speech and by action the pleasures of sin, and immediately fill the vacuum with praises and thanksgivings to God for His mercies. The key is immediacy (a delay in this transfer of imaging favors evil). Practice the new thought pattern until it becomes spontaneous.

(**Gal. 5:13-14**; **Rom. 6:3-6**) Having been 'buried' with Christ in our baptism, we are 'made alive' with Him by the Spirit. See self in the spiritual realm as a member of the household of God, endued with the Spirit of God, now enabled to live by God's commandments to be a blessing and a servant to others on earth: This is the true you.

(**Gal. 2:20**) As a result of your union with Christ (**Eph. 4:1**; **Eph. 4:20-21**; **Eph. 5:6**), you are compelled to speak truthfully (**Eph. 4:25**), to build up (**Eph. 4:29**), to die to self (**Eph. 5:1**), and to not be ruled by self, passion or anger (**Eph. 4:31**) in relationships especially in marriage.

(**1 John 4:7-8**; **1 John 1:6-9**) God says if my heart is kept pure by continually meditating on the word in the context of God's sanctifying work, I will have the power to overcome temptation that leads to indulgence, pornography, masturbation, and similar actions. It is not psychological techniques, not a problem of dealing with our drives but of sanctifying our hearts in communion and intimacy with God and with others: the purification of our intellect, our memories, and our wills.

Work Out Your Salvation (Phil. 2:12-13)

Memory Verse(s):
>**1 Tim. 4:7**

Devotion:
>BSAF on **2 Tim. 2:22**; **Phil. 2:3-4**; **1 Tim. 4:7**.

Put-Off/Put-On:
>Review and briefly answer the following questions:

- **Lust Objects:** What controls or possesses you— magazines, x-rated films, quest for power, status, wealth, etc. ?

- **Relationship Lusts:** What are your relationship desires? What do you want out of a relationship? Do you want to be close? distant? Do you want to get

195

involved in the lives of others? or do you want nothing to do with people?

- **Life Meaning Lusts:** What do you believe makes life work? What's important? What isn't? What do you believe you must have in order for your life to work, to function, to be successful?

Key: Reprogram your life so that God's honor and glory and the welfare of others are to be foremost.

Note: In order to penetrate and understand the workings of the self, keep a journal of times when you are tempted. Review for trigger mechanisms such as stress, disappointments, rejection, bitterness, resentments and similar reactions. Use **Appendix A.9, "Contingency Plan"** to counteract. Review worksheets **Section 11.13, "Life-Dominating Sins"** and **Section 5.1, "Cleansing and Purifying the Soul"**.

11.3. Feelings/Faith

(**Heb. 10:38**) Christian is to walk by faith (God in the present moment), not by feelings or emotions. We are naturally disposed to live by our feelings and emotions, and to react according to life's confrontations. When emotional we react according to the emotion; when we feel bad, we react irresponsibly: grumble, complain, murmur. If we feel good, we act happy. Our behavior is determined by how we feel and react to emotional experiences. Living by one's feelings is contrary to God's will. "The just shall live by faith." This is God's will. Faith is to control our lives and to face life's particular problems according to God's word and wisdom—not by our feelings.

(**Rom. 8:29**; **Heb.4:9-10**; **10:22-23**) When memories of the past influence us, the past directs our lives, and we become our own god. We are to be in control by keeping our memories pure regardless of what is happening. Only in this spirit of a pure heart and memory do we allow God to work through us in order to conform us to His Son.

How does a believer live by faith? What does it mean to live by faith? It means to do four things, and that, consistently.

1. The believer is to commit his life and his problems to God all day long—throughout his waking hours: a life of prayer and meditation. He is to take his experiences and his problems of the day and commit them to God, immediately and once for all. He is to believe that God hears his commitment and gives strength to walk triumphantly throughout the day. He is to know that God does not like a whining, whimpering child begging and begging for strength, wallowing around in self-pity (**James 1:5**).

2. The believer is to deny self: the feelings, the emotions, and selfishness of his flesh, to put off these reactions. He is to put on and clothe himself with the new and better self resembling God in the righteousness and holiness of the truth (**Eph. 4:22-24**) (See **Appendix A.5, "Dying to Self"**).

3. The believer is to act as though he has made a commitment to God, to keep on, keeping on regardless. His feelings are immaterial. He is to act responsibly. He is to do what God's word says to do, to behave as he should: that is, to respond to life daily forgiving all offenses with a heart full of benevolence and compassion (**Matt. 5:43-48**).

4. While he is doing what he should be doing, he is to ask God for strength and grace. He is to acknowledge God in all his ways throughout the whole day: walking in prayer, asking forgiveness when he slips and falls, and to praise and to thank God for His mercy and grace. It is when the believer is going about his affairs in a responsible manner that God directs his path. When a believer chooses to follow God's way rather than to follow his feelings or fleshly instincts, then God enters into the situation and provides the wisdom and strength and grace to perform and complete an appropriate biblical response (**Gen. 4:7**) (See **Appendix A.9, "Contingency Plan"**).

The Description of Faith

The key to any of us being great in the eyes of God is faith: faith in His Son, the Lord Jesus Christ.

Faith (wisdom of God, His word) is the substance, the actual possession, of things hoped for (eternal values), the evidence and reality of things not seen. It is both an act and a possession of the thing believed. It is believing and trusting in that which actually exists. We may not be able to see it, but it is real and existing, and we can possess it by believing and having faith in it. We can possess it now. We cannot see it, but we can actually possess the very substance of it by believing and entrusting our lives to it.

To be possessed and influenced by what we see is to live by 'natural grace'— Tree of the Knowledge of Good and Evil—following the pattern of the 1st Adam which leads to futility.

But what you see is made from what is unseen which is the true reality. Thus, we are to attain to possess Christ from whom all things proceed. In Him, we possess 'all things' in its true form, that is, we act and live by supernatural grace—Tree of Life—by which we give honor and glory to our Lord.

Intellect and Memory Possessed

Thus, anything that possesses us and controls us other than the word of God, to that extent it keeps us from being possessed by Life itself—Christ. To the extent we keep our intellect and memories pure and current (not possessed or occupied by the past, by things, by people, by circumstances), to that extent we are possessed by God.

The first step to take to insure that we are moving from natural grace to supernatural grace is to turn our will over to God the Father, to allow His will to be our will, which is His word. Regardless of what is happening, declare "Thy will be done!" This declaration will raise us above ourselves and the circumstances that surround us (**Matt. 26:42**).

The second step is to keep our thoughts and images from being polluted and desensitized by the world's influences (TV, movies, and the like). We are to keep our memory fresh and pure by focusing our mind on eternal values, and, thus, looking at, and seeing life from God's perspective (**Col. 3:1-3**).

Faithfulness

Being a committed christian is a 24 hour affair. Thus, be aware that life is but a training exercise and the battle field is what you allow to occupy your mind: living by the Tree of sight and sense—the lower nature; or the Tree of life—faith, the unseen but the true reality, the higher nature. Faith must be tested because it can only become your intimate possession through conflict (**Rom. 12:1-2**; **James 1:2-4**; **2 Pet.1:3-10**).

Approval

Accordingly, the reward of faith is God's approval, and when God approves us, He accepts us into His eternal Presence. The approval of God means that God fulfills all His promises to us, and the promises of God become a living reality in our experiences. This means that God looks after and cares for us, giving us victory over all the enemies of this world. As we speak, it is God speaking through us establishing His kingdom and His will on earth (**John 5:19**).

Review **Section 15.1, "Mind"** and **Section 15.2, "Abiding"**.

11.4. Bondages

Perspective

(**John 8:31-32,36**) Good news of the Gospel is that the christian is free to become like the person God wants him to be, to achieve the goals God wants him to achieve, to obtain maximum enjoyment of life in Christ. Many, however, are slaves to bondage of sins, habits and thought patterns that keep the inner man bound. There are three major areas of bondage that rob us of our freedom: bondage of **inferiority**, of **insecurity**, and of **inadequacy**.

Hope

(**2 Pet. 2:17-22**; **2 Tim. 1:7**; **Rom. 8:11-18**; **Isa. 58:12**; **Heb. 10:17-19**) Oppressive influences are to be dealt with by your position in Christ, and not by blaming others or circumstances. Inferior people try to impress others to cover up their sense of inadequacies. Inferiority can only be overcome by righteousness. We need to build up the waste places of our lives and establish firm foundations of God's word. Jesus' blood forgave us and cleanses us once and forever. The blood frees us from all inferiorities.

(**James 5:15-18**; **Isa. 32:15-20**) Exercise of prayer is the exercise of power. Rule your environment on the inside and the outside. Be ruled by peace, quietness, assurance; live in sure dwellings and quiet resting places and know that in all adversities His fruit remains regardless. Believe your beliefs, doubt your doubts.

(**2 Cor. 5:21**; **Rom. 5:12**; **Isa. 53:10**; **Heb. 12:1-3**) Jesus broke sin's dominion over us. It is sin that makes us inferior, inadequate and thus full of fear. But we are free, and free to reign in righteousness. We cannot lose for winning. Christ is unlimited and so are we in Him (**1 John 4:17**).

Change

(**1 Sam. 11:1-5**; **Jer. 10:2-7**) We are more than a conqueror because nothing has the power in and of itself to subjugate us, but only one's perception of it. See yourself living in the shelter of the Most High, under shadow of the Almighty who delivers you from the lies of the devil: this is the true reality, the whole of one's personality centered in God.

(**1 Chron. 4:9-10**) Whatever has you conquered, call on God and come free. Whatever names you were called by your parents, whatever experiences in life made you feel ashamed, guilty and condemned, all the patterns of thought developed over the years which have led to inferior ideas and images, come out from under and be on top in Jesus.

Work Out Your Salvation (Phil. 2:12-13)

Memory Verse(s):
> **Col. 2:9-10**

Devotion:
> BSAF on **Ps. 112**.

Put-Off/Put-On:
> Practice these truths until they become a living reality in your spirit! Takes time, in fact, a lifetime—be patient.

> 1. Read chapter one of Ephesians, identify and personalize each "In Him" by inserting your name: "In Him, I, (your name) have redemption through His blood";

> 2. How were you placed in Christ? (**1 Cor. 1:30**; **Rom. 6:4-6**)

> 3. What does Paul say about our inadequacies? (**2 Cor. 3:5,6**)

> 4. How do we know the truth that sets us free? (**John 8:31**)

> 5. Why must we be careful to stand daily in our freedom in Christ? (**Gal. 5:1**)

> 6. How do we keep standing firm? (**Gal. 5:16**)

11.5. Eating Disorders

Perspective

Labels tend to type anorexia and bulemic conditions as 'disease'. This provides and gives one an excuse for sin; therefore, God needs to heal them of this disease: it is God's fault. We turn away from the truth to a deception, a problem of wrong thinking and doing as defined by the Bible.

Common Characteristics of Eating Disorders

Habits and the desire for instant gratification (to be as the world says you are to be):

- Compulsion to binge and purge can be defined as greed and self-promoting satisfaction.
- Looking for triggers of this action reveals lust of both mind and body (**1 Cor. 10:13**; **Nu. 11:4, 6, 13-24, 31-34**; **Ps. 78:17**).
- The issue is clearly trusting in God and not in circumstances.
- Compulsions can also be related to excessive worry, anxiety, etc. (**Matt. 6:25-32**; **Col. 3:5**).

Ungodly desire for a 'surface' perfection and pride; "The Pharisee within."

- **Matt. 23** says a lot about living for one's outward image.
- Apt to cover up and hide binges and purges. The healing requires confessing to God and others.
- And maintaining a journal depicting eating habits—when, where, how much, etc..

Desire to save herself for her sins:

- Purging can be an act of penance or self-flagellation.
- This penance is sinful as it exposes the heart which trusts in its own efforts instead of in Christ and His provisions (**Phil. 3:7-9**; **Gal. 2:16**).
- Becomes one who serves the law rather than grace.

Laziness and desire for instant solutions:

- Putting off and putting on takes effort and time (**Prov. 13:9**; **Prov. 21:25-26**).
- The lazy way (purge) leads only to more cravings (binge) and ultimate death.
- slothfulness and laziness are shortcuts and may be pervasive in other areas that need investigation.

How to Help

1. Be sure of their salvation.

2. Set the agenda. Anything that is less than pleasing God is unacceptable.

3. Plan to deal with resistance to the truth (**Prov. 26:16**).

4. Establish accountability—give and check homework. Maintain a journal and review same, and have person accountable to someone in their family.

5. Teach them how to handle temptations to binge (See **Appendix A.9, "Contingency Plan"**).

6. Cry out to God for help and identify motives that tempt her.

7. Draw near to God for both mercy and grace to help in time of need (**Heb. 4:16**).

8. Avoid places that trigger binges.

9. When tempted, keep on the move, change locations, leave house if necessary.

10. Remember that the escape of purging is no longer opened to her. At that point she is to call upon her Saviour for the true way of escape (**1 Cor. 10:13**).

11. Call a friend for prayer.

12. If she has already started to binge, cry out for His help.

13. Read **Isa. 53:3-7**. Become aware of particular 'triggers': e.g., moods, time of month, difficult situations, etc.. Anticipate and be ready for them.

Work Out Your Salvation (Phil. 2:12-13)

Memory Verse(s):

> **2 Cor. 5:15**

Devotion:

> BSAF on **2 Cor. 5:1-10**.

Put-Off/Put-On:

> Prepare **Appendix A.9, "Contingency Plan"**, guided by paragraph above, **How to Help**. Work out **Appendix A.4, "Victory over Sin Worksheet"** for entrenched patterns. A day at a time will do it! Review **Section 10.1, "Self Hatred"** and **Section 10.2, "Self-Acceptance"**.

11.6. Out of Control

Perspective

(**Eph. 1:17-23**; **Rom. 6:22**) Jesus is head over all principalities and powers, and so are we in Him. We were formerly subject to death by process of impurity, lawlessness and absolute corruption. Now we are no longer in union with Satan, we are now in union with the Spirit of God.

Hope

(**Rom. 6:1-7**) When you are willingly or unknowingly under control of something other than God's Spirit, you are in bondage to sin. However, God has broken the power of sin through the Lord Jesus Christ. You can overcome sin's power by depending on His strength and being obedient to His word.

(**2 Pet. 1:3-4**) We live in a new dimension of truth, of principle, of thought, of action by our partaking of the divine nature: by this we escape the corruption of the world of lust. With this new mindset, I need to develop this new attitude through practice, that is, to add virtue to faith, to this add knowledge, to this self-control, follow this with perseverance, godliness, and brotherly kindness. With practice and commitment, you will not fail in life.

(**Eph. 1:17-19**) God's strength is united with mine, and He will never leave or forsake me, His strength is always there: all I need to do is to act in faith, choose God's way, and victory is mine.

Change

(**2 Cor. 10:3-5**) To change a thought pattern is to invite a challenge. Regardless of any thought whether good or bad, check it out with God first. Turn it over to Him and receive from Him the right thought and subsequent action to follow. Respond with God's answer, not react by your feelings which are death.

(**Rom. 6:11**; **Phil. 2:5**) I live in a new dimension of thought, the supernatural. From this level I speak being dead to sin. As I practice this on a regular basis—the life of Christ—His thoughts and action begin to take over until I live regularly in the spirit, no longer controlled by the flesh in that area of temptation. As a spouse and a parent, I realize whatever I think can and will affect my children—good or bad.

(**Prov. 25:28**; **Eph. 4:26-27**) You are to control your spirit by being slow to anger, by putting-off wrath, abusive speech, strife, and by putting-on patience, humility, and bearing with one another.

Work Out Your Salvation (Phil. 2:12-13)

Memory Verse(s):
>   He: **2 Cor. 10:3-5**; She: **Eph. 4:29**.

Devotion:
>   BSAF **1 Pet. 2:9-12**.

Put-Off/Put-On:
>   From failure list begin working out a plan of action to overcome
>   via **Appendix A.4, "Victory over Sin Worksheet"** and/or
>   **Appendix A.2, "Think and Do List"**.

11.7. Sexually Abused

Symptoms

- Authority principle ruptured, distrust and fear of all authorities.

(**Ps. 130:7**; **Isa. 51:3**) Because authority figure cannot now be accepted as a sanctuary or hope for reliable direction, there are no eternal truths to rest in. Thus, abused person is left with nothing but the 'idol of feelings'. Her mind works frantically to justify those feelings (**Deut. 29:17-19**).

- **Root:** Fear and inability to trust any authority figure.
- **Confusion of Identity:** Abused by father-role reversal-replaced mother's functions: female, daughter, wife or mother; thus, tattered and torn. Sense of glory, dignity, and worth destroyed instead of celebrating her femaleship.

Remedy

(**Heb. 7:25**; **Matt. 18:4**) God forever cleanses us even the past we can't remember. Seek hidden memories of being abused and any statement and vows made to defend and protect self (**1 Cor. 12:8**; **1 Cor. 4:5**).

(**John 20:23**) Wash away the filth of the past, and expose the memories of the spirit of the person to light (**Phil. 3:13-14**; **Luke 11:46**; **Luke 6:45**; **Eph. 5:13**).

(**Rom. 6:10-14**) Allow the Lord to expose our hearts, to the light of His grace, compassion and forgiveness, and apply the cross to our practical responses and reckon them as dead (**Isa. 51:3**; **Prov. 20:5**; **1 Cor. 13:11-12**; **Eph. 1:18**; **1 Cor. 4:15-16**; **Eph. 5:8**; **Isa. 61:1-3**).

Calling to Life

(**Luke 4:18**; **John 11:44**) We, ourselves, are called by God and commanded to "unbind them, and let them go!" Don't resort to gimmicks, techniques, or methods, abide in the Presence of the Lord, grow daily in skills of listening and the gifts of discernment.

Suggested formulas, use only as a guide:

- Intercessory prayer is the most powerful tool (**Isa. 30:18**; **Eph. 1:18-19**; **Eph. 3:16**; **Ezek. 36:26**).

- Prepare the heart of the wounded (**Ps. 139:8-10**; **Prov. 1:29-33**; **Ps. 112:7**; **Phil. 1:6**).

- Prayers of intercession are not to be manipulative, but only to help others to restore their will to be free from captivity and to equip her to make her own choices.

- (**Heb. 12:14-15**) Regardless of horrors, we must eventually, by our will, forgive the offender so that we can regain the freedom in Christ.

- (**Luke 6:45**) Since we see and hear and speak from that which fills our hearts, unforgiveness, hatred, lodged in the treasures of our heart perverts all perceptions and adversely affects our relationships.

Review **Chapter 12,** *Bold Love Series* and **Chapter 13,** *Armor of God Series*.

11.8. Sexual Abuse (2)

Perspective

(**Eccl. 3:11**; **Heb. 2:18**; **Heb. 10:11-23**) Use washing of the word, rather than the blood in dealing with sexually abused.

(**1 Cor. 6:16-20**) Husband and wife become one flesh? An unholy union with child, the spirits reach out to latch on. Intercessory prayer required to break this unholy union. Child needs to feel especially chosen and loved. A deposit of confusion exists in her spirit, an unwanted identification of her spirit with the one who molested her. Woman abused needs the critical factor of faithfulness, integrity, and purity of motives in relationships especially with counselor—this must be displayed and conveyed.

(**1 Thess. 2:7-11**; **2 Cor. 1:3-5**) One must be there with the wounded with tenderness and respect. Don't challenge their excesses in emotions, of their behavior, be calm, not judgmental. Understanding and unconditional acceptance is itself comforting. Use comforting Scriptures, such as **Isa. 40:11**; **Ps. 23:2-3**.

(**Matt. 18:18**) Vows or self-curses made in the past can be broken by the power of Christ: "I am no good", "never be intimate with any man", etc..

(**1 Pet. 2:24**; **Rom. 6:6-7**; **Rom. 6:11-14**; **Rom. 8:11-13**) Break old habit patterns, self-opinions. Begin to walk in the 'new you'—not go back to old thoughts and habits.

(**John 19:30**) When Jesus died He accomplished the finished work, and so are we in Him, but we must walk it out daily. Renounce old habit structures, flight patterns, sinful self protection: to trust the Lord to be her defense.

(**Gal. 5:24**; **Gal. 2:20**; **1 Cor. 15:31**) When tempted to freeze-up, say, "NO! This died on the cross with Jesus. I will be open to my husband, thank you, Lord, for your enabling power and grace." The healing itself is done by the Lord as He is invited in by prayer to do His good works.

(**Eph. 3:14-19**) This is our intercessory prayer for those still suffering.

(**Col. 2:5-7**; **Isa. 51:3**; **Isa. 61:1-3**) Working with the Lord, healing process depends upon quality of ministry and response of the wounded.

Starting with the New Birth

209

(Heb. 10:14) Positionally made perfect, made alive, sitting in heaven.

(Eph. 2:4-6; Phil. 2:12-13) Work it out in experience and grow in Him.

(Col. 3:9) Put-off old and put on new, my inheritance made possible by the finished work of Jesus' death and resurrection.

(Gal. 2:20; Gal. 5:24) Living totally in Christ.

Armor

(Eph. 6:13-18) Either we have God's armor of righteousness or we have a fleshly one, no neutral area. Putting on God's armor by His word and His action leaves no room or house for demons to dwell in: they must leave.

Work Out Your Salvation (Phil. 2:12-13)

Put-Off/Put-On:

>Review and apply the approaches in **Section 11.13, "Life-Dominating Sins"**; **Section 10.1, "Self Hatred"**; **Section 10.2, "Self-Acceptance"**.

11.9. Life-Dominating Sins

Drunkedness, Drug Addiction, Homosexuality

People with these problems need total restructuring. Drunkenness, drug addiction, and homosexuality are life-dominating sins, that is, they usually affect every area of life.

1. These problems are sin: **1 Cor. 6:9**; **Gal. 5:19-21**.

2. These problems are life-dominating sins: **Eph. 5:18**; **1 Cor. 6:12**; **Deut. 21:21**; **Prov. 20:1**; **Prov. 7:6-23**; **Prov. 23:29-35**; **Isa. 5:11,13,22**; **Joel 3:3**; **Joel 1:5**; **Amos 6:6**; **Hosea 4:11**.

Accordingly, these sins affect the person's

- … Home relationships,
- … Sleep,
- … Job,
- … Friends (social life),
- … Church attendance and service,
- … Emotions (self-pity, anger),
- … Finances,
- … Health,
- … Character and practices (deceitfulness),
- … Marriage and family life.

Insecure and Unhappy

These people are insecure, unhappy—people who are looking for satisfaction. They often do not know how to cope with life and are riddled with guilt. They turn to the bottle or drugs for quick satisfaction. For example, when Joe performs poorly at work, he feels bad, so he turns to the bottle for satisfaction. Then he performs worse and feels worse. So he drinks again, and in time, his health suffers and his relationship with his wife becomes strained. This causes him to feel worse, and he turns again to the bottle for relief.

Hope

(**1 John 1:7**; **1 Cor. 6:9-10**; **Rom. 6:14**; **Eph. 5:18**) Since the problems are sin (not disease), there is hope.

Change

(**Eph. 5:18**) God's solution to life-dominating sin is the filling of the Holy Spirit. To be filled with the Spirit means to submit to the Spirit's directions in every area of life. It means to be filled with right things. It means to put-off the old man and to put-on Jesus Christ. It means restructuring your life according to God's word. It means submitting to God's directives concerning work. It means handling your problems God's way. It means handling money in a God-appointed way. It means learning to relate to people according to the Scriptures.

(**Eph. 4:17-22**) To be filled with the Spirit involves replacing the unbiblical behavior and attitude with biblical behavior and attitudes. It involves reorganizing and reorienting your responses into a new pattern (**Rom. 6:19**).

It may involve probing into every area of your life to discover concrete ways you are failing God and others. Honesty and thoroughness are essential.

(**1 Cor. 15:33**; **Prov. 13:20**) Then, having discovered the ways you are operating unbiblically, you must repent and adopt biblical patterns. You probably will need to replace certain friendships. You must avoid all close contact and associations with companions with whom you have indulged in this practice.

(**2 Tim. 2:22**; **Heb. 10:24-25**) You will also have to stay away from those places frequented by people engaged in the same practice. Conversely, you will need to deepen or develop friendships with christians who are strong in the Lord. Your whole life may need to be restructured; how you do your work; where and how you spend your time; how you relate to people; how you spend your money, etc..

You will need to institute a meaningful program of Scripture reading, prayer, Scripture memorization, and church attendance and fellowship. You may also need assistance in setting biblical goals for living and for attaining them. You should establish a regular schedule, making sure you have time for all your God-given responsibilities.

You may also need to keep a daily journal of times when you are tempted; what you do when you are tempted; where you are; with whom you are; what you are thinking about. This journal may be of immense value in overcoming your problem.

(**Rom. 12:17**) You must devise a specific plan to use whenever you are tempted and put that plan into practice immediately and regularly when the temptations comes. You must exercise (discipline) yourself for the purpose of godliness (**1 Tim. 4:7**).

Work Out Your Salvation (Phil. 2:12-13)

Memory Verse(s):
      Eph. 4:22-24

Put-Off/Put-On:

      To assist in developing and restructuring the mindset (attitudes) and in order to attain and maintain godly habits and patterns of thought, speech and actions that are pleasing to God, use and apply any or all of the forms and worksheets listed in the Appendix. Review and apply **Appendix A.12, "Anchor Posts"** and **Appendix A.9, "Contingency Plan"** as standard guides and directions for life. Review **Chapter 5,** *Soul Dynamics Series,* ***Part B***; **Chapter 10,** *Self-Acceptance Series*; **Chapter 11,** *Overcoming Lust Series*; **Chapter 12,** *Bold Love Series*; and **Chapter 13,** *Armor of God Series*.

Reference: See [Mack3] and [Sanford2].

11.10. Perfectionism

Perspective

(**Gen. 1:26-28**) God's word is the source of life which enables man to exist in a blessed state. To reject God's word is to default to the word of Satan who says we can be complete in ourselves. To reject God's word is to allow fear to enter as a constant because we can never be complete unless we live by God's word.

(**Gen. 3:1-5**) Be as God, be perfect and independent. Shame came as they realized they were not perfect. Without God in their consciousness—separated from His Spirit—now on their own, trying to be god by their own wisdom and strength, they allowed the spirit of competition, the spirit of self-consciousness, the spirit of self-interest to prevail.

(**Luke 9:23-25**; **Phil. 2:3-4**) The issue is a quest for completeness. Man is designed by God to focus on and to help complete others. By so doing he completes himself. The need to be complete is inherent in man but this is only possible when man lives by the word of God. By the power of the Holy Spirit, man is enabled to apply the word which conforms man to the image of Christ. Accordingly, this image is one of self donation in the Spirit of Christ to consider others as well of great value and importance.

(**Gal. 2:20**; **Col. 1:27**) This is accomplished as we put-off self-effort and rely on the Holy Spirit to lead and guide us in all of life's functions in a spirit of purity and holiness—being God conscious—revealing the character of God through us to the world. The emphasis, therefore, is to stop trying to be god, and let God be God for us, in us, as us.

Humanism

(**1 John 2:16**) Who I am is my performance as rated by someone. Since God is not or no longer in the scheme of life, there is a constant need to be accepted and approved by others, a never ending cycle to be perfect and complete in their eyes. Rejection and shame, a sense of incompleteness, awaits at every corner. To counter this state of anxiety, man looks to himself, to his accomplishments, to the things of the world, and to the approval and acceptance of others to fulfill his needs. This quest for gratification, for the longings of the mind, for assurance of one's own resources and reliance on earthly things leads to emptiness, futility and destruction.

Elements of Perfectionism

- Independence: Make myself perfect as God without God.

- Shame: Looking at myself, seeing imperfection, brings on shame and embarrassment.

- Rejection: Emphasis is on my own needs, and I will do anything to save myself even to the point of destroying others.

- Perfectionism: Who I am now is dependent upon my performance and the rating of my performance. Need acceptance and approval of others even of God.

Solutions

(**Col. 2:10**; **John 16:8-13**) We can be complete only in God.

(**1 John 1:7**; **Phil. 2:12-13**) As we obey His commandments, He works in us to complete us.

(**Eph. 4:22-24**) Our job is to put-off the obsession with the self, and put-on the true self: Jesus Christ.

(**Matt. 22:37-39**) The emphasis is on God to fill us with His Presence. As we allow His divine wisdom to penetrate our intellect, our memories, our emotions and our wills, we will be able to love as He loves.

Key: We are imperfect. God uses trials and temptations to reveal these imperfections in order to prompt us to turn to Him to complete the process began in the 1st Adam. Through our human spirit, the Spirit of God fulfills and completes our souls, clearing away the areas of imperfection, to enable us to do the things Jesus did: to bless others and to destroy the works of the devil.

Review **Section 4.2, "Sins of the Flesh/Self of the Flesh"**; **Section 10.8, "Creative Thinking"**; **Section 10.9, "Mental Obsessions"**; and **Section 10.10, "Breaking Physical Habits"**.

215

11.11. Schizophrenia (Double-Mindedness)

Perspective

(**Isa. 29:13**; **Matt. 6:22**; **James 1:8**; **Amos 3:3**; **2 Cor. 6:14**) Double minded man is a man who minds on two souls, a man of two minds—hesitating, dubious, irresolute—unstable and unreliable and uncertain about everything (that he thinks, feels, decides). Forces acting upon the person causing problem behavior are forces distorting one's ability to perceive or evaluate the world as it is in reality or self-induced forces that cause one to misread or mislead one's self or others.

Schizophrenia is a disturbance, distortion or disintegration of the development of the personality resulting in a **split personality**.

Hope

(**Prov. 28:1**; **1 John 1:7-9**) The behavior of any given counselee stems fundamentally from organic defects or from sinful behavior. In case of bizarre behavior careful medical examination may be in order to detect any glandular or other chemical malfunction—brain damage, toxic problems, etc.. If problem is not organic or not only organic then counsel may be made on the supposition that such behavior must stem from sinful life patterns.

(**Eph. 4:26**; **Prov. 28:13**) After careful medical examination to detect any glandular or other chemical malfunction, and reasonably assurance that (at base) the problem is not organic, one will counsel on the supposition that such behavior must stem from sinful patterns. What is due to sin can be changed; there is no such certainty if schizophrenia is largely due to other factors.

(**Jere 17:9**; **Rom. 5:20**; **1 Pet. 3:12-16**) Man is largely responsible for his behavior, even when it is of a bizarre nature. It is not impossible to command the control of one's emotions. By prayer, one can change in attitude and actions. A christian can control his bodily functions and states as God intended him to. Counselor deals with schizophrenia in the same manner as he would in confronting those who have other problems occasioned by sinful living patterns.

Change

Overcoming three personalities: **(1) Rejection, (2) Rebellion, (3) True Self.**

(**Jer. 3:12**) Schizophrenic needs time to adjust and to fall out of agreement with the false demonic personalities, point by point. He must come to loathe the schizophrenic personality, and fall out of agreement with it.

(**James 1:8**; **Matt. 6:22**) The core problem of the schizophrenic is 'rejection' and 'rebellion'. Rejection is usually the **first** personality that emerges. There are many 'doors' that lead to rejection. It commonly begins in childhood or infancy and sometimes while the child is still in the mother's womb. One can be rejected and not be schizoid, and still manage to form a healthy personality and be secure in themselves. To the contrary, the schizoid is always floundering "Who am I?" The identity of the true self is confused and lost.

Love Deprivation

(**Luke 6:45**; **Ps. 120:2**) Rejection depicts a withdrawn type personality. It is a feeling within—it is agony within ... it is a starvation of love ... it is insecurity ... it is inferiority ... it is fantasy ... it is unreality ... it is all in the inside.

The **second** personality that emerges is rebellion. When a child does not have satisfactory love relationships in life, he grows up being unable to feel and share in love relationships. Rebellion sets in. He begins to fight for love. Or he lashes out to those who have starved him of love.

Rebellion asserts itself in stubbornness, self-will and selfishness as one personality. Or it begins to be aggressive, lashes out in anger, bitterness, resentment, hatred and retaliation as another personality. The schizoid is literally under these two opposite powers—passive, resistant, withdrawn; or aggressive and violent. He can switch from one type of personality to the other in a moment's time.

There are really three personalities—the true self, the rejection, and the rebellion personalities. All three can be manifested at any time. The rejection and rebellion personalities are fueled by a root of bitterness. Thus, one must deal with three factors: rejection, rebellion, and bitterness.

True Self

(**2 Cor. 5:17**; **Gal. 2:20**) The emphasis in dealing with schizophrenics is to concentrate on the true self, to draw it out, to relate the true self to Jesus. Jesus must start growing in the person, developing that personality and making it what He wants it to be. Identity with the 'true self' takes time. The person does not know who he really is. Until he does he will fall back to the false 'self' as a refuge. He must be weaned away slowly until the wounds within can be healed.

Biblical Approach

(**Eph. 4:22-24**; **Rom. 12:1-2**) Put-off the old man and put-on the new man is the basic tool. The root of all sin is lust. And the root of lust is thought. Therefore, the basic change involves the spirit or attitude of the mind. Godly thoughts begins the process of healing.

The inward self and the outward self must be dealt with. The goal is for the person to change his focus from self to God and to others. The following provides an insight into the immensity and complexity of the schizoid personality:

- **Rejection/Inward Personality:** Fear of Rejection; Fantasy/Lust; Harlotry; Perverseness; Self-rejection; Insecurity; Inferiority; False compassion; False responsibility; Self accusation; Suicidal; Perfectionism; Unfairness; Compulsive confession; Jealousy; Envy; Fear of judgment; Self-pity; Depression; Despair; Hopelessness; Guilt; Pouting; Pride; Vanity; Ego; Intolerance; Frustration; Impatience; Withdrawing; Vivid imagination.

- **Rebellion/Outward Personality:** Rebellion; Self-will; Selfishness; Accusatory projection; Stubbornness; Suspicion; Self-deception; Persecution; Self-delusion; Confrontational; Self-seduction; Distrust; Pride; Judgmental; Unteachable; Controlling; Possessiveness.

Setting the Captive Free Process

(**Matt. 7:5**; **Luke 4:18**; **John 14:21**; **Rom. 8:28-29**) Understand the past but do not deal with it. Deal with the present moment, where the person is at the present moment, and that with the concrete reality. Discard and do not even discuss or refer to any illusions/distortions. Objective is to draw out the true self, bit by bit.

(**Matt. 12:34-37**) The person lives by his diseased and entrenched attitudes, the broken spirit of the mind. He walks alongside himself. He is his own god, constantly listening to his perverted self for guidance and direction.

(**Luke 11:1-4**) The total emphasis from this point on is to relate the person to God the Father. Healing process begins at this point. He has been worshipping a false god—himself. Therefore, until he acknowledges God as the source of his life, healing cannot begin. The first step is to teach the person to love God and that by simply obeying His commandments: to begin to think right and to do right, to practice daily devotions, to judge himself and not others, to forgive others and act forgiven and to be reconciled within self, with God and with others.

(Luke 9:23-24; Rom. 12:1-2; Rev. 12:11) This is a long term process, and it begins with renewing the mind. The person may appear to improve but falls back to zero, time and time again. For the counselor persistence is the key coupled with gentleness, kindness and goodness. God's love through the counselor touches the person. God's Spirit thus is being manifested in the situation.

(John 16:8-13) Our responsibility in dealing with the severely disturbed and damaged personalities is to present and confront with the truth, to comfort and to exhort. We are not responsible for the results. We are to rest by faith in God's words of wisdom, that God will do what His words say He will do. The Holy Spirit is responsible for changing the individual and for the final results.

Review **Chapter 4,** *Soul Dynamics Series, Part A*; **Chapter 10,** *Self-Acceptance Series*; **Chapter 11,** *Overcoming Lust Series*; **Chapter 12,** *Bold Love Series*; and **Chapter 13,** *Armor of God Series*.

Reference: [Adams1] and [Hammond1]

Part III.b. Life Study: Anger and Bitterness

Table of Contents

Chapter 12. Bold Love Series

12.1. Forgiving Love

Perspective

(**Matt. 5:23-24**) Forgiving love is this inconceivable, unexplainable pursuit of the offender by the offended for the sake of restored relationship with God, self and others. What we call love might be little more than a slightly veiled, self-interested demand for appreciation and respect or avoidance of the offense in order to achieve an end other than biblical reconciliation. Love offers life, forgiveness enables love.

Hope

(**Gal. 5:14**; **Rom. 13:8-10**; **John 13:34-35**) Love is the summary of the Old Testament law and is the central measuring rod by which one's life will be judged. Therefore, the exercise of biblical love brings meaning and fulfillment in life. The meaning of love is found in the person of Jesus Christ and gives fleshly definition by His death and resurrection. His presence within enables love to flow, not a life bent toward success in finances and cares: but a sacrifice of soul for the sake of giving others a taste of God.

(**Matt. 6:13-14**; **1 John 1:9**; **2 Tim. :6-7**; **Luke 7:43**) Love cannot last long or live out its eternal purpose in human relationships without a foundation of forgiveness: forgiveness from God when we fail to love with a pure, and other centered heart: and forgiving when the recipient of our love spurns our gift or uses our soul in an unloving fashion. When this is done, love will suffer the corruption of denial, hardness, cynicism and eventually hatred. But, obedience to God's word, God continually, second by second, covers our sin under the blood of His Son. He forgives us our sins for not loving, which enables us by our choice to love in His power. Gratitude for forgiveness is the foundation for other-centered love. A stunned and grateful heart is free to love because knowing he is so unlovely, yet is loved and freed to love others without condemnation.

Change

(**Rom. 8:7**; **Rom. 5:10**; **Titus 3:3**; **Rom. 7:22-23**; **Rom. 8:5-7**) All of us tried to deal with life apart from depending on God which blocks our desire and commitment to love others. The battle to subdue sin in our members still rages and it is intense. At this point you are hostile to God. However, in the deepest part of your being, the new identity in Christ, you love God and His law. We are a mixture of life and death, good and evil, love and hatred (**2 Cor. 5:17**).

(**John 15:5**; **Matt. 6:24**) We are grafted into a new vine but it takes time for branches to grow and bear fruit. At times we feel close to God, at other times when irritated we feel separated from God. We are one or the other, there is no gray area.

(**Rom. 1:18**; **Heb. 3:13**; **Rev. 3:15-16**) We have the capacity to suppress truth and become deceived. A cold or hot heart is more pleasing to God than a lukewarm one. Sin or hatred of God is a defiant movement, sometimes unwittingly, other times quite conscious, refusing to depend on God for His direction and strength.

(**1 John 3:2**) The battle to replace hatred with love will be over only when we see Jesus in the flesh and become one as He is. Crossroads of choice in the face of injustice is where hatred may bloom.

(**James 4:1-4**) Self-protection is the self-centered commitment to act without courage, compassion, boldness and tenderness for the sake of the other. Self-protection can be dressed either in co-dependent maneuvering that lacks self-identity, freedom of choice and strength; or in counter-dependent distancing that alienates through self-assertion, demanding control and intimidation.

In our flesh, we want to be free of choice and its consequences, to be passive or seeking the perfect choice. We try to avoid the consequences of choice. We act impulsively or procrastinate so that excuses can be made. But we are commanded to love and to love perfectly. God expects us to choose life and love over self-protection and self-centeredness.

(**Rom. 12:9**; **Ps. 45:7**; **Phil. 4:8**) Our regenerated hearts are built to cling to what is good and to hate evil, to hate all that is wicked, and to enjoy what is lovely.

Work Out Your Salvation (Phil. 2:12-13)

Memory Verse(s):
2 Cor. 10:3-5

Put-Off/Put-On:

Study **Appendix A.3, "Love is an Action"** and **Section 5.2, "Sin, Self, Suffering"**. Prepare **Appendix A.4, "Victory over Sin Worksheet"**.

Reference: [Allender2]

223

12.2. Vicious Thoughts

Perspective

(**Eph. 6:10-18**; **Rom. 7:21-24**) The Scripture confirms that our everyday experiences in living are but a battle. Our christian growth is a battle against Satan in our own hearts, a battle against our own vicious and destructive thoughts, memories, emotions, and actions. However, in the ultimate it is God against whom we struggle. It is God who fights for us. The battle is the struggle between God and Satan: it is waged in our hearts. It is through recalling the past that activates the destructive emotions. Thus, our memories are to be dispossessed of the past by renewing of the mind and by acting according to the will of God. This process now allows God to direct our lives and not the god of our emotions.

Hope

(**Eph. 4:22-24**; **1 Cor. 10:13**; **Rom. 8:18**) The Bible calls us to the life of a warrior in a world of conflict. We don't fight on our own. Jesus won the battle on the cross: the way of victory is through love and sacrifice, not hate and greed. Our growth is always developmental, we grow slowly over time. God Himself will lead and direct us to comprehend the personality of God.

(**Phil. 1:21-25**; **Heb. 11:13-16**) We are to realize that the christian life on this planet is one where we are confronted with evil in all its forms: that the reality of life here is awful, that this world is not our home: but we should look beyond. This place is but one of a pilgrimage, a temporary stopping place.

Our permanent home is in heaven; thus, we are to take advantage and not be concerned about ourselves, but use our lives to advance other's progress and joy in Christ: to prepare them for a city without foundations. Courage comes when we challenge the evil in our lives and not accept it as part of living on this earth. But face it and begin to be free in the Spirit of Christ: to replace evil with goodness in the memory, in the intellect, in the will.

(**2 Cor. 2:14-15**; **Rom. 6:15-23**; **Prov. 6:16,19**) We are called to be servants—warriors unto righteousness. We are called to hate sin and the hatred of evil in others will deepen our hatred of what is evil within us. This, in turn, deepens our wonder of a God who forgives much. Our increased hatred and wonder will, over time, increase our wisdom in dealing with evil.

Change

(**Matt. 10:16**; **Luke 16:8-9**) We are to be as clever and cunning as the devil and as good-hearted and intentioned as God. Instead of reacting sinfully to an abuse or offense, see it as sin on your part and of others: then establish redemptive sorrow and deal with the situation without contempt for yourself or the other. The fallen human heart is continually attempting to predict and control. When we respond in a biblical fashion—choosing to do good to those who have done us harm—we outwit the enemy: making him powerless, as we make an offer of restoration to those who offended. A brutal father may want love and recognition, but he wants revenge even more.

(**Matt. 6:9-15**; **Matt. 18:21-35**; **Luke 17:3-4**) To forgive another means to cancel the debt of what is owed in order to provide a door of opportunity for repentance and restoration of the broken relationship. Reconciliation is not withheld when there is deep repentance, a radical redirection of life taking place: but an offer of restoration and peace is not extended to someone who has not repented. Forgiveness involves a heart that cancels the debt but does not lend new money until repentance occurs. A forgiving heart opens the door to anyone who knocks but entry into the heart does not occur until the muddy shoes and dirty coat have been taken off. Forgiveness is more than a business transaction. It is the sacrifice of a heartbroken Father who weeps over the loss of His child, and longs to see the child restored to life and love and goodness.

Work Out Your Salvation (Phil. 2:12-13)

Memory Verse(s):
> **Matt. 6:14-15**

Put-Off/Put-On:
> Review **Appendix A.3, "Love is an Action"** and **Section 5.4, "Transforming the Natural Self"**. Examine self in areas of forgiveness, fear, contempt and self-protection. List failures and process **Appendix A.4, "Victory over Sin Worksheet"**.

225

12.3. Reconciliation

Perspective

(**2 Cor. 7:11**) A hatred of evil deepens our passion for repentance that increases earnestness and produces eagerness to clear ourselves, and to see that justice is done. But a hatred of the hope of restoration is a hatred of beauty because it saps one through contempt, bitterness and cynicism. This produces hardness resulting in denial of emotions and distorts our ability to experience moments of joy and exaltation. Once beauty of restoration is denied then nothing exist but my own selfish pleasures in the present.

Hope

(**Matt. 10:39; Luke 9:24**) Refusing to forgive or to be reconciled is to lose one's life. To see that all the trials, the pains and the sufferings of this life are but means for me to die to my own self-centeredness and self-importance, and to better understand what God has for me to learn about loving others and Him: this is the meaning of the struggles we have in life. To do otherwise is to fill the empty parts of our soul with food, sex, people-pleasing or people hating activities.

(**Rom. 8:28-29**) Good hope is that greater good will prevail no matter how awful the awful remains. Good hope, regarding any tragedy, is in the present power of the moment to press us beyond the struggle of the day, to the day of beauty and justice. A rich vision of hope intensifies our desire to live courageously today. Thus, take pressure off self, it is God alone who causes redemptive changes in people and/or circumstances. Changes occur through repentance and a touch of God's grace, no one can produce repentance in another's heart but God.

(**Prov. 20:30**) Love may pardon an offense but does not ignore the ugliness and arrogance. To pretend is to distance truth: but love may demand change. Love may bring consequences for a failure to change. Love may withhold involvement until beauty is restored. Love may limit the other for the sake of a greater good.

Change

(**Rom. 12:19**) Illicit revenge is making someone pay now without any desire for reconciliation. But revenge can be legitimate when it involves a desire for justice, to see ugliness destroyed, wrongs righted and beauty restored. It is not 'getting even' but 'getting restored'.

(**Matt. 7:21-23**; **Rom. 12:17**) Desire for revenge is legitimate, people must pay for their sins either on earth or in hell. Many who call themselves christian may not be. In any case, our position should always be one toward brokenness and restoration since the unrepentant will be destroyed in God's final sweep of wrath. We who have been forgiven much should be compelled to prod evildoers—christian or not—toward brokenness and restoration.

(**Rom. 12:20-21**; **Ps. 69:22-28**) Don't pretend that you do not desire revenge because it is a reflection of longing for justice. It is a battle cry that asks God to intervene to destroy that which mars beauty and bring the offender to repentance.

(**Matt. 7:1-5**) Don't seek to destroy evil in others until you seek first to destroy evil in yourself.

(**Gal. 6:1**; **John 22:23**) Don't withhold good from those who do you harm. Do good in order to unnerve evil.

Work Out Your Salvation (Phil. 2:12-13)

Memory Verse(s):
  Matt. 5:23-24

Devotion:
  BSAF on verses dealing with forgiveness in the concordance. Select at least 6 verses.

Put-Off/Put-On:
  Process **Appendix A.4, "Victory over Sin Worksheet"** dealing with someone you need to forgive and to be reconciled with. Review **Section 4.2, "Sins of the Flesh/Self of the Flesh"** and **Chapter 15, *Supernatural Life Series***.

227

12.4. Conquering Evil

Perspective

(**Rom. 12:9-10**) When a victim is full of frenzied and vulgar desire for vengeance, an evil person can easily control the victim who is reacting in sin thereby influenced by the sinful spirit. But a hatred that despises evil and clings to truth and beauty infuriates evil and draws forth its most compelling assaults of shame. If evil at this point cannot control or shame, then it loses its effectiveness.

Hope

(**Phil. 3:18-19**; **Rom. 8:1**) Evil will not be conquered as long as our hearts live to obtain immediate relief or to escape profound loss. Only when we have little or nothing to lose will we be willing to love. It is then possible to be face to face with the most shaming accusation of the Evil one and find the Lord's mercy sufficient to withstand the brutal assault of contempt. His mercy will enable us to survive any attack and offer freedom from condemnation to those who choose to trust in the blood of Christ.

(**Heb. 12:1-12**; **1 Pet. 4:1-2**) We must practice daily being trained in righteousness to respond biblically regardless in order to align our hearts with truth and to be strengthened by discipline. In due season we will yield a harvest of righteous fruit. If we follow God's purposes in the midst of pain and suffering, we will grow in the knowledge of God in a deeper fashion. Accordingly, God will then control us regardless of the externals of life or the circumstances that surround us. Thus, evil is enraged when it is faced with strength and mercy.

Change

(**Luke 17:3-6**) Forgiveness can be defined as a continuous process of hungering for restoration, revoking revenge, and offering good gifts. We are to forgive until there is reconciliation. But restoration should not occur until there is repentance. Repentance on the part of the evil person will include a renunciation of rage and mockery. He needs to be willing and humbled and broken by guilt for his use of shame and contempt.

(**1 Cor. 5:5**; **2 Thess. 3:14-15**) Gift of excommunication is withholding of relationship for it removes immediate opportunity for sin and opens door to loneliness and shame. It destroys sinful inclinations and intensifies shame. The task of loving an evil person requires supernatural intervention. The battle is not ours, it is the Lord's.

Work Out Your Salvation (Phil. 2:12-13)

Memory Verse(s):
>   **Luke 17:3**

Devotion:
>   BSAF **1 Pet. 3:9-12**.

Put-Off/Put-On:
>   Review **Section 7.9, "Holding Self Accountable"**. Make a list of failures, and begin to process them one at a time by completing **Appendix A.4, "Victory over Sin Worksheet"**. Practice the new pattern for 6 weeks or so. Keep on, keeping on, and begin anew until a sense of the Presence of God becomes apparent. Obedience is our part in "fighting the good fight of faith". As we obey, God will do the rest.

12.5. Doing Good to Your Enemies

Perspective

(**Matt. 5:40-42**; **Eph. 4:29**) Loving your enemy means feeding your enemy what he desperately needs. In many cases, bold love will unnerve, offend, hurt, disturb, and compel the one who is loved to deal with the issue that is robbing him and others of joy. Our job is to continually learn and relearn what it means to offer what the other person needs. All humans need love and honor. Thus, the emphasis is to increase a desire for love and honor, and to decrease the penchant to pursue false paths to satisfaction.

Hope

(**2 Cor. 7:8-16**; **Rom. 12:27**) Kindness is the gift of thoughtfulness, looking for ways to serve others in compassion. Tenderness is a response of mercy that can see through the sin to the parts of the human heart, a heart that was designed for more. Strength involves a willingness to bleed in the midst of unpleasant, undesired conflicts. Strength is needed to expose violations of relationship, and does not fear the loss of relationship. We are to feed our enemy because we love beauty and hate arrogance.

(**Matt. 26:17-35**; **John 21:15-19**; **Matt. 27:3-5**) Goodness exposes the nakedness and hunger of the enemy, shames the enemy, and then offers the opportunity for restoration. Evil cannot bear the intrusion of goodness. What unnerves evil more than any one thing is someone who is not controlled by shame and yet is not shameless.

(**Luke 6:27-31**) Need to pray for wisdom to learn how to apply truth to different situations and people we encounter. How should I use my tongue? What should my attitude be toward the person? How am I to deal with fools?

Walk with God and discuss with Him how to respond in varied situations. Rehearse some scenes, ponder out loud with God what might be going on in the heart of the person, review your behavior and responses. Accordingly, wisdom is defined as skillful kindness and strength, tempered with shrewdness, armed with courage, clear about the calling and hungry to see arrogance destroyed and beauty enhanced. To bless one, words are to be used to arouse legitimate longing, expose emptiness, and deflects the enemy's attempts to shame or intimidate. Blessing should be designed to open the heart of the enemy to astonishment and curiosity.

Change

(**Matt. 5:40-46**) Walk a mile, turn other cheek, involves shrewd sacrifice: for it is giving that which is designed for an enemy, not a friend. The enemy expects that his intimidation and shaming will get him what he wants because it gives him a sense of control and fantasy of being like God. To respond with kindness and generosity causes the enemy to stumble because the act bears a redemptive bite. Shrewd sacrifice is a gift of grace that exposes hatred and rage, and invites the enemy to wrestle with his sin. Good words and deeds are the elixir of life, the antidote against death (**Prov. 1:22**). There are 3 kinds of enemies in our lives: evil people, fools, and simpletons (normal sinners).

(**Heb. 10:24**) Goodness involves a desire to see someone or something grow in strength, freedom and beauty. An arrogant heart is hardened by its own sin and blinds the hearts of those it controls. Mockery is the language of accusation and it is the weapon that evil uses powerfully to strip the victim of a sense of self and life. Evil steals faith, hope, and love for it disseminates dis-information: pinning the blame on the victim, robbing the person of the adventure found in faith. It creates bondages, a form of slavery, it dulls the senses, and steals from the soul a vision of what could be.

Work Out Your Salvation (Phil. 2:12-13)

Memory Verse(s):
> **1 Pet. 3:9**

Devotion:
> BSAF on **Rom. 12:9-23**.

Put-Off/Put-On:
> Review **Matt. 5:3-12**. On the basis of these truths, process **Appendix A.2, "Think and Do List"**, visualize what you can be as you allow God to will and work in you for His good pleasure, conforming you to His Son.
>
> (**1 Pet. 2:21-23**) Turn over all your hurt, pain, all potential offensive reactions to God. Allow Him to deal with the offense and the offender. Prepare yourself to be free from all bitterness when tempted by following the steps in the Contingency Plan and:
>
> 1. Call on God for 'help'.

2. 'Give up' trying to handle the situation your way. Ask God to intervene totally.
3. Ask God to make good come out of the situation.
4. Ask God to make good come out of whatever harm you may have caused.
5. Pray for the health, the wholeness of your enemies. Pray for the salvaging of all that is good, beautiful and true within them.
6. Finally, whatever happens, confess: "Thy will be done", and stand firm.

12.6. Loving a Fool

Perspective

(**Prov. 12:15**; **Prov. 18:2**; **Prov. 28:26**; **Prov. 30:32**) Proverbs describe a fool as one who is angry, arrogant and self-centered. Some of us blame ourselves primarily or we blame others for our problems. In either case, the focus is on the self, on one's own needs and purposes. A fool's anger is to intimidate and frighten in order to establish his pre-eminence and independence, and to gain compliance and control.

Hope

(**Ps. 14:1**; **Ps. 53:1**; **Luke 12:19-20**; **Ps. 73**) The fool normally uses arrogant pride as a shield against the shame provoked by exposure. It is an intense self-centeredness. His heart is empty, but feels full because it finds satisfaction in the material world. He does not say God doesn't exist but that God does not matter. What does matter is what he can lay his hands on to fill his soul. A fool is self-sufficient, and is easily satisfied but morally stupid. A fool is insatiable but easily pleased. But the only true fulness comes from humble dependence on the mercy of God.

(**Phil. 2:12**; **Heb. 2:10**; **Heb. 5:8-9**; **1 Pet. 4:1-3**) Fools seek easy resources in order to fulfill their own selfish desires regardless of the cost or damage done to themselves or others in the process. Fools hate the pain of discipline and the inherent fear involved in growing in wisdom and knowledge. Growth always involves fear and trembling and suffering and death. The fool hates anything that exposes the ugliness of his own heart, and he avoids the pain that produces lasting beauty.

(**Prov. 15:5**) Discipline involves loss and emptiness, whereas the fool is committed to pleasure and fulness. Discipline is personal engagement with thorns and thistles that moves to subdue the unruly chaos of the Fall. And it is a battle against the effects of the Fall. The fool refuses to struggle with the issues of character, he lives for pleasure. The fool disputes wisdom because he must abandon his anger and bravado, and experience the shame of helplessness.

Change

(**Prov. 26:5**) A fool's folly must be exposed, consequences experienced, and the failures of love discussed and worked through toward repentance. We are called to

233

use the highest degree of wisdom in knowing whether to rebuke or to remain silent. The essence of love is not foolhardy sacrifice, but judicious, well-planned disruption.

(**Luke 18:18-25**; **John 4:1-30**) Jesus did not allow Himself to get pulled into the quicksand of arrogant presumption or shame or based defensiveness. In dealing with the rich ruler, Jesus instead challenged his understanding of the word 'good' in order to expose what he really desired: affirmation or radical change. At the well, Jesus did not get involved in the woman's defensive maneuver but continued to deepen her curiosity and hunger for what she knew she had not possessed: life-satisfying refreshment. He used data of the moment and used it to expose the heart of the woman rather than merely condemn her behavior and exhort change.

(**Rom. 12:9-21**) When we 'set up' the fool for further exposure, as above, we set ourselves up for attack. Be prepared to step aside lightly, but not in fear. Be prepared to respond in tenderness and in strength, not succumb to shame or intimidation. This will surprise the fool who no longer will be in control of you or himself. Respond to him gently, be full of wit, passion, sorrow, strength and tenderness. A fool cannot repent unless he feels pain.

Work Out Your Salvation (Phil. 2:12-13)

Memory Verse(s):
> **Rom. 12:9**

Devotion:
> BSAF on **2 Pet. 1:3-8**.

Put-Off/Put-On:
> Process **Appendix A.8, "Freedom from Anxiety"**. Judge and establish yourself in the grace of the Lord, then proceed to face the fool and win him over to the Lord. Remember only God can change the heart of another. Your job is to assess the behavior (not motives) and not to react impulsively but practice applying **Appendix A.9, "Contingency Plan"** until a biblically structured pattern becomes spontaneous. Do not give up, this takes time. Even if the fool never changes, by practicing godly responses you will change and grow in the image of Our Lord.

Chapter 13. Armor of God Series

Table of Contents

13.1. Injustices

Perspective

(Gen. 3:15; Matt. 5:10-12; Gal. 1:12-13; Col. 2:13-15) God's people have been at war with the enemy since the Fall. From this point on and for the rest of history, there is a vicious conflict between God and Satan, between those who follow God and those who reject Him. Central theme of Old Testament holy war is that God is present with His people as a warrior. Jesus came as the divine warrior to rescue His people from the devil himself by waging the greatest war of all: the war against the devil. He did this not by killing but by dying. When Jesus died on the Cross, He incisively defeated Satan and all of his evil hordes.

Hope

(Matt. 24:30-31; Rev. 19:11-16) Before He died, Jesus told His disciples: that He would return in the future with a full display of power: that He will return to earth as a glorious warrior who will once and for all bring evil to a violent end.

(Eph. 6:10-18) Before He comes to end it all, we, in Him, are to stand and fight against the spiritual forces of evil. And that we will have victory only as we allow God to use us, realizing that our strength comes only as we put on the 'armor of God'.

(Matt. 7:5; Rom. 7:21-24; Rom. 8:18) Our christian growth is a battle against Satan in our own hearts: for we have to battle against our own vicious and destructive thoughts, emotions and actions. The struggle between God and Satan is waged in our very hearts. This is a spiritual battle that is won not by physical but by spiritual weapons: prayer, faith, hope, and love. We use prayer as a weapon against our abusers by praying for their repentance. Faith is a deep trust in our

235

Commander-in-Chief, Jesus Christ, who does the battling, which is already accomplished on the cross. And love: we are to love our enemies to the point we move into their lives to open the door of their repentance. Jesus defeated evil by dying on the cross. He shows that the road to victory is through love and sacrifice—not hate or greed.

Change

(**Ps. 25:7**; **Jer. 31:34**; **Ps. 103:12**; **Matt. 6:9-15**; **Matt. 18:21-35**) As christians we are told to be like God, who does not remember sin but forgives wickedness. Likewise, we are to cancel the debt owed to us, and provide a door of opportunity for repentance and restoration of broken relationships.

(**Luke 17:3-4**) We are not to rebuke unless a sin has been committed, nor are we to restore unless true repentance has occurred. Reconciliation is not to be withheld when repentance, that is, deep, heart changing acknowledgement of sin and a radical redirection of life takes place in the one being rebuked. Reconciliation is not to be extended to one who has not repented. Forgiveness involves a heart that cancels the debt, but does not lend new money until repentance occurs. Cheap forgiveness—peace at any cost—that sacrifices honesty, integrity and passion—is not true forgiveness.

(**Rom. 12:16-18**; **2 Cor. 7:11**) It is for joy that Paul tells christians to be at peace with everyone by developing a desire for beauty and harmony to reside within all of us, and to seek reconciliation to all those who offended us. Our hatred of evil will produce a passion to live righteously in accord with restored relationships.

(**Matt. 10:39**; **Luke 6:27-28**; **2 Cor. 5:18-20**) We want others to change for our pleasure, convenience and vindication which leads away from restoration. This only deals with the symptoms. God tells us to go beyond, to love our enemies, to do good to those who persecute us. We are to do good as God does to us. We were His enemies, but we were reconciled and commissioned to do as He did.

(**Prov. 20:30**) God's love may demand change: it brings consequences for a failure to change, withholds involvement until harmony is restored: and may hurt another for the sake of a greater good.

Work Out Your Salvation (Phil. 2:12-13)

Memory Verse(s):
>   **1 Pet. 2:23**

Devotion:
BSAF on **Matt. 5:3,5,7,9,10,13,14**.

Put-Off/Put-On:
Select verses dealing with 'vengeance' particularly involving the
characters of King Saul and Ahithophel, advisor to King David,
both destroyed themselves with bitterness. Meditate on verses
dealing with forgiveness until your heart is changed to enable you
to see the other person through the eyes of God. Let God deal with
the vengeance part, you deal with the forgiveness part to save your
own soul. See verses **James 1:19-21**; **Heb. 12:19-21**; **1 Pet. 2:23**.

Reference: [Allender1]and [Allender2].

13.2. Revoking Revenge

Perspective

(**Deut. 32:35; Rom. 12:17-21**) Illicit revenge is making someone pay—Now!—for a real or perceived wrong without any desire for reconciliation. Vengeance is part of the character of God and is not in contradiction with His love and mercy. Revenge involves a desire for justice, to see ugliness destroyed, wrongs righted and beauty restored.

Hope

(**Ps. 69:22-28; Rom. 2:20-21**) Our goal is to conquer evil, and this is done by 'doing good'. However, it is appropriate to pray for a person to be broken, humbled and brought low in order to see their evil destroyed. We pray for the death of arrogance and self-sufficiency.

(**Matt. 7:1-5; Gal. 6:1; Jude 22-23**) Don't seek to destroy evil in others until you first seek to destroy evil in yourself. If someone slights or deceives you, then you imply that the same tendency to slight and to deceive is in you. We must live with the on-going work of removing our log without neglecting to remove the specks in the eyes of others. Thus, part of the answer to destroy evil is to do good by rebuking and restoring others after we judged ourselves.

(**Luke 6:27-28**) Evil cannot comprehend goodness: for goodness offers life and evil death. Goodness is a force of power that is designed to surprise, supplant, and shame evil. To hate others is to reveal the sin that is in our own hearts. To love godly, one must hunger for restoration plus revoking revenge.

Change

(**John 3:16; Eph. 4:29**) We are to restore others as God has restored us. God gave us what we needed and not what we deserved. Likewise, bold love involves feeding those who have done us harm. To honor and worship God, and give glory to Him is for us to respond and meet the needs of others as God has done for us. We die to our own sense of revenge, to get beyond being offended, in order to destroy the evil that is in the other, and open the way for godly responses and actions.

(**Luke 6:27-28; Rom. 12:9-21**) Basically, you start doing 'good' simply by being thoughtful and kind, looking for ways to serve another, seeking ways to be of help to another in need. Love feels the pain of the offender's sin and ugliness. To think ill of the person is to be guilty of the same offense, that is, taking care of self and neglecting the other.

(Ps. 140:9-10; Rom. 12:20-21; Rom. 1:16) It takes strength to love and it takes grace of God to love tenderly. Giving love should be with a strength that does not fear the loss of the relationship. Our enemy is anyone who intentionally or unwittingly harms us for his gain. Doing good or heaping coals are means to bring the offender to a point of shame, to surprise our enemy and invite him to deal with his offense. Goodness exposes the nakedness and hunger of the enemy, and offers clothing and food: it shames the enemy and then offers the opportunity for restoration.

Work Out Your Salvation (Phil. 2:12-13)

Memory Verse(s):
> **James 1:2-4**

Devotion:
> BASF on **Ps. 142**.

Put-Off/Put-On:
> List your failures, your fleshly reactions to offenses of life, the hurts and pains as manifested by defensive coldness, harshness and withdrawal. On the basis of principles stated herein, devise a plan of biblical responses in which God is glorified and the old self put to death. Process **Appendix A.4, "Victory over Sin Worksheet"** for this purpose. Review **Rom. 12:9-21** and **Section 5.2, "Sin, Self, Suffering"**.

13.3. Responding to Difficult People

Perspective

(**Rom. 1:16**; **Luke 9:23-24**; **Ps. 1:1-3**) Doing good is accomplished by words and deeds, by praying and blessing, and by turning and giving. To bless is to give words of life that nourish the soul and deepen its desire for truth. The wisdom to do this must be developed to learn how to apply truth to the differing situations and people we encountered.

Study of God's word is the only way and means to have wisdom. The godly skill to respond to life is mastered only after the expenditures of heart, soul and strength and mind grow in ability and performance.

Hope

(**James 1:5-8**; **Prov. 18:21**) "How am I to use my tongue?"..."What should my attitude be to my neighbor?"... "How am I to deal with fools?"... These questions and others as when to hold my tongue and when to speak, how to avoid unnecessary conflicts and how to confront when necessary. To live shrewdly in a fallen world with love and integrity requires much wisdom: God is our source. In any and all situations take a long walk to talk with God, rehearse typical scenes, ponder out loud with God how to handle various relationships. By praying this way, we invite God to use us and to teach us what it means to love boldly.

(**1 Pet. 2:23**; **Matt. 5:38-48**) The Lord did not use contempt or intimidation to shame and frighten His accusers. Turning the other cheek is to thwart the enemy's attempt to intimidate and shame by which he controls the situation. Kindness and generosity causes him to stumble because you did not fight or flight. Thus, a gift of grace exposes hatred and rage and invites the enemy to wrestle with his sin.

(**Rom. 12:9**; **1 Cor. 13:8**; **Rom. 8:1**) Love conquers and love foils the evil person to win. Evil's strength lies in its ability to dominate. Frustrating these attempts will weaken its position. But one must be willing, without flinching, to face shame and hatred.

Change

(**Heb. 12:1-2**; **1 Pet. 4:1-2**) God promises in due season we will yield a harvest of righteous fruit if we keep in mind God's purposes in the midst of pain. If we desire to know God in the midst of suffering, growth will be our reward.

(1 Cor. 5:5; 2 Thess. 3:14-15; Titus 3:10) If reconciliation is not possible due to an unrepentant heart, then separation from the individual may be in order. It is not loving to continue an evil relationship with a person who consistently and perniciously sins against you without some sign of repentance and change.

(2 Chron. 20:12; Josh. 1:1-9; John 15:5) In all evil confrontation, the battle is the Lord's who will be with you: for it requires supernatural intervention. It is the mighty God who can change your heart as well as the evil person. Accordingly, you may pray the following…

1. Pray that the eyes of all who surround these persons be opened to see the situation as it really is.
2. Pray that their associates will be given ways to speak truth and light into the situation.
3. Pray that any demonic power within these persons or within the situation manifest itself—that it may be clearly discerned and seen by all the people.
4. Ask that what can be salvaged (in this situation and in the lives of your enemies) be saved, humbled, blessed by the Spirit of God.

Work Out Your Salvation (Phil. 2:12-13)

Memory Verse(s):
    2 Chron. 20:17

Devotion:
    BSAF on **Rom. 12:9-21**.

Put-Off/Put-On:
    You are to be influenced by the Holy Spirit in all of life's activities, and not controlled by people or circumstances. Accordingly, select verses on the Holy Spirit, list areas where you are in bondage, meditate on verses that apply to the situation. Study the principles on this sheet, and visualize yourself confronting life in the wisdom and power of the Holy Spirit. Pray for the health, the wholeness of your enemies. Pray for the salvaging of all that is good, humbled, and true within them.

    Note: The key is cleansing and purifying your intellect, memory and will of all offenses to allow the Holy Spirit to occupy the cleansed area and to empower and direct your biblical responses henceforth. Review **Section 5.1, "Cleansing and Purifying the Soul"**.

13.4. Assaults of Shame, Rage, Hatred

Perspective

(**1 Tim. 4:7-9**; **Heb. 12:5-11**) Being conditioned by guilt, shame, fear and loneliness and seeking to alleviate the pain by things other than what God proposes, we need to discipline ourselves and restructure our attitudes and patterns of behavior. This to be done in accord to God's standards by which we pursue a course of personal holiness. We are to worship God first: then we can have healthy relationships with others later.

Hope

(**Prov. 1:7**; **Prov. 26:5**; **Col. 1:9-12**) Knowledge of God provokes a personal response towards what is known and demands a change to whatever would keep deeper knowledge from taking root in the soul. Knowledge points to God and compels change. Realization that what you have been depending upon for security or satisfaction is false and empty and must be replaced. It takes time to fill the void, and we are no longer in control. But God is now in sole control over every area of our lives. God's word is to be rooted in our being gradually filling in the ruts of sin patterns and behavior. From these godly roots, we recreate a pattern of biblical responses to honor God and to please Him.

(**Luke 18:18-25**; **John 4:1-30**) Our hearts need to be exposed to show to ourselves the need for radical change, Jesus confronted both in tenderness (mercifully seeking the other to repent) and strength (not succumb to a challenge of being merciful and tender) and to sustain the pursuit regardless. Confront with a word what is matter-of-fact, strong and benevolent either with self or with others, with emphasis on the freedom of choice.

(**2 Cor. 7:11**) True repentance will lead to feelings of indignity and anger at the past damage, followed by a desire to make restitution, and a renewed longing for purity and godliness. Repentance without reversal is not repentance.

Change

(**James 1:2-4**; **James 3:16**; **James 4:1-3**) Envy seems to be one of the major causes of conflict and disorder in relationship. The demand of our soul is for satisfaction now or relief rather than to pursue spiritual growth in facing trials and tribulations. To work out our self-centeredness, we are to change our emphasis from self on to God and others.

The task of growth is to pursue real honesty about self, the world and God—no matter what. And not hide behind denial or deceit. Be aware of self defensive and self protective postures for this reveals the 'old man' covering himself, refusing to ask for help outside of himself—pride! This is what Adam and Eve did in the garden: they defended themselves by blame shifting rather than to confess and to repent. Accordingly, avoid excusing, justifying self and putting the blame on others.

(**Prov. 14:15**; **Prov. 22:3**; **Prov. 27:12**; **1 Pet. 4:8**; **Prov. 10:12**) When we cover over sins of others, we make a conscious choice to wait, prayerfully and patiently, for the right moment to deal with an observable pattern of sin. Covering over sin is waiting for the right opportunity for interaction. We should cover over sin unless we are called by God to deal with it directly.

(**1 John 4:20**) To the extent we face evil, foolishness and simple ways in others, we will see those ways in our own hearts. Thus, open our hearts to the relief of forgiveness and the wonder of the meaning of the Cross.

Work Out Your Salvation (Phil. 2:12-13)

Memory Verse(s):
    1 Pet. 4:8

Devotion:
    BSAF on **1 Pet. 3:9-18**.

Put-Off/Put-On:
    Review **1 Pet. 2,3,4** and **2 Pet. 1:3-11**. This is God's approach to how we should view life, how to contend with evils of the world, people and circumstances. We must free ourselves of being a victim, and be open to being empowered by the Presence of the Holy Spirit so that we can be a blessing instead of a curse (**Rom. 6:1-11**). Accordingly, be renewed in the spirit of your mind and realize that you are a child of God, and not a victim of the world (**James 1:2-4**).

    Apply **Appendix A.9, "Contingency Plan"** and **Appendix A.12, "Anchor Posts"** on a daily basis to keep self cleansed and to break self defensive and self protective patterns (excusing, justifying self and blaming others) incurred by slights, resentments, spites, grudges, annoyances, ill feeling, ill will, irritations and the like. If the offenses of life are taken for granted and not dealt with immediately, you will eventually forfeit the grace of God, and allow the noxious weed to grow and poison self and infect those with whom you associate (**Heb. 12:14-15**).

13.5. Forgiving Enemies

Perspective

(**Ps. 66:18-19**; **Luke 11:4-5**) Repenting of sins, forgiving others their sins against us, and gaining deliverance in temptation, all of this is central to Christianity. Without forgiveness or freedom from evil, we are subject to sickness of spirit, soul, and, eventually, body as well.

Repenting, forgiving others, and gaining deliverance in temptation are three vital petitions that are to be incorporated in our prayer life. Accordingly, failing to receive forgiveness, to forgive others, and to gain the great virtue of self-acceptance are three great barriers to personal healing and wholeness.

Hope

(**Luke 11:4-5**; **Ps. 139:23-24**; **Ps. 51:6**; **Ps. 32:1-2**) As we pray as Christ has taught us, we trust Him to shine His light on any unconfessed sin in our lives so that we can repent of it instantly. We also ask Him to show us if we need to forgive others. By faith, we trust His radiance will shine into any space in our hearts and lives—inner or outer, conscious or unconscious—and free us to pursue holiness.

(**Mark 11:25**; **Luke 23:34**) We will benefit greatly by allowing the Lord to shine His light over our entire lives. We can do this by taking our lives in manageable segments, such as: seven year periods, or early childhood, grade-school years, junior-high years, and so on—and spread before the Lord any memory of our sin or our grievous reactions to the sin of another. In this way we root out unforgiveness, fully confess our sin and carefully receive God's forgiveness.

Change

(**James 1:13-15**; **1 Pet. 5:8-9**; **Matt. 26:41**; **1 Cor. 10:13-14**) Satan is the author of temptation, not God. Satan stimulates our carnal desires which leads to sin and death. Many people, angry with father or mother or church or life and circumstances, transfer their anger to God. Problem of denial, unforgiveness, anger and unbelief need to be dealt with.

Also, we must watch out for worldly desires and things: for power, for pride, for material gains and possessions. We are to give thanks for gifts and things, but we must be watchful for the shift from thankfulness to an idolatrous dependence on things or people.

(**2 Tim. 4:18**; **1 Pet. 1:5**) We need to know when to work with God—listening to Him—in the midst of a spiritual battle and to act in the power of His love, righteousness and wisdom. Relying on God we will be 'kept' by the power of God. The Lord protects us from the evil that strikes. As it is both through others (human evil) and through demonic spirits that we normally strive by human effort. We are to practice His presence, together with listening prayer: This takes all wrongful striving out and releases our faith.

(**Prov. 8:13**; **Rom. 12:9**) We hate evil but we find grace to forgive those in the grip of evil. We begin by confessing specific sins against us. Hating evil while releasing the evil doer from unforgiveness on our part which means that we not remain under his or her power to destroy us. Instead we gain Christ's strength to defeat and utterly overcome the effects of that evil on ourselves. We have the privilege in Christ of breaking the power these sins continue to have over us. However, the sinner is not released from his evil deeds: This can be done only by his or her personal repentance.

(**Micah 7:6**; **Matt. 5:39**; **Rom. 12:9-21**) If we are to be victorious in spiritual conflicts we must move forward not only in the knowledge of Christ's presence with us, but in the gifts of the Holy Spirit as they operate through listening prayer. Speaking the truth in love born of God is the greater part of the gift of battle: the gift of divine love that comes from God's life within us.

Remember: Christianity is God in the soul of man.

Work Out Your Salvation (Phil. 2:12-13)

Memory Verse(s):
> **1 Tim. 6:11-12**

Devotion:
> BSAF on **Rom. 12:9-21**.

Put-Off/Put-On:
> Whenever tempted to judge, criticize, gossip, when evil is being done, being sinned against at home, at church or in the world, speak the following prayer: "Lord Jesus Christ, Son of God, have mercy on us." Prepare self to be a blessing instead of a curse by practicing His Presence. Review **Section 12.3, "Reconciliation"**.

Meditate on the following: "Save, O Lord and have mercy upon those that envy and affront me and do me mischief, and let them not perish through me, a sinner."

Steps to take to forgive and to be forgiven:

1. No matter what others have done to us, we are responsible only for how we acted. We are not responsible for what others do, but responsible for harboring bitterness and withholding forgiveness.

2. It is our will that directs our actions, not our 'feelings'. We must choose to forgive and release offenders to God, no longer be their judge.

Method to release offenders:

1. Make a list of all who offended you.

2. Beside each name, note the offense, what they did or fail to do, what they owe you.

3. Visualize the sins cancelled by the Blood of Jesus. Cancel the debt and release them by destroying the list (**1 Pet. 2:24**). Leave it up to God to deal with them.

4. When thoughts of anger/bitterness come, exercise your authority over them, declare the person forgiven, and refuse to think on the events of the forgiven past. In time, these experiences will become distant memories without the hurt and anguish.

…Then **John 10:10** will be yours.

Reference: [Payne2]

Part III.c. Life Study: Fear

Table of Contents

Chapter 14. Freedom from Fear Series

Table of Contents

14.1. Origins of Fear

Perspective

(**Gen. 1:26-28**; **Ps. 111:10**; **Gen. 3:10**) Mankind was created to know God, the Almighty, infinitely wise, all-knowing, and unconditionally loving One. Man was to live all of his life in the consciousness of His presence. Man was to be in awe of the magnificence of the Lord and to be the container and revelator of God on earth. In our everyday lives, we were to be constantly a visible manifestation of the invisible God, the purpose for our existence on the planet, the meaning of life.

After man decided to be his own god, the center and the source of his own life, sin entered and fear followed. Fear becomes the driving energy of man's life: anxiety, worry, fret, dread and panic become part of man's vocabulary.

> Man who was created to fear the One who unconditionally loves him, now potentially fears all persons, spirits, and created things—except the God who alone gives him life.

Hope

(**Matt. 22:37-39**; **John 14:21,27**; **1 John 4:18**) To return from a self-loving-self to self-loving-others, one must resume the dependent attitude, to 'stand under' God in obedient faith, to again actually partake of Him, to be a participator in His love, His very life. Man was created capable of receiving and becoming the dwelling place of divine love, and revealing that love in his behavior within creation which leaves no room for fear.

(**Isa. 42:7**; **Isa. 61:1**; **Luke 2:10**; **1 John 4:18**; **Rom. 8:15-16**) The Gospel is the message of what God has done in the person of the Lord Jesus Christ, His death, His resurrection, the Conqueror of death. And in His exaltation He sends the Holy Spirit to come and dwell within us, returning us to the original design. From this position He wills to bring us all out of the dungeon of fear where we are tormented by worry and anxiety.

Change

(**Phil. 4:6**; **John 14:1,27**; **Isa. 8:12-14**; **Isa. 26:3**) Worry centers on present and future problems as if there is no God. Standing in terror and awe, worry gives honor, respect and reverence to the power of evil.

However, the fear of God centers on the character of God, His unchanging presence within us: His promises. Deliberately taking and acting on His promises by obedient faith, we demonstrate His love and express His peace. In this mode, we confront, work through, and rise above all of life's adversities. Thus, fear is primarily in the mind and behavior, which we can change. You cannot command your emotions.

> Regardless of your feelings, you act by the Word in your mind, and your behavior will follow suit: victory awaits.

(**Eph. 4:18**; **2 Cor. 4:4**) Fear and worry describes us totally absorbed in ourselves, in self-preservation, self-interest, and self-pity. Accordingly, we see neither God nor man except as they can be used to further 'our' meaning of life. We either fear God as He designed us to do, resulting in our living in His love, or we fear the forces that we perceive as hostile to us, taking away the illusion of our meaning of life.

(**Matt. 6:32-33**; **John 16:33**; **2 Tim. 1:7**) We must accept responsibility for our fears. God command us to 'Fear Not' numerous times in Scriptures. Jesus commands us to "be anxious for nothing", and He placed the responsibility in our hands when He said, "Let not your heart be troubled."

> Christians feel fear, but they make it the springboard for faith to fear offending God. The answer to fear is the greater fear of God. Believers feel fear but know it is a lie. They replace the feelings of fear with the truth of their relationship to God and the presence of God within themselves.

251

Work Out Your Salvation (Phil. 2:12-13)

Memory Verse(s):
> **1 John 4:18**

Put-Off/Put-On:
> Process **Appendix A.8, "Freedom from Anxiety"**.

Reference: [Smith4]

14.2. Presence of Fear or Faith

Perspective

(**Gen. 1:26-28**; **Isa. 8:12-14**; **Rom. 1:16**; **Rom. 5:17**; **Eph. 4:1**) The only answer Scriptures gives to fear is the greater fear of the Lord. Isaiah describes how the believer transfers his fear of people and situations to the Lord who is always with him. As believers we are to 'walk worthy' of our calling, i.e., to walk in harmony with what we believe. The Gospel is good news of our restored relationship with God, and a return to live in God's presence. According to God's original design, we are to rule in love and in righteousness.

Hope

(**Josh. 1:6-9**; **1 Pet. 3:13-15**; **Heb. 13:5-6**) In Scripture, the presence of God is equated with the fear of God, and this is always expressed in our behavior. A person living in the fear of God demonstrates a lifestyle of love, joy and peace, and above all, freedom from fear.

(**Isa. 41:10**; **Ps. 23:4**; **Ps. 3:18,27**) The presence of God is the logic behind a life, a life without fear. God's command to change our anxious behavior is based on the reality of His presence. Freedom from worry, fretting, and anxiety is not a miracle in our emotions but is a result of the conclusion of a Holy Spirit enlightened mind.

(**Ps. 62:1-2,5-6**; **2 Cor. 13:14**) Living in the fear of God means not only that Christ has died and is risen from the dead, but also that He is exalted and has sent the Spirit to dwell in our heart: He is the center of our true self. Thus, our biblical hope is born of a living relationship with God. And we know we are in covenant with God who is love, and who is active on our behalf.

Change

(**Luke 9:23-24**; **Rom. 8:5-9**) We have practiced the presence of our flesh so long that we are on 'automatic' in the presence of a hostile situation. We react rather than act. We either deny there is a reason to fear, or we are immobilized and paralyzed, or we lash out in anger, afraid of our helplessness.

To counteract this tendency, we have to understand that we must act in faith, and practice the consciousness of God's presence within and with us. This does not just 'happen' to us! Notice **Ps. 23:4**. It is David's determined faith and determined response to God's announcement that He is with us!

(**Rom. 8:26**; **Phil. 4:6-7**; **Isa. 26:3-4**; **Isa. 40:31**) The Holy Spirit is our prayer partner. We share every detail with God in prayer, and leave it with Him. We praise and give thanks, knowing it is the way faith anticipates His actions in our unknown future. This leads us to wait upon God which results in supernatural strength. We take time to simply sit in His presence and confess that 'Thou art with me' and share the things that are the object of our worry and anxiety. When we do so, He promises that we will know the peace of God that is beyond all human comprehension.

(**2 Cor. 10:5**; **Prov. 16:25**; **Prov. 18:21**) Every thought that comes to mind, give immediately to the Holy Spirit who will return the right word to your mind to digest, to understand and to apply in love and truth through your tongue. Thus, the anointed word addresses life and rejects death.

Work Out Your Salvation (Phil. 2:12-13)

Memory Verse(s):
> **Ps. 62:1-2,5-6**

Devotion:
> BSAF on **Ps. 31:24**; **Ps. 39:7**; **Ps. 71:4-5**; **1 Thess. 1:3**; **Rom. 5:5**; **Rom. 15:13**.

Put-Off/Put-On:
> Read **Ps. 3**; **Ps. 18**; and **Ps. 27**. Personalize your own situation, and visualize your fears replaced with the fear of the Lord, that is, practice the presence of the Lord. Review this worksheet to reinforce God's truth, and think God's thoughts after Him. We have the victory already, it is a question of walking and working it out (**John 16:33**; **1 John 5:4-5**).

14.3. Learning Truth Talk

Perspective

(**Phil. 2:5**; **Eph. 4:23**; **Col. 1:8-10**; **Phil. 4:8**; **2 Cor. 10:5**) The New Testament teaches that the source of our behavior is the mind. The salvation we have received through Christ begins to be established and worked out in our thoughts before it becomes our lifestyle. It is in the mind that we look at ourselves and form a perception of who we are. We have a mental mirror that images to us who we believe ourselves to be. Accordingly, before Christ, the false images we had of ourselves: patterns of anxiety, acting on feelings and resultant fretful behavior, are to be changed to new patterns that reveal the love, hope and peace of God, i.e., learning to think with the mind of Christ.

Hope

(**Matt. 13:1-9**; **Matt. 8:23**; **Jer. 31:33**; **Ezek. 36:26,27**) We now have a new center, a new magnetic north. Christ has put His life into us, we have a new heart, and His law written on that new heart, a heart of flesh, not stone. We have new soil to receive the word of God in order to conform to his image.

(**Matt. 18:3**) To hear the Gospel is usually a passive act. At the surface level, it may make sense to us so that we accept it. At the same time, we may still believe in our deepest being the prompting of the Lie, and we self-talk ourselves and fail to translate the Gospel into behavior. Having a new heart means to turn around and go in the other direction, facing the fact that we now have to build our lives on a totally new foundation. Like children, we have to relearn the meaning of our lives and how to live it. Is is a question of choice—choosing to change, to repent, which opens the door to being Christlike.

(**Eph. 1:18**; **Eph. 4:23**; **Col. 1:9-10**) The 'heart' in Scripture is never the seat of emotions, but the center of a man's person. The heart of a man is his mind, the way he thinks and believes about life: from his beliefs he makes his decisions. The spirit of the mind speaks to the direction the mind thinks in. As we study the word of God, we progress in being filled with godly knowledge. This wisdom and understanding originates in the spirit, moves to our intellect, and this becomes the source of our behavior which pleases God.

Change

(**2 Cor. 4:3-4**; **Rom. 12:1-2**) Our genealogy, life's experiences and encounters formed us to a self-focus, and a self-defensive posture to guard us against the fears of living. From this we established a belief bank which fashioned and determined the course of life. The basic cause of all our fears is not how other people view us and how we measure up in their eyes, but how we view ourselves and measure up to our own standards.

We talk to ourselves from our source, and by it we judge ourselves and everyone else. It is by this self-talk with its endless commands, requirements, and patterns of fear that directs our lives. It is this thinking that we base our actions or inactions. This belief bank and resultant self-talk is to be renewed.

(**Gen. 3:5**; **Rom. 8:6-7**; **Eph. 4:17**; **Rom. 1:18-27**) The Satanic lie of Eden 'You shall be as God' was first injected into the mind and introduced a new and totally false belief system. It reflected to man through the inner mirror that he was to find the meaning to life in his created flesh. By this lie Satan gained legal access to the mind. Thus, man outside of Christ has a mind that is blinded by flesh feelings, he is led by passion, not logic: believing man is the center and the meaning of life.

(**2 Cor. 10:4**) The foundational belief system and the image of our self that arose from it were fashioned and given definition in our childhood. They were laid down and built up by our forefathers and parents, and were passed into our hands to build upon and updated to pass on to our children.

(**2 Cor. 10:5**; **Rom. 12:1-2**; **Rom. 8:29**; **Rom. 10:9**; **1 Cor. 2**) Daily we replenish the mind to eventually realize that we were created capable and responsible to receive a revelation of who God is, who we are, and the meaning of our existence. We are responsible to look to the 'One' who made us and ask, "Who am I?" He tells us. We are dependent upon the creator God who is unconditional love. We derive our lives from Him. In the ability of the Holy Spirit, we are to express that life—His love in our behavior, glorifying Him in creation. This is the belief bank we are to live from: the truth of God's word embedded in our human spirit which directs our lives to being a blessing on earth as Jesus was, and is. By this we subdue and are separated from the world, the flesh, and the evil.

Work Out Your Salvation (Phil. 2:12-13)

Memory Verse(s):
      Eph. 4:22-24

Put-Off/Put-On:

Study and apply **Eph. 4:25-32**; **1 Pet. 3:9-17**. Review **Section 7.14, "Mind Control "** and apply **Appendix A.7, "Problem/Solution Worksheet"**.

14.4. Applying the Truth

Perspective

(**2 Cor. 6:16-18**; **Eph. 4:20-21**; **Phil. 3:12-14**) Understanding the true foundational beliefs, the inner image of ourselves arising from these beliefs, and the inner talk that continually directs our lives, will help us to attack and destroy the lies that are behind all of our fears. The new birth does not neutralize the effect of what we tell ourselves. If we think with only the flesh—feeling input—we return, in fact, to life under the flesh, directed by the Lie. We effectively silence the mind and the revelation of the truth as it is in Jesus.

Unless we understand what is going on, we will continue to live by leftover feelings and a view of life—a way of thinking—rooted in the Lie. These old lies are the factory where new lies and distortions to fit the new situation are manufactured. They are the landing strips for Satan's flying missiles to land on.

Hope

(**Eph. 4:20-21**; **2 Cor. 10:3-5**) It is the Holy Spirit who renews the mind. As we study the Scriptures, we learn by Jesus, hear of Jesus, and be taught of Him. The Spirit would totally renew our mind and outmoded way of thinking, and would establish in us the mind of Christ—a new way of thinking.

(**Rom. 5:5**; **Phil. 4:6-7**; **Heb. 13:5-6**) When we take a stand of faith with the truth, the Holy Spirit then works in us mightily, pouring out and communicating the love of God to us. The love of God reaches into our fears, and surrounds and engulfs us. He enters our soul, where our emotions and thoughts are in turmoil, and speaks His peace-giving presence. We hear Him affirm us in the stand we take. He tells us He will never leave us, and we realize that He is our strength to face all our tomorrows.

(**John 14:6**; **1 Pet. 1:22**; **2 John 2**; **2 John 4**; **3 John 4**; **3 John 8**) We are those who have become confronted by the Truth, the Lord Jesus Himself, and have renounced the Lie and obeyed the Truth. The Truth has come to take residence within us by the entrance of the Spirit of Truth. We now walk in the Truth. We are actively participating in the Truth and aggressively promoting the Truth.

Change

(**Phil. 4:6-8**; **Matt. 6:25-32**) Because I am a child of the Father, I do not have to be anxious over anything. Whatever is beginning to bother me, I choose with prayer and supplication with thanksgiving to make my requests known to my Father. I do now and in all hours of the day and night, choose to direct my mind to dwell on whatever is honorable, right, pure, lovely, of good repute, of excellence and of praise.

(**Col. 3:1-3**; **Matt. 5:14**) I have been raised up with Christ, and I choose to keep seeking the things that are above, where Christ is seated at the right hand of God. I choose to set my mind on the things that are above, not on things that are on the earth, because I have died and my life is hidden with Christ in God. Christ is my life and in Him I am the light of the world. I am a city set on a hill that cannot be hidden.

(**John 1:12**; **Rom. 8:16**; **Gal. 4:6-7**) I have received Jesus Christ and, therefore, have been given the right to become a child of God. The Spirit Himself bears witness with my spirit that I have been born of God. And because I am His son, the Father has sent forth the Spirit of His Son into my heart. I am no longer a slave, but a son and an heir-an heir of God, a fellow-heir with Christ.

Work Out Your Salvation (Phil. 2:12-13)

Memory Verse(s):
> **Gal. 2:20**

Put-Off/Put-On:
> Read and dwell on the following Scriptures to reinforce who and what you are in Christ:
>
> > **John 15:1,5,15-16; Phil. 1:2; 1 Pet. 2:5;**
> > **Rom. 6:18; Eph. 3:4-10; 1 Pet. 2:9;**
> > **1 Cor. 6:15-20; Eph. 4:21-24; 1 John 3:1-2;**
> > **2 Cor. 5:17; Col. 1:12-14; 1 John 5:18;**
> > **Gal. 6:18; 1 Thess. 5:5; Matt. 5:13.**
>
> Review **Section 15.9, "Union with God"**.

14.5. Out of Control (World of Non-Existence)

Perspective

(**Matt. 6:34**; **Isa. 33:2**; **Ps. 90:4**; **Lam. 3:21-24**) Sin is man choosing to be independent of God's love. It is taking sides with Satan in defiance of God, turning to one's own way. When man came out from under God to live in the Lie of "I can be independent and alongside of God," he walked out of God's shalom. The first words of man were "I was afraid." When we seek to be in control of our lives, independent of God, we create a world of fear and anxiety. Believing the Lie that he is the source and master of his own life, his world and all his futures, man seeks to create shalom independently of God. To do this he must have control over all that happens in life, today and in all tomorrows, in his own life and in the lives of those who affect his happiness.

This leads to compulsion to control every detail of his existence and that of everyone around him. If he is a god, then he must be in control. This is the world of non-existence, the territory of the Lie, that exists only in our darkened imagination and in the minds of demons.

Hope

(**Matt. 6:34**; **Isa. 33:2**; **Ps. 90:14**; **Lam. 3:21-24**) Jesus commands believers to live life in increments of one day at a time, and within that, one hour at a time. We have grace for today to be used entirely on today's quota of problems and challenges. The only action we can take today is to use that grace to do what must be done today in preparation for tomorrow. We then place all the problems of tomorrow in God's hands. Scripture advises us to receive from God in the morning the grace that is needed for that day.

(**Ps. 23**; **Heb. 13:8**; **Isa. 26:3**; **Deut. 33:25**) David spoke of God in the present tense, giving him the strength and enablement he needs in the present moment. Resting in the fact that God is now his Shepherd gives him the wisdom to handle the problem when he actually faces it. We don't try to imagine the changing future or what we will do with it; we focus our attention on the unchanging Christ, the Ruler of history. Instead of imagining a tomorrow without God, we concentrate our picture-forming ability on who God is to us, and in us now. As he is, so are we.

Change

(**Luke 22:31-34**; **John 15:10-11**; **John 16:33**; **Phil. 4:7**; **Ps. 91:11-13**) In our flesh, we not only want to control tomorrow, but all the people who are part of our lives, who fill our todays and tomorrows. We believe it is our responsibility to heal all the wounds and hurts of our family and associates. We must have the answers to all their problems. We are responsible to provide for family and to counsel and discipline children. These thoughts are flawed. God commands us never to manipulate others or try to live life for others. We must repent of our sinful attempts to control the lives of others, and release them to God who is responsible for them.

(**Num. 13:25-14:35**; **Phil. 4:6-7**; **James 4:6-8**; **1 Pet. 5:5-6**) We are afraid of change, the fear of the unknown that causes anxiety. We procrastinate learning a new skill, driving a car, fear changing jobs, meeting new people, moving to a new area, afraid of success and new challenges: fear of being found wanting. We worry over things that we have no control over: the life or death of loved ones, their joy and their sadness, and the choices they make. We worry because the Lie has taught us we should control them. The fear of death is the ultimate fear of the unknown and uncontrollable.

These types of fear lead to murmuring and complaining and often directed at God. We must do as Joshua and Caleb in not fearing the unknown. They self-talked the truth, confronting themselves and their fears in the presence of God. They knew God's presence with them, and they knew God's track record.

(**Rom. 6:3-6**; **2 Cor. 5:17,21**; **Rom. 8:1-2**; **Heb. 11:1**) The only way to be free from all fear, especially the anxiety arising from the compulsion to control, is to pass through the ultimate fear, fear of death. We must become new persons, no longer dominated and controlled by the Lie and the liar. The only way that can happen is for that lie-controlled self to die! Jesus took our place in death and resurrection. Our response to that announcement is to repent and renounce the Lie, specifically in the area of control. Faith means death to the controlling self because the act of faith in the Gospel is admitting we can do nothing to save ourselves from ourselves and our sin. Faith abandons all efforts to make self right with God and rests with thanks in what God has done in Christ.

Work Out Your Salvation (Phil. 2:12-13)

Memory Verse(s):
>> **Eph. 5:18**

Devotion:

Read this worksheet and verses daily, develop a sense of consciousness of the Presence of God.

Put-Off/Put-On:

List those areas, people and circumstances, that cause your anxiety. List areas which you try to control. See yourself dead to the old fleshly reactions, see yourself filled with the Presence of the Holy Spirit. With Him you confront the old fear-filled patterns of the flesh and the controlling spirit. See the life of these lies evaporate in the Light and the Presence of Christ who now directs your life.

He is constantly at work within us, changing the old programs of behavior that conformed to the Lie, that we may be conformed to the very image of Christ in whom we are more than conquerors. Thus, we allow Him through us to be God in the lives of others and in the circumstances of life.

Accordingly, we put away anxiety and control, place ourselves as intercessors in the spiritual realm, and put our trust in God that He will intercede in the lives of those for whom we pray. We rest in Him (not in ourselves) that He will do according to His word. Review **Section 4.4, "Union with Christ"; Section 5.4, "Transforming the Natural Self"** and **Appendix A.8, "Freedom from Anxiety"**.

Chapter 15. Supernatural Life Series

15.1. Mind

Perspective

(**Isa. 55:1-8**; **Rom. 12:1-2**) Cease from thinking of the self and the willing of the self, keep your intellect and will quiet, then you are ready to receive the impressions of the Eternal Word and Spirit. See your soul above all outward senses and let your imagination be locked up by Holy Thoughts, opening the way for the Eternal Hearing, Seeing and Speaking to be revealed in you. Now you are the organ of His Spirit, and so God speaks in you, whispers to your spirit, and your spirit will hear His voice.

Hope

(**2 Cor. 5:17**; **Rom. 4:13,15,17-20**; **Rom. 5:1-2**) If you can stand still from self-thinking and self-willing, then you may arrive at length to see the great salvation of God, being made capable of all manner of Divine sensations and Heavenly Communication.

(**Gen. 2:7**; **Gen. 1:26-27**; **Rom. 6:17-18**; **2 Cor. 4:16**) Man was descended and derived from the earth, given Eternal life by the breath of God. This life was given before man could think and will for himself. God initiated and activated man's thinking and willing. Man's life is in God, and this life came into the body. Thus if you remain quiet and silent as when God made man's nature, then you will hear God speak.

(**Col. 3:1-3**; **James 4:6-10**; **Matt. 10:37-38**) To hear God, three things are required:

1. Resign your will to God and realize you exist simply by the mercy of God.
2. Hate your own will and resist from doing what your will drives you to do.
3. Put your soul under the Cross and die daily to temptations of the flesh and things of life.

(**John 1:1-4,10,16**; **1 John 2:16**; **1 John 5:1-5**) The world is but an image, a shadow of the Substance and the Reality which is Christ: for all things came into being by Him. Of His fulness we have received which is a state of living above images, figures and shadows of this created world. We rule over creatures in Jesus from whom all things came into being. Therefore, we are to be ruled by Christ and in Him rule all things.

Change

(**Matt. 18:3-4**; **John 15:4-5**; **Luke 9:23-24**; **Phil. 2:12-13**; **1 John 5:19-21**) We are to lean upon the Lord for all things. As we depend upon the Author and Fountain of all things and become like him in all dependence by union of my will with his will, as I give my desires and will to the Lord, and I receive no new thing unto my self: then I will be free of all things and will rule over them as a Prince of God.

(**Matt. 28:18-20**; **John 15:5**; **1 Cor. 1:30**; **Phil. 4:13**; **Prov. 14:12**; **Prov. 21:1**) Christ is the strength of my salvation and the power of my life. I can do all things by the faith which He works in me. But I must give up my entire life and resign my will wholly to him and desire nothing without Him. I am not to be delighted by my own reasonings, and abilities, but put them all under the Cross of the Lord Jesus Christ. Thus my will will be walking in Heaven, I will behold all things outwardly with my reason, and inwardly with my mind. Therefore, I will rule in all things and over all things with Christ unto whom all power is given both in heaven and on earth.

Work Out Your Salvation (Phil. 2:12-13)

Memory Verse(s):
>**John 15:5**

Put-Off/Put-On:
>View whatever you desire or possess whether it controls or possesses you: talents, gifts, skills, ambition, wealth, career,

family, children, homes, pleasures, appetites, etc.. To the extent they control you, you are in bondage and enslaved. Bear this principle in mind: the meaning of life is for God to reveal His life through you to others according to the talents and gifts He has given to you. Evaluate and measure your thoughts, speech and actions accordingly. Work out **Appendix A.4, "Victory over Sin Worksheet"** and **Appendix A.9, "Contingency Plan"** for those things that control and influence you inordinately. Review **Section 4.2, "Sins of the Flesh/Self of the Flesh"** for additional insights.

Reference: [Boehme1]

15.2. Abiding

Perspective

(**Col. 1:13**; **2 Tim. 4:17-18**; **1 Cor. 6:16-20**; **Phil. 3:17-20**) Our spirits have been translated into the highest of Light but our bodies still exists with the creatures. Spiritually, we walk with God knowing in our minds we are redeemed from the earth, separated from the creatures, to live the life of God.

We can will in our mind that we are separated from creatures and go forth from them. Therefore, in my mind's eye, I am with God and He directs and guides me on how I should respond in my body on the earth in my relations with creatures. If we are the Temple Of God, the Spirit of God dwells within me. Thus, the Holy Spirit who dwells within, dwells in the 'will' of the mind.

Hope

(**John 15:5-7**; **Matt. 16:24-25**; **Eph. 4:22-24**) To make this a reality, let your 'will' abide in the words of Christ, then His word and Spirit will abide in you. If your will goes into creatures, then you will be separated from God because creatures still live in you, that is, in your bodily appetites. Daily we must be aware that we can descend quickly into the shadow of things. Thus, we must daily die to creatures, and exercise a daily ascending into Heaven in our wills

(**Gal. 6:14**; **Matt. 10:34-39**; **John 16:3**; **1 John 2:2**) To remain in a state of repentance and humility, you must leave that which loves you, and love that which hates you. All things that please and feed you, your will feeds on it and cherishes it. All visibles and sensuals by which the imagination or sensual appetites are delighted or refreshed, the will of your mind must leave and forsake, even count it as enemies. At the same time, you are to love that which hates you and even to embrace the reproach of the world. To do this, you must learn to love the Cross of the Lord Jesus Christ, and for His sake to be pleased with the reproach of the world which hates and derides you. Being crucified to the world and the world to you, you shall have continual cause to hate yourself in the creature and to seek eternal rest which is Christ. In Him you may have rest and peace: but in the world you will have anxiety: for the world gives only tribulation.

(**Col. 3:1-3**; **1 John 2:15-16**; **2 Cor. 5:19-20**; **1 Pet. 4:19**; **2 Tim. 1:12**; **Matt. 26:8-9**; **1 John 1:7**; **Phil. 3:10**) To accomplish what God desires requires meditation on the word of God for, at least, half-hour to an hour a day. By faith, you will throw yourself beyond all creatures, above sensual perceptions and apprehensions and move into the sufferings of Our Lord, into the fellowship of His interceding. From this you will receive power from above to rule over death and the devil, and to subdue hell and the world when you endure in all temptations.

By the practice thereof of being in the Presence of God, we allow ourselves to be penetrated and clothed upon with the supreme Splendor of the Divine Glory. By this, we would taste in itself the most sweet love of Jesus. Then our spirit would feel in itself the cross of the Lord Jesus Christ, to be very pleasing to it. And thereupon, love the cross more than the honors and goods of the world.

Change

(**Rom. 12:1-2**; **Phil. 2:5**; **Phil. 3:10**) You must be willing to offer your body, the right of yourself, and to renew the mind in order that the mind can have dominion over the body according to the will of God. The body is to die without to the customs and fashions of the world, and within to the lusts and appetites of the flesh. Now there is a new mind being subject to the Spirit continually and directed to God. The body becomes the Temple of God and of His Spirit in imitation of the Lord's body.

(**1 Pet. 2:23**; **1 Pet. 3:13-18**) By offering our souls and spirits up to God when bombarded from within and without, the body would penetrate into itself and would sink into the great love of God. Thus it would be sustained by God and refreshed by the sweet name of Jesus. The body would find within itself a new world springing forth as through the anger of God into love and joy eternal which will clothe the body as with a garment.

Therefore, the world and the creatures can't touch him while he remains in this love: because this love makes him invulnerable both from within and without. Whether he is in heaven or hell all is alike to him: because his mind resides in the greatest love of God. Now he has God for his friend... Angels are his friends... God is his helper which is sufficient for anything in this world—under it or over it.

Work Out Your Salvation (Phil. 2:12-13)

Memory Verse(s):
> **Phil. 3:10**

Put-Off/Put-On:

Read Hebrews chapters 3 and 4. List areas in which you seek approval, acceptance, sense of value and purpose, that is, trying to find the meaning of life through creatures, things or possessions (the world, the flesh, and the devil). Check for emotional dependency (co-dependency) on others for acceptance and approval rather than focusing on God and His word.

Note: All things and creatures bound to the world compete with God and are enemies of God (See **James 4:4-5**; **Col. 2:9-19** and **Matt. 10:37-39**).

15.3. Virtue of Love

Perspective

(**Gen. 1:1,31; Rom. 8:31,32,39; 2 Cor. 5:18-21; Eph. 2:4-5; Eph. 3:18-21; Titus 3:4-5; 1 John 3:13,16,19; Rev. 3:12**) The virtue of God's love is the principle of all principles; its power supports the heavens and upholds the earth. Love being the highest principle is the virtue of all virtues. It is the holy root from which all things flow, the holy power from whence all the wonders of God have been wrought by the hands of His elect servants. Whoever finds this love finds all things.

Hope

(**Gen. 1:26-31; Zech. 7:9; Acts 1:8; Acts 2:1-4; Rom. 12:1-2; Eph. 1:17-33; Phil. 3:10**) When you go forth from the creature and that which is visible, and have become nothing to all that is natural and creaturely, then you are in that Eternal One which is God Himself. Herein you will perceive within and feel without the highest virtue of love. God's love—its power—is in and through all things. And as you perceive the power in your soul and body, the fire will burn away all the dross and enlarge the soul as wide as the whole creation of God: for God's love abides in all of His creation. To realize this is to set the Throne of love in your hearts.

(**Deut. 3:24; Job 9:4-10; Ps. 84:8,9,13; Prov. 21:30; Isa. 40:12; 1 Cor. 13:7; Eph. 3:17-19; 1 John 4:16-19**) This virtue which is love is the very life and energy of all the Principles of Nature. It reaches to all worlds, to all manner of beings. The workmanship of Divine Love is the first mover: both in heaven above and on the earth beneath and in the water under the earth. Love's power supports the heavens and upholds the earth. Should this love fail or recede the world would disperse as loose dust before the winds.

God's love is higher than the highest heavens. The Throne of God is higher than the highest, so must love also be, which fills all things and comprehends them all. Thus, this love when permitted to manifest to the soul—the Light of Godhead—darkness is broken through and the wonders of the new creation will be successfully manifested.

Love is indeed the virtue of all virtues, worker of all things. It is a powerful vital energy that passes through all power, natural and supernatural, through the whole creation of God, inspecting and governing all things.

Change

(**Deut. 30:19-20**; **Josh. 24:15**; **Matt. 26:29**; **John 6:38-40**; **John 14:23**; **1 Cor. 10:3-5**; **Phil. 2:12-13**) Two wills exist: the false self of flesh and appetites; the other the true self, human spirit in union with the Holy Spirit. The will is the partition wall that exists in the soul which divides between the two principles or states of heaven and hell. The creaturely will can be broken by nothing but by the Grace of self-denial which is the entrance into the true fellowship of Christ. And this is totally removed by nothing but a perfect conformity with the Divine Will.

Not by self-effort but by the Light and Grace of God received into the soul will the darkness be broken and one's own will be melt down and brought into the obedience of Christ. Then the creaturely will is removed between you and God and the true self. All we need to do is to be obedient and passive to the Light of God shining through the darkness of the creaturely being.

(**Ps. 84:1-2,10,12**; **Prov. 14:12**; **John 6:63**; **Gal. 5:16-18**; **Heb. 5:13-14**) We are not to resist the Sun of Righteousness—the Light of the Grace of God—to be received in our souls. To receive or not is our decision to choose. Therefore, by our choice we seek the Fountain of Light—the Sun of Righteousness—which illuminates the properties of our natural lives and leads the sensual and rational lives into the most perfect order and harmony. This is done by ceasing of our own activity and concentrating our eyes on one point—the promised Grace of God. Gather all your thoughts and by faith press into the Center, the Presence of God, laying hold upon the word of God. Be silent before the Lord, sit alone with Him, your mind being centrally united in itself and attending His will in the patience of hope.

(**Matt. 6:22-24**; **2 Cor. 5:7**) How you see determines light or darkness. There are two wills within: one that sees through the false self of flesh and appetites, the left eye; the other, the true self in union with the Holy Spirit, seeking holy things, the right eye. The left eye, the eye of Time competes with the right eye, the eye of Eternity. The soul of man determines which eye he will follow. The left eye always seeks to satisfy the self nature, and must be controlled. You must permit your right eye to command the left eye to desist and to follow godly standards. The left eye will be trained to follow the right eye, and in time both can exist together and be of mutual service to each other. This unity can be accomplished only by entering fully into the will of Our Saviour Christ, and thereby bringing the eye of Time into the eye of Eternity and then descending by means of this unity through the Light of God into the Light of Nature (See **Chapter 4**, *Soul Dynamics Series, Part A*).

Work Out Your Salvation (Phil. 2:12-13)

Memory Verse(s):
Matt. 6:22-24

Put-Off/Put-On:

For the next week or so, maintain a journal and note what you see and how you look at what you see, the judgments you make, how things affect your spirit, whether good or evil. Make a list of those things that reflect the left eye of the flesh and its appetites, and correct same by seeing as God sees via **Appendix A.4, "Victory over Sin Worksheet"**

Review **Section 15.9, "Union with God"** for additional insights.

Note: We are to look at all of life from God's perspective. This is a lifelong effort and activity which leads to a pure heart and a humble spirit.

271

15.4. Will of God

Perspective

(Isa. 26:3; Isa. 40:6-7; Matt. 12:50; Matt. 13:22; Rom. 8:5-6; Rom. 12:2; 1 Cor. 2:1-16; 2 Cor. 4:18; 2 Cor. 6:17-18 : 1 Pet. 4:1) Develop a single eye that concentrates upon the Center, the Presence of God within your soul. From this Center, the eye of Time looks at nature through the eye of Eternity. Resign yourself to the Eye of God in your spirit, then you can labor with your hands or head and allow your heart to rest in God. God is a Spirit, dwell in the Spirit, work in the Spirit, pray in the Spirit, do all things in the Spirit. Remember you are a spirit, created in the image of God. Present yourself as a naked spirit before God in simplicity and purity. In this position the world, the flesh and the devil, the temptations of life, and the fashions and customs of this world will not be able to draw you out... Mind them not... They can't hurt you if you choose to abide in His will.

Hope

(Rom. 8:29; 2 Cor. 3:18; 2 Cor. 4:17-18; 2 Pet. 3:10-14; 1 John 4:16-17) The world of naked matter, of corruption and decay, the lusts thereof, lead to frustration and anger, and darkens the root of our being. Do not let the things of the world even enter into your imagination. Your hope lies in beholding God's Light and seeing your soul being divinely illuminated.

(Eph. 4:24) Let not your eye enter into matter or fret yourself with any thing whatsoever either in heaven or earth. But let it enter by naked faith into the light of His Majesty and so receive by pure love the Light Of God. This Light attracts the divine power into itself, putting-on the Divine Body, and thus, we grow up in it to the full maturity of the Humanity of Christ.

(Ps. 37:7; Ps. 91:15-16; Phil. 2:12-13; Phil. 4:13; James 4:6-7; 1 Pet. 5:6-7) Nothing is required of us but let our will be in the will of God. We are to stand still and see the salvation of the Lord. If you have followed so far you have nothing to care for, nothing to desire in this life, nothing to imagine or attract. All you need to do is cast your care upon the Lord who cares for you. And let him do with you as He wills according to His good pleasure. God knows what is best for us if we but trust Him.

(Matt. 26:39; Luke 11:2; John 4:34; John 5:20; John 10:10; Rom. 6:13; Col. 3:1-3) When you imagine after anything other than God, then it enters into you. In time it will take over your will, overcome it, and lead to darkness. But when the will imagines or lusts after nothing but God, to give glory to Him, it receives the will of God into itself. And there it dwells in Light and begins to work the works of God.

Change

(John 5:30; Acts 17:25,28; Gal. 6:14) The resigned will of a truly contrite spirit which is crucified to the world, the center of this will is impenetrable by the world, the flesh and the devil. Nothing in the world can enter or adhere to it because the will is dead with Christ unto the world. The will is alive and quickened with Christ in the center of this life. When the love of self is banished, there dwells the love of God. For as so much of the soul's own will is dead unto itself, even so much room has the will of God to take over.

(Matt. 13:36-46; John 4:34; John 5:30; Rom. 6:11-23; Gal. 2:20) You cannot enter the spiritual realm by comprehending it but only by a complete surrender and the yielding up the will: then the love of God becomes the Life of your nature. You live now by God's will forasmuch as your will has become His will. It is no longer your will but the will of God. No longer the love of self but the love of God, which moves and operates you. You will become dead to self but alive unto God. So being dead, you live rather God lives in you by His Spirit. This love therefore apprehends and comprehends you: there the Treasure of Treasures is found.

(John 16:33; Rom. 5:3-5; Rom. 12:9-23; James 1:2-4; 2 Pet. 1:3-10; 1 John 1:7) It is the love of God as it penetrates into the dead self that burns and purifies the ego, the greed and envy, the deceit and vanities, and the false and treacherous ways. In the world you must have trouble and your flesh will be disturbed. In this anxiety of the soul arising from the world or the flesh, the love of God will enkindle itself and its conquering fire is made to blaze forth with greater strength for the destruction of that evil. For the way to the love of God is folly to the world but it is wisdom to the children of God. Whosoever obtains it is richer than any on earth. He who gets it is nobler than any emperor can be, and more potent and absolute than all power and authority.

Work Out Your Salvation (Phil. 2:12-13)

Memory Verse(s):

2 Pet. 1:3-4

Put-Off/Put-On:

See **Matt. 12:50**. Bear in mind your relationship to the Lord as His brother/sister and spouse. Review areas of your life still influenced, controlled or manipulated by the world, the flesh and the devil. Review **Appendix A.5, "Dying to Self"** and prepare a plan (**Appendix A.9, "Contingency Plan"**) to deal with these failures.

15.5. That Which is Perfect

Perspective

(**1 Cor. 13:9-11**; **Isa. 40:3-8**; **1 Pet. 1:7,14**) That which is perfect is a Being: Christ. He is the substance of all things. He is unchangeable, immovable, and without whom and beside whom there is no true substance, in whom all things have their substance. The fallen self, the creature, the I, the self, the me, the mine, must all be lost, and done away. As long as we think of the interest of the self, so long remains the Perfect unknown to us. That which is Perfect is come, by the pure word of God, and through the word may be known, felt and tasted by the soul. Thus, we are nurtured and grown into complete salvation which is the substance of Christ Himself: all of Him, none of the self.

Hope

(**2 Pet. 1:4**; **2 Cor. 5:17,21**; **John 3:3-6**; **2 Pet. 1:2-4**; **1 Cor. 1:30**; **1 Cor. 3:11**; **Gal. 2:20**; **Col. 2:10**) God took human nature or manhood upon Himself and was made man, and man was made divine; thus, healing was brought to pass. As I accepts this, I die to the self, the I, the me, the mine, and move from the flesh to the spirit. A new creature emerges entirely, washed and cleansed, made righteous. The center of my being replaced by God Himself from whom I live and breathe and have my being: all that I need to live the righteous life, giving glory to His Holy Name.

(**John 15:5**; **2 Cor. 12:9-10**; **John 8:31-32**) Man should acknowledge that in himself, he neither has nor can do any good thing. None of his knowledge, wisdom, will, love and good works come from himself. But the righteous acts are of the eternal God, from whom all good things proceed. When we recognize this and refrain from claiming anything for our own, we shall have the best, fullest, clearest and noblest knowledge that a man can have as well as the purest love, will and desire. When the vain imagination and ignorance are turned into an understanding and knowledge of the truth, the claiming of anything for our own will cease of itself: all goodness is of God.

Change

(**1 Cor. 13:9-11**; **2 Tim. 3:16-17**; **1 Cor. 2:7**; **1 Cor. 4:4**) Accordingly, we are to make judgments, discriminate, and discern all outward things on the basis of inward truths. It is of sin that we do not love the best. As the inward man holds to the truth of God's word, he will see that the Perfect is without measure, better and nobler than all which is imperfect. Thus, that which is imperfect and in part would become tasteless and be as nothing to us.

(**Matt. 19:17**; **1 Cor. 2:9-16**) All manner of virtue and goodness and even the Eternal Good which is God Himself can never make a man virtuous, good or happy: so long as it is outside the soul, so long as man is holding conversation with outward things by his senses and his reasons. The like is true of sin and evil. Sin and wickedness, can never make us evil: so long as it is outside of us, so long as we do not commit it, or give consent to it.

The Goodness of God resides within and as we live in pure submission to the Eternal Goodness, we will live in the perfect freedom of fervent love. To partake of the Goodness, we must cease always seeking ourselves and our things. Let God draw us up to something higher, that is, to an utter loss and forsaking of our own things, spiritual and natural. And even to withdraw His Presence from us in order for us to learn to seek alone the Honor of God.

Work Out Your Salvation (Phil. 2:12-13)

Memory Verse(s):
> **Heb. 13:16**

Devotion:
> BSAF on **Luke 9:23-24**; **Eph. 6:6**; **Phil. 2:12**; **James 1:25**.

Put-Off/Put-On:
> God is in all that He created. Ascertain the extent that your happiness is found in created things, and not in God Himself, that is, the extent you seek God's hand rather than His Face. Ask the Holy Spirit for the wisdom to know the difference, and what to do about it.

15.6. Listening to God

True listening is obedient listening. To listen to God is to obey Him. Wisdom from above is received by those who are prepared to obey it. To listen in prayer for the voice of the Lord is to find the mind of Christ. It is to gain transcendent wisdom: a wisdom that includes understanding, guidance, knowledge, exhortation, and consolation.

To be born from above is to be drawn up into this Union of the Holy Trinity by listening obedience. This love calls forth the real 'I' in each one of us. And from this real 'I' or true self, praise is called forth. Love then flows down from the Uncreated into the created, and then into all other created beings (Note: the 'Uncreated' is God, the 'created' is us) .

(**John 17:23**) "I in them and you in me." This is the ultimate point of everything for which Christ came to earth to accomplish. The incarnation and the cross was for this. All He suffered on our behalf was to bring us back present to the Father.

When Christ says to the Father that He has given us the glory that was given to Him, He speaks of the Father's presence. The glory of God is the presence of God. Listening to God is an important part of the presence of God we are to practice, that is, acknowledge always. Just as we learn to practice His presence within, without, and all around, so we must learn to open the eyes and ears of our hearts and recognize His voice.

(**1 Thess. 5:17**; **Luke 2:52**; **2 Cor. 4:18**) Practicing the presence of God is a way of praying continually as Scripture exhorts us to do. The practice of His presence, then is simply the discipline of calling to mind the truth that God is with us. In this listening we come out of our spiritual adolescence—our immaturity—and begin to mature in Christ. To listen to God is to receive wisdom from above. Like Jesus, we grow as we continue to receive it.

To fail to listen to God is to be listening to other voices that are not of God. It is to miss the vital walk in the Spirit and our immensely creative collaboration with Him. This collaboration requires the new self—one in union with Christ—to be always maturing in Him.

The Secret of Guidance

Promises for guidance are unmistakable...

277

- **(Ps. 32:8)** "I will instruct thee and teach thee in the way which thou shall go."
- **(Prov. 3:6)** "In all thy ways acknowledge Him and He shall direct (or make plain) thy paths."
- **(Isa. 58:11)** "The Lord shall guide thee continually."
- **(John 8:12)** "I am the Light of the world: he that followeth me shall not walk in darkness, but shall have the light of life."

1. Our motives must be pure

(Luke 11:34) "When thine eye is single, thy whole body also is full of light." So long as there is some thought of personal advantage, some idea of acquiring the praise of men, some aim at self-advancement, it will be impossible to find out God's purpose concerning us. Ask the Holy Spirit to give you the single eye, that glorifies the Lord, not self.

2. Our wills must be surrendered

(John 5:30) "My judgment is just because I seek not mine own will, but the will of the Father which hath sent me." We are not to extinguish our will but surrender it to the Lord so that the Lord can take, and break, and make us. If and when you are not willing, confess that you are willing to be made willing. Hand yourself over to Him to work in you to will and to do of His good pleasure.

3. We must seek information for our mind

God uses the faculty of our mind to communicate His purposes and thoughts. No need to run to others for their opinions or ideas as to what we should do. But there is no harm in taking pains to gather all reliable information on which the flame of holy thought and consecrated purpose may feed and grow strong, acting on the materials we have collected. God may act miraculously to guide us, and other times allow ordinary light of reason to be adequate for the task. He will leave us to act as occasion may serve.

4. We must be much in prayer for guidance

The Psalms are full of earnest pleadings for clear direction: "Show me thy way, O Lord, lead me in a plain path, because of mine enemies." It is the law of God's house that His children should ask for what they want: "If any of you lack wisdom, let him ask of God, that giveth to all men liberally, and upbraideth not."

5. We must wait the gradual unfolding of God's plan in providence

God's impressions within and His word without are always corroborated by His Providence around, and we should quietly wait until these three focus into one point. Thus, meditation, prayer, and acting upon and applying faith precedes God's power and provision.

Note: Review **Section 15.8, "Inordinate Desires"**. It is the corruption and pollution of the world's many voices (TV, movies, magazines, etc.) which crowds out and dampens the 'fire' of God's voice and His presence in our souls.

15.7. Center of the Soul

Three Greatest Gifts

At conversion and baptism, our human spirits are regenerated and receive the grace of life in terms of faith, hope and love. These theological virtues are the center and the core of our being in the spiritual life process: the substance by which we are being conformed to the image of Christ (**Rom. 8:29**). Being adopted as children of the Father, we share in the nature of triune God within by the virtues of faith, hope and love (**1 Cor. 13:13; 1 Thess. 1:3**).

The Gift of Faith enables us to believe that God 'is', and enlarges our capacity to believe God's word and His promises. Faith affirms what cannot be understood by the intellect (transcends human wisdom) and partakes of godly wisdom (**Heb. 11:1**).

The Gift of Hope provides the capacity to trust God: that His promises will be fulfilled, that He is with me in trials and difficulties, and that eternal life is mine now and in heaven. Hope empties itself of all natural possessions in order to be possessed by the divine. To the measure our intellect, memory and will are dispossessed of things, to that measure we possess God (**Rom. 8:23-25; Matt. 10:34-39**).

The Gift of Love is the capacity to love God above everything: to respond to all of life's encounters (especially the unlovely) in patience, kindness and goodness (**Luke 14:33; 1 Cor. 1:30**).

Four Cardinal Virtues

Within the mansions of faith, hope and love reside the virtues of prudence, justice, fortitude, and temperance. These are the cornerstones or pillars, which provide a framework for our spiritual growth:

Prudence is a state of being in Christ. Prudence is the expression of this being—the truth. Prudence precedes truth, and truth precedes goodness. The intrinsic goodness of man, his true humanness, consists of his reason being perfected in cognition of the truth. "Reason" means nothing other than a regard for and openness to reality, and the acceptance of reality. Thus, prudence is concerned with the means to the end, not the end itself. Accordingly this virtue prepares our conscience (the voice of our spirit) to distinquish good from evil, and conditions our conscience to be docile, sensitive, and capable to respond to the slightest promptings of the Holy Spirit.

Justice, fortitude and temperance are the properties or abilities of prudence which give form and substance to the truth.

Justice is to establish God's will on earth, to care for the widow and orphan, to defend the defenseless, to secure and exercise honor, integrity and equity in the economic, political and social arenas of life.

Fortitude is the development of the muscles of the will to remain faithful, to resist temptations, to endure trials, to overcome fear and anxiety, and to undergo challenges and persecution: to abide in love regardless.

Temperance is the tightrope on learning how to balance and control the skills in the use of passions, impulses, instincts, and, thus, to bring order and harmony to our desires and reasonings.

Thus we are enabled to move in consonance with God's grace to establish His kingdom and will on earth (**2 Pet. 1:3-10**).

Seven Gifts

Wisdom, Understanding, Counsel, Fortitude, Knowledge, Piety, Fear of the Lord: These gifts are the embodiment, the dynamic expression of prudence, which enlightens our soul. We become filled with the Light of the Holy Spirit which speak to the inner recesses of our soul giving beauty, light, and wonder to our being. The more we enter the light, the more it increases and partakes of the radiance of the Holy Spirit—the divine nature—thus, escaping the corruption of the world (**Isa. 11:1-5**).

The Fruit of the Spirit

Love, Joy, Peace, Patience, Kindness, Goodness, Fidelity, Gentleness, Self-Control: The sanctity of the Glory of God invades the soul and drives out darkness and sinfulness, and, thus, the soul is being filled with His grace in all mansions. The fruit of the Holy Spirit reflect this overflowing. As virtues are practiced, it gives glory to God, reveals love of God and our love to God and to all others. Thus, we become encircled by light, by wonder, being lost in waves of endless adoration in clouds of angels (**Gal. 5:22-26**).

Review **Appendix A.12, "Anchor Posts"**.

Reference: [StTeresa1]; [StThomas1]; [Pieper1].

15.8. Inordinate Desires

Soul Conditioning

A prerequisite for the journey of the soul is a 'still' house. To attain to this stillness is to rid the soul of any desires, which impede the entrance of God's grace and His Presence. Desires are not to make loud demands and to engage our will. Thus, it has to be free from inordinate 'desires', namely all those "for the external things of the world, the delights of the flesh, and the gratification of the will." (**1 John 2:15-17**).

From birth our souls were 'empty slates'. Over the years, our senses deposit abundant 'writings' upon the slate. In receiving information from all five senses, the soul becomes aware of the broad range of objects in the external world, which become imprinted on the soul. It is then in the power of the soul to desire what it has experienced. In so doing, it draws the will to what it desires. Objects themselves can never damage a soul, but the turning of the will toward them in any excessive manner can (**1 John 5:21**).

Desires can damage the soul in two ways. First, they deprive the soul of grace and its working; second, they influence the soul in a variety of ways: all harmful. By their nature, these desires are ever demanding and restless. Satisfying them does not remove them. To the contrary, the more they are satisfied, the more demanding they become. As they grow, they harass the soul and prevent it from functioning well. What they affect in particular are the intellect, memory, and will (**Phil. 2:2-5**).

Soul Standards

St John also indicates the ideal activities of these three faculties: the intellect is to receive "the illumination of God's wisdom"; the memory is to take on "serenely the impression of God's image"; and the will to embrace "God within in pure love." Each faculty is to be totally open to God. The intellect is to be filled with only divine 'wisdom'—its knowledge is to be God-centered; the memory is to reflect perfectly God alone; the will is to choose God solely—human and divine will becoming one (**John 17:23**).

This is not the usual state of the soul. Desires (lusts) clutter it and prevent it from acting in grace with a single goal and single focus: God. The greater the number of desires and the more varied their objects, the less focused the soul can be, and less freely it can act under the impulse of grace (**Col. 3:5-10**).

Matt 11:28-29 summarizes this teaching. Reflecting on this passage, St John says, All you going about tormented, afflicted, and weighed down by your cares and appetites, depart from them. Come to me and I will refresh you and you will find the rest for your souls that the desires take away from you (Ascent, p. 134 [StJohn1]).

Soul Examination

St John urges us to see desires (lusts) at the root of negative behavior—to discern, and to resist them. To identify those controlling forces is the first step: Then you locate them and place them in a position to be removed from your life. To do this, the following practical steps may prove helpful.

1. Make a failure list of 6 or so desires that we suspect are harming our spiritual growth. This list could include such things as an excessive need for affirmation, approval, acceptance, power, success, and possessions. These factors lead to guilt, shame, greed, envy, impatience, intolerance, anger, resentments, and various forms of addictions. To bring to light this darkness clarifies its hold on us. With a sense of hope, we can look forward to either their disappearance from our souls or to our deft control of them.

2. Carefully examine why we have an excessive or inordinate desire for those objects. By assessing the source of our behavior, we may be able to understand more fully why we act as we do.

3. We bring the desire, with its origins and manifestations to prayer. Placing ourselves in the presence of Jesus, we can ask, "Free me from this desire." When we pray, "Let me not desire this", we are inviting grace to work. Gradually we may find that the desire no longer takes control of our soul in any degree. On the contrary, now it is our will united with God's will that controls the desire.

4. To work out this healing process for each inordinate desire or lust, recognize that God has given us everything we need for life and godliness. As we share in His divine nature, His power enables us to escape the corruption that sinful desires cause in the world (**Rom. 5:1-5; 2 Pet. 1:3-10**).

But it is up to us to work out our salvation by adding on to what He has done for us on the cross. Accordingly, as God's grace enters our lives, we are responsible to:

- Add **integrity** to our faith, and this by moral excellence and goodness of character, moral strength and moral courage (**1 Thess. 4:1-7**).

- Add **knowledge**: practical intelligence, insight. It means knowing what to do in every situation, and doing it; it is practical, day to day knowledge that sees situations and knows how to handle them. It is seeing the trials and temptations of life and knowing what to do with them and doing it (**John 8:31**; **Rom. 12:9-21**).

- Add **temperance**: to master and control the body or the flesh with all its desires and lusts. It means self-control, the master of desire, appetite, and passion, especially sensual urges and cravings. It means to stand against the lust of the flesh, the lust of the eye, and the pride of life (**1 John 2:15-16**).

- Add **patience**: endurance, fortitude, steadfastness, constancy, and perseverance. It is the spirit that stands up and faces life's trials, that actively goes about conquering and overcoming them. It is trials in life that teach one how to be patient (**Luke 21:19**; **Rom. 12:1-2**; **James 1:2-4**).

- Add **godliness**. This actually means to live in the reverence and awe of God; to be conscious of God's presence that one lives just as God would live if He were walking upon earth. It means to live seeking to be like God; to seek to possess the character, nature, and behavior of God. Man is to seek to gain a consciousness of God's presence—a consciousness so intense that he actually lives as God would live if He were on earth (**2 Cor. 3:18**; **2 Pet. 2:3,11**; **Titus 2:12-13**).

- Add **brotherly kindness**. This means to love others unconditionally as God loves us. This selfless or agape love is a gift of God. It can be experienced only if a person knows God personally, only if a person has received the love of God, that is, Christ Jesus, into his heart and life.

Soul Values

A response to these virtues and godly values, and the exercise of these qualities will gradually replace and force out the inordinate desires that beset many lives. " (**Eph. 4:22-24**; **Rom. 8:29**) The road to spiritual growth is open before us. We can advance as we become less dominated by desires within our souls, and more open to the working of grace. As St Paul describes, "You were taught to put away your former way of life, your old self, corrupt and deluded by desires, and to be renewed in the spirit of your minds, and clothe yourselves with the new self, created according to the likeness of God in true righteousness and holiness".

The Holy Spirit has been given; the Lord is glorified. Our waiting is not dependent on the providence of God, but on our own spiritual fitness. Thus, we need to look at ourselves and work out our salvation daily. Review **Appendix A.5, "Dying to Self"** and **Section 15:9, "Union with God"**.

Reference: Article "Desires: Guidance from St. John of the Cross", by Shirley D. Sullivan, 'Spiritual Life' magazine. 2131 Lincoln Road, NE, Washington, DC 20002)

15.9. Union with God

Fallen Nature

We are creatures, God is transcendent. We are made in the image of God, but fallen. Human nature is inclined to evil, how can God unite with evil? The Incarnation made this union possible. Becoming man, Jesus took our punishment for sin to free us. His living sacrifice defeated sin, and He became the mediator between heaven and earth. Gates of heaven opened to man through Jesus' human nature. Now man through Christ can approach God without being destroyed by His Holiness: Human nature united to God.

Transformation

Upon conversion, man's spirit is united to God, but the residuals of the old self-life still remain in the corrupted soul. This is man's responsibility, he must choose to put-off the old man and put-on the new man by the renewing of the spirit of the mind (the memories), moment to moment, day by day, year by year (**Eph. 4:22-24**).

Growth Stages and the Seven Mansions

There are three stages of this union: justification, sanctification and glorification. Justification is the movement from dark to light, becoming sons of God; sanctification is the process of becoming conformed to the image of God through His Son; glorification begins at death (**Rom. 8:29**).

Matt. 5:48 states we are to be complete as the Father. **Matt. 7:13-14** states any way other than our single focus on the Lord Jesus Christ will not do it (**Gal. 2:20**). **Col. 3:1-10** states that we are to put to death anything that is rooted on earth. Sin becomes a god which controls us and must be totally eradicated. To effect spiritual growth, we must pursue a dynamic course of action (a conscious self awareness) to separate ourselves from the world, the flesh and the devil. Accordingly this gives rise to...

1. The purgation of gross sins.

2. We begin to receive illuminating light and insight and sensitivity to sins and to be aware of God's Presence.

3. In addition to our own efforts, God begins to take the initiative in our lives.

4. This leads into the union stage, which is stable and consistent.

First Mansion

This is the initial turning to the Lord, seeing the horror of sin, and opening self to the mercy of God. Sense of humility and a sense of self knowledge develops but a great danger of falling back exists because serpents, lizards, and other poisonous vipers abound.

Second Mansion

Struggle continues here in battling the gross features of snakes and vipers of all sorts: but in the process one becomes aware of less gross sins. The practice of prayer emerges to counteract falling away. Here one is learning to turn away from the occasions of sin, hearing God's voice in His words. Distractions and discouragements are common but one becomes sensitive to the Presence of the Holy Spirit who encourages and strengthens, and prompts to confess and repent in failures, and to start again. Here determination to proceed is critical. Don't look for sensations or feelings, go by faith that God is with you. It is in the dry periods where spiritual growth is deepened. Ask God for a spirit of determination.

Third Mansion

This is a life of basic order and stability, living a consistent christian life of serving, giving, helping the poor, judging self, exercising mercy, daily devotions, etc.. However, watch out thinking the Lord owes you something. Develop an attitude that the Lord owes you nothing. All that we have are gifts to begin with. Our salvation and all that it means are merciful gifts that we are to exercise to His glory. Don't look for consolation in periods of dryness. Dry periods are means to purify us. Dryness reminds us what is it like to live without God. Thus, as we become rooted in God, we will be set free in time from the need of wealth, reputation, and power: all that is of the world, the flesh and the devil.

However, many remain attached to things of the world, and are subject to falling back when great trials come their way. Folks who live this ordered and stable life may be inclined to look down and judge those who live a weak spiritual life instead of being the means of encouragement.

Fourth Mansion

The first three mansions represent our self-effort, and self-emphasis. At this fourth stage, God begins to take the initiative—supernatural life begins here (**Song 1:4**).

This fourth area is one of recollection and quiet entering into the realm of the supernatural life. We are to recollect who and what we are in Christ Jesus, not focus on what we are or have done in the world. Here we begin to discern the false values of the flesh and the world and the true values of the Kingdom.

However, poisonous creatures are still hanging around, and these temptations keep us from being anchored to God. One major danger is thinking that we are better than others. The other fault is trying to figure out all things. Through prayer, worship and meditation, one is to seek God in all things, who will direct every thought henceforth. Our job is just to obey. God is responsible for the results, He knows the end from the beginning.

This requires a quiet time in the Presence of the Lord, an inner calling of the Lord to help us dwell on Him. Distractions will come, don't fight them, let them come, concentrate on the Lord. Open one's heart to the Presence of the Lord, and not on our own preoccupations. Here let God fill us, make room for Him, be not inclined to talk but just listen. Be in a state of thanksgiving, being grateful that you know God.

Fifth Mansion

As we give up self and make room for God to enter our soul, recollection and quietness leads to this mansion of full union and complete dependence on God. This is the passive night of the senses: The Lord strips and detaches us only to fill us with His Presence: The Holy Spirit works to rid self of its old ways of selfishness and self-concerns.

Here we pray to bring our will into the union of God's will. From this point on God takes the initiative to drive out the self-will. Even in the midst of deep trials, deep peace will prevail but one must press forward and not fall away. Union of our will with God's will is the major event. The danger again is pride that we are superior to others. However, the evidence that this union is real is an increase of our loving our neighbor, which is a reflection of our loving God.

Sixth Mansion

This stage is one of spiritual betrothal (**Song 2:7**). God will not give Himself until we strongly desire Him. We will be subject to many tests and trials. Trials will increase which is God's favor to deepen the union. Things will get tough. God will not cast pearls before swine. Sufferings of various dimensions in the physical and mental arenas will come, convincing you that you are back to zero, spiritually. You will be accused of many sins, you will be slandered, treated unjustly: all this to challenge the self-life. The Lord will give the devil license to try you, to make you feel lost and abandoned, lose faith and have no sense of God (**Job 1:12**). In the midst, we continue in this dark night, the passive night of the spirit, waiting for the mercies of God until the light of His Presence penetrates and disperses the darkness.

Seventh Mansion

Now we come to the stage of the spiritual marriage. All that Christ is, we are (**1 Cor. 1:30**). His virtues are mine, His wisdom and strength are mine. **Gal. 2:20** is not just of the mind but of the heart and ought to be lived out in all of life's activities. The Spirit of God fills the mind, the memory, the will and emotions and directs the conduct and behavior of the body. No more fears and doubts but we are tested time and again to remind us of our complete hopelessness without God and our complete dependence upon Him (**John 15:5**).

Review **Appendix A.12, "Anchor Posts"**.

Reference: [Kavanaugh1] and [StTeresa1].

Appendix A. Forms and Worksheets

Table of Contents

A.1. Bible Study and Application Format (BSAF)

This worksheet is used extensively in this manual and is abbreviated as **BSAF**. BSAF is an exercise to renew your mind and attitude as you train yourself in the application of God's word.

How to Work on BSAF

Follow the steps (A), (B), (C), (D), (E) described below to complete this form. Two examples are given to help you visualize how this form works.

Bible Study and Application Format (BSAF)				
Biblical Reference	**Teaching— What is the command or principle?**	**Reproof— How did I fail to keep the principle?**	**Correction— What do I need to do?**	**Training in Righteousness —How do I do it?**
(A) Choose a Bible verse that you want to work on.	(B) List the teachings of this verse that God speaks in your spirit. This is the area that God wants you to work on.	(C) **Be specific** on how you have failed in this area of your life. Give a brief description of a recent event that God convicted you in your heart.	(D) What is the **biblical response** to this situation according to God's word? If you are fuzzy about how to fill this column, try to just reverse what you wrote in the previous column.	(E) Specify a **detailed plan** to act on this situation in the future. God will bring up the same situation again and again until you are refined in this area.
Training in Righteousness—How do I do it? (Cont.)				
(E) (Cont.) It should be **a step by step** or **point by point** list of action. Pay attention to this area in the following week and use every opportunity to exercise your plan of response.				

Example I of BSAF

This is a short example using **Psalm 103**.

The counselee, full of self-pity, was constantly thinking of problems in his life. He was instructed to study Psalm 103 using the BSAF form. While studying Psalm 103, he began the practice of praising the Lord which, through practice, will help break the negative thinking process (**Ps. 103:1**; **2 Cor. 10:3-5**).

Bible Study and Application Format (BSAF)				
Biblical Reference	Teaching—What is the command or principle?	Reproof—How did I fail to keep the principle?	Correction—What do I need to do?	Training in Righteousness—How do I do it?
Psalm 103	Bless the Lord whenever I think.	Been dwelling on problems, self-pity, hardly on God.	Whole of me is to thank, praise, dwell on the Lord, not on self.	Each time I think negative, I will use the thought as a springboard to remind me to thank and praise the Lord.

Example II of BSAF

The second example is a longer example using **1 John 3:17**. The counselee is a young christian. He became aware of a woman at his church in need of winter clothes. He was convicted by his conscience to help, but he rationalized it away. Later while he was counseled by the biblical counselor, he was instructed to study **1 John 3:17** using the BSAF form on this event. He made a detailed plan based on his conviction.

Bible Study and Application Format (BSAF)				
Biblical Reference	**Teaching— What is the command or principle?**	**Reproof— How did I fail to keep the principle?**	**Correction— What do I need to do?**	**Training in Righteousness— How do I do it?**
1 John 3:17	We do not demonstrate God's love in us if we are not willing to share our lives as well as material goods with others.	I became aware of a woman at church whose children needed new winter coats. Her husband is disabled and unable to work and can not afford to buy coats. I reasoned that my kids and I also needed new coats, and I can't be responsible for everyone.	In reality, only one of my children really needs a coat. The others only want new ones of a more current style. I need to buy the one needed coat for my child and use the rest of the money to buy coats for this family in need.	1. Pray for God's guidance and strength in carrying out a plan to help this family. 2. Call a family meeting. Explain the need to my family and my plans to help another family. (Cont. next page)

Training in Righteousness—How do I do it? (Cont.)

3. Get my family's input.

4. With my family, review verses on sharing.

5. Contact the leaders in my church to alert them of the needs of the other family and tell of my plans of help.

6. Call the woman in need. Explain to her how my sharing shows my love to the Lord and provides a blessing for her family as well as my own.

7. Schedule a shopping trip so her family can pick out coats they like.

8. Perhaps take their family to lunch as part of the shopping trip.

More Examples

Bible Study and Application Format (BSAF)				
Biblical Reference	**Teaching**	**Reproof**	**Correction**	**Training in Righteousness**
1 Sam. 16:7	God is more concerned with our motives than our behavior.	Making impulsive decisions or responses and do not act on the first thought that comes. **James 4:14**	Call upon the Lord as an automatic action then take every thought into capitivity unto the Lord. **1 Cor. 10:3-5**	1. Call upon the Lord whatever the situation, **Prov. 3:5-7**. 2. Recall a scripture, dwell on it, **John 6:63**, and ask God for wisdom and strength for the moment. 3. If necessary, seek counsel of others—fellow christians. 4. Seek personalized counseling, if necessary. 5. Practice this spiritual discipline that brings the soul under the government of God each day.

Bible Study and Application Format (BSAF)				
Biblical Reference	**Teaching**	**Reproof**	**Correction**	**Training in Righteousness**
Matt. 6:14-15	Not to forgive is to destroy yourself.	Retaliation and hateful thoughts.	Discuss and give the hurt to God to deal with the person. Then rely on God via scriptures to soften my heart.	1. Resolve to never let offenses fester. Forgive daily offenses. 2. Replace hateful thoughts with blessings for the person. 3. Remember God has already forgiven the person. All he/she has to do is ask. 4. When hurt returns, praise God that He is working in me to enable me to forgive and growing me into the image of His Son.

Blank BSAF Form

Bible Study and Application Format (BSAF)				
Biblical Reference	Teaching—What is the command or principle?	Reproof—How did I fail to keep the principle?	Correction—What do I need to do?	Training in Righteousness—How do I do it?

A.2. Think and Do List

This worksheet is used to examine a particular problem area of sinful thoughts or temptations. Since the spiritual battle starts from the thought, a new thinking pattern has to be established. New thinking patterns result in new behavior patterns over time.

Think and Do List		
Problem: (Describe your problem area briefly.)		
My temptations and sinful thoughts (Matt. 15:19; James 1:14-15).	**What I should be thinking in this situation (Ps. 19:14; Phil. 4:8).**	**What I should be doing as a result of my new biblical thinking (Phil. 4:9).**

298

A.3. Love is an Action

Love is an Action

According to **1 Cor. 13:4-8** ...

Love is patient:

- It is long-tempered, opposite of 'short fused'.
- Love is learning how to put up with others.
- It has restraint of anger, wrath, temper in all sorts of life situations.
- Patience is the key factor which is required in order to take a biblical course of action.
- Lack of patience is evidence of a lack of love.
- Love thinks of the other person first; lack of patience puts oneself first.
- Love shown to be giving of one's self, time, interests to another while giving up on one's rights, privileges, concerns, etc..
- Love is never in the abstract, it involves relationship with God and neighbor. It never stands alone.

Love is kind:

- Kindness is the opposite of all that is cruel and severe.
- It is thoughtful of other's feelings.
- It is gentleness in action, not passive.
- It cares about others and actively helps in a concrete way.

Love is not jealous:

- It rejoices in other's good fortune.
- It has no desire to lessen the desires, virtues, achievements or happiness of another.
- It puts others first before self.
- He shares what he possesses and enjoys helping others develop their assets.

Love does not boast:

- It does not parade one's self before others.
- It does not need personal significance in the eyes of others, but gives praise to others.
- It makes no odious comparisons.
- It does not put down others in order to lift self up.
- It keeps quiet about even genuine achievements, but deflects from self to give praise to God

Love is not proud:

- It acknowledges God's hand in all his achievements; always has an attitude of thankfulness to God, in all things.
- It exhibits a sense of humility recognizing God is all.
- It does not demand rights, privileges, significance, praise, etc..

Love does not act in an ugly way:

- An unloving person will do things, say things, assume attitude of which he later will be ashamed.
- It never offends by indelicate or crude acts and words that are violent or foul.
- It is concerned about manner as well as matter.

Love is not self-seeking:

- It seeks the other person's welfare and does not calculate what benefits he may accrue, no boomerang thinking.
- It does not do for others as a gimmick to gain certain personal ends.
- It does not say "what's in it for me", but does what God says to do in order to please God first.

Love is not easily irritated:

- This refers to 'rousing to anger'.

- It considers and thinks carefully before being irritable, thus, checking his spirit and sacrificing self, his plans, schedules, etc. for others.

Love does not keep records of wrongs:

- It is one who does not count up, recall and throw up to another all the offenses that he has committed.
- Forgiveness is the key problem for one who keeps records.

Love is not happy about injustice, but happily stands on the side of truth:

- It does not sit idly by when God's word is attacked.
- It is not mute about unfair actions against others.
- It takes a stand for what is right and against what is wrong.

Love covers all things:

- Rather than make a point of every offense against himself, the lover bears wrongdoing patiently.
- Out of love, he even covers what was done to him or others.
- Not every wrong should be made an issue, but love covers every little rub between believers and covers these from his own eyes as well as from others.

Love believes all things:

- When others doubt, the one who loves firmly believes.
- Only hard evidence would make him doubt another's words.
- Love thinks first of others, not himself; thus, involves himself in risk.
- He would rather injure himself than to injure another.
- His disposition is always to believe another if it is at all possible.

Love hopes all things:

- It always gives the other fellow the benefit of the doubt.
- It hopes for the best in others.
- It does not go around looking for wrong in others.
- This optimism does not grow out of faith in men, but in God who can change them.
- Whereas, a spirit of hopelessness or resignation, can be further occasion for the person to fall.

Love endures all things:

- This means that every sort of offense, pressure, affliction, and persecution can be endured in love (**1 Cor. 10:13**).

The essentials of love in verses 4-8 all boil down to this: **Love means putting others first**. Every positive quality examined can only be destroyed by self seeking. Each can be enhanced by giving one's self more and more to others. The route to love, therefore, is essentially the route to discipleship, to deny (crucify or put to death) the desires of self for Christ's sake and then to follow Him by losing one's life for His sake and the gospel's. Losing life this way, one indeed finds it.

A.4. Victory over Sin Worksheet (VOSWS)

This worksheet is to define a proactive plan to implement biblical change in your life. Especially it targets a particular sin or problem area and develops a put-off and put-on plan based on **Eph. 4:22** (**1 John 5:4-5**).

Victory over Sin Worksheet (VOSWS)			
My Specific Unbiblical Thoughts, Words, Actions (Matt. 7:1-5)	**Put Off and Biblical Reference(s) (Eph. 4:22; Col. 3:5-9)**	**Put On and Biblical Reference(s) (Eph. 4:23-24; Col. 3:10-17)**	**My Plan Not to Repeat This Sin and to Respond Biblically Instead (Titus 2:11-14)**
(A) List a specific sin or problem area that God convicts you in your heart. An area that is either obviously sinful or that you can do better in your christian walk.	(B) List thoughts, words, actions that you want to put off. List Bible verses to support your point—this is very important because it is in vain if we do these from our own ideas, but not according to God's word.	(C) Thoughts, words, actions that you should put on. List Bible verses to support your point.	(D) Detail an action plan to reinforce the put-on. God will bring up the same situation again and again until you are refined in this area. It should be a step by step or point by point list of actions. Pay attention to this problem area in the following weeks. Use every opportunity to exercise this action plan.

Note: VOSWS 4th Column Help

The VOSWS is usually applied to entrenched sin patterns. Unless biblical change occurs in the thoughts and belief systems, one is doomed to repeat the offense. For the 4th column, the plan of action, the use and practice of **Appendix A.9, "Contingency Plan"** may prove sufficent for a plan of action in most situations.

It would be wise to memorize the eight steps of your Contingency Plan to assist you to "walk in the Spirit" all the day long and to counteract spontaneous fleshly tendencies. Or one may use any of the forms in the appendix or worksheets for the 4th column.

As an alternate to this form (VOSWS), one may also use **Appendix A.6, "Problem Solving Worksheet"** to restructure and condition a biblical response to life's challenges.

Example (4th colume is moved to another row due to space limitation)

Victory over Sin Worksheet (VOSWS)		
My Specific Unbiblical Thoughts, Words, Actions (Matt. 7:1-5)	Put Off and Biblical Reference(s) (Eph. 4:22; Col. 3:5-9)	Put On and Biblical Reference(s) (Eph. 4:23-24; Col. 3:10-17)
I didn't feel like going into work yesterday because there was a difficult assignment coming to me from my supervisor. Thus, I called in sick and stayed home all day watching TV.	I have committed the wrong of: 1. Lying (**Eph. 4:25**); 2. My selfish interests (**Phil. 2:3**); 3. Not doing my responsibilities (**James 4:17**); 4. Living by my feelings (**Gen. 4:7**); 5. The idea that I just work for supervisor (**Col. 3:23**); 6. Wasting time (**Eph. 5:15-16**).	I should be: 1. Speaking the truth (**Eph. 4:25**); 2. The interests of others on my job (**Phil. 2:4**); 3. Doing my responsibilities (**James 4:17**); 4. Living obediently to God (**Gen. 4:7**); 5. Working heartily for the Lord (**Col. 3:23-24**); 6. Redeeming the time (**Eph. 5:15-16**).
My Plan Not to Repeat This Sin and to Respond Biblically Instead (4th col)		

1. Reconcile by **a)** confessing my sins to God (**1 John 1:9**); **b)** telling my supervisor the truth about why I was not at work (**Matt. 5:23-24**).
2. When tempted to call in sick, recite **Col. 3:23-24**.
3. When faced with a difficult assignment at work, I will:
   a. Pray for God's wisdom on how to handle it (**James 1:2-8**);
   b. Speak the truth (in a loving way) to my supervisor about how to complete the assignment (**Eph. 4:15,25**);
   c. Recognize that I am to be doing the best job I can because I ultimately work for the Lord (**Col. 3:23-24**).		

Blank VOSWS Form

Victory over Sin Worksheet (VOSWS)			
My Specific Unbiblical Thoughts, Words, Actions (Matt. 7:1-5)	Put Off and Biblical Reference(s) (Eph. 4:22; Col. 3:5-9)	Put On and Biblical Reference(s) (Eph. 4:23-24; Col. 3:10-17)	My Plan Not to Repeat This Sin and to Respond Biblically Instead (Titus 2:11-14)
My Plan Not to Repeat This Sin and to Respond Biblically Instead (Cont.)			

306

A.5. Dying to Self

When you are forgotten, or neglected, or purposely set at naught, and you don't sting and hurt with the insult or the oversight, but your heart is happy, being counted worthy to suffer for Christ.

THAT IS DYING TO SELF

When your good is evil spoken of, when your wishes are crossed, your advice disregarded, your opinions ridiculed, and you refuse to let anger rise in your heart, or even defend yourself, but take in all in patient, loving silence.

THAT IS DYING TO SELF

When you lovingly and patiently bear any disorder, any irregularity, any unpunctuality, or any annoyance; when you stand face-to-face with waste, folly, extravagance, spiritual insensibility; and endure it as Jesus endured.

THAT IS DYING TO SELF

When you are content with any food, any offering, any climate, any society, any raiment, any interruption by the will of God.

THAT IS DYING TO SELF

When you never care to refer to yourself in conversation, or to record your own good works, or itch after commendations, when you can truly love to be unknown.

THAT IS DYING TO SELF

When you can see your brother prosper and have his needs met and can honestly rejoice with him in spirit and feel no envy, nor question God, while your own needs are far greater and in desperate circumstances.

THAT IS DYING TO SELF

When you can receive correction and reproof from one of less stature than yourself and can humbly submit inwardly as well as outwardly, finding no rebellion or resentment rising up within your heart.

THAT IS DYING TO SELF

Are you dead yet? In these last days, the Spirit would bring us to the Cross.

"That I may know Him, and the power of his resurrection, and the fellowship of his sufferings, being made conformable unto his death" **(Phil. 3:10)**.

Others May, You Cannot!

If God has called you to be really like Jesus, He will draw you into a life of crucifixion and humility, and put upon you such demands of obedience, that you will not be able to follow other people, or measure yourself by other christians, and in many ways He will seem to let other people do things which He will not let you do.

Other christians and ministers who seem very religious and useful, may push themselves, pull wires, and work schemes to carry out their plans, but you cannot do it, and if you attempt it, you will meet with such failure and rebuke from the Lord as to make you sorely penitent.

Others may boast of themselves, of their work, of their successes, of their writings, but the Holy Spirit will not allow you to do any such thing, and if you begin it, He will lead you into some deep mortification that will make you despise yourself and all your good works.

Others may be allowed to succeed in making money, or may have a legacy left to them, but it is likely God will keep you poor, because He wants you to have something far better than gold, namely, a helpless dependence upon Him, that He may have the privilege of supplying your needs day by day out of an unseen treasury.

The Lord may let others be honored and put forward, and keep you hidden in obscurity, because He wants to produce some choice, fragrant fruit for His coming glory, which can only be produced in the shade. He may let others be great, but keep you small. He may let others do a work for Him and get the credit for it, but He will make you work and toil on without knowing how much you are doing; and then to make your work still more precious, He may let others get credit for the work which you have done, and thus make your reward ten times greater when Jesus comes.

The Holy Spirit will put a strict watch over you, with a jealous love, and will rebuke you for little words and feelings or for wasting your time, which other christians never feel distressed over. So make up your mind that God is an infinite

Sovereign and has a right to do as He pleases with His own. He may not explain to you a thousand things which puzzle your reason in His dealings with you, but if you absolutely sell yourself to be his love slave, He will wrap you up in a jealous love, and bestow upon you many blessings which come only to those who are in the inner circle.

Settle it forever, then, that you are to deal directly with the Holy Spirit, and that He must have the right to tie your tongue, or chain your hand, or close your eyes, in ways that He does not seem to use with others. Now, when you are so possessed with the living God that you are, in your secret heart, pleased and delighted over this peculiar, personal, private, jealous guardianship and management of the Holy Spirit over your life, you will have found the vestibule of Heaven.

A.6. Problem Solving Worksheet

This worksheet is to help you examine a problem area or situation where you have failed to act biblically.

Problem Solving Worksheet	
(A) What Happened? (Describe the problem)	**(B) What I did?** (Describe my response)
(C)What should I have done? (Cite biblical references)	**(D) What I now must do?** (What steps must I take to rectify matters?)

A.7. Problem/Solution Worksheet

There are three worksheets in this appendix:

Problem/Solution Worksheet I, Part A and B
Problem/Solution Worksheet II, Part A and B
Final Session Review

These worksheets are to be used in conjunction with the counseling sessions. After the initial review of personal data and after every subsequent counseling session, the counselor should use **Problem/Solution Worksheet I** to organize his observation and analysis in **Part A**, and a plan of action in **Part B.** Then he can follow up with **Problem/Solution Worksheet II** to lay out topics to be discussed for the next session. The counselor can either use **Worksheet II, Part A,** as a handout to the counselee, or write up a more formalized page for the session as he/she wishes. **Worksheet II** also includes a homework section in **Part B.** Counselee should be expected to complete the homework assignment to demonstrate his/her commitment to work on the problem area. **Final Session Review** is used in the last session to lay out a future direction for the counselee.

Problem/Solution Worksheet I

Review counselee's personal data sheet or results from last week's homework. Make note of judging others, blame shifting, self-will, weak or no commitment, lack of sensitivity to sin, defensiveness, bitterness, sin patterns (**Gal. 5:16-24**; **Col. 3:5-15**).

Problem/Solution Worksheet I, Part A: Analysis
Data from Session: _____ Date: _____
Feeling: (Gen. 4:7; Ps. 38:3-10; Ps. 38:17-18) (The spirit in which self was expressed)
Doing: (Eccl. 12:13; Luke 6:46; John 3:21; John 14:15; 1 John 2:3-6)
Thoughts (What person was thinking before, during and after the incident) **Speech** (Manner and content of spoken words)   **Actions** (Verbal/physical)
Root: (Mark 7:20-23; Luke 6:45; Heb. 12:15)

Problem/Solution Worksheet I, Part B: Plans
Data from Session: _____ Date: _____
Plans for next session; topics to be discussed:

1. Laying aside the old self and its practices (**Eph. 4:22**; **Col. 3:5-9**)

2. Renewing the mind (**Rom. 12:2**; **Eph. 4:23**)

3. Putting on the new self and its practices (**Eph. 4:24**; **Col. 3:10-16**)

Problem/Solution Worksheet II

Problem/Solution Worksheet II, Part A: Handout
Session: _____ Date: _____
Perspective: [1]
Hope: [2]
Change: [3]
[1] See Self-Confrontation Manual: Lesson 22 [BCF1] [2] See Self-Confrontation Manual: Lesson 6 [3] See Self-Confrontation Manual: Lesson 7 And/or refer to appropriate verses from a concordance; And/or passages from a related worksheet.

Problem/Solution Worksheet II, Part B: Homework

Session: _____ Date: _____

Work Out Your Salvation (Phil. 2:12-13)

Memory Verse(s):

Devotion:
1. **Daily Devotional Practices:** See **Appendix A.12, "Anchor Posts"** to insure one is walking a godly path by daily examining one's conscience, developing a sensitivity to sin, and practicing being in the Presence of the Holy Spirit from moment to moment.
2. **BSAF:** Selected verses related to the problem area.
3. **Word Study:** Use of concordance to study the problem area.

Put-Off/Put-On:
1. Appropriate worksheets and forms related to the problem area may be given as handouts (See **Table of Contents** and **Appendix**).
2. Other suggested put-off/put-on action items.

Final Session Review

Final Session Review
Confirm and reinforce biblical changes and patterns: (**Luke 9:23-24**)

Set goals of short-term, medium, and long-range plans:
 	
    • See **Matt. 6:33**; **Luke 6:36-38** for short-term goal:
 	
    • See **James 4** for medium-term goal:
 	
    • See **Rom. 12**; **Rom. 8:29**; and **1 John 3:8** for long-term goal:

A.8. Freedom from Anxiety

This worksheet is to help you examine your concerns that have caused you anxiety. Anxiety paralyzes a person and wastes significant amount of time in idleness. Persistent anxiety will result in mental and physical illnesses.

Freedom from Anxiety Worksheet (A biblical action and prayer plan based on Phil. 4:6-9)		
My Concerns (All the things about which I am tempted to worry)	**The Lord's List** (Those things about which I can do nothing)	**My List** (My responsibilities to fulfill in faithful obedience to The Lord)

A.9. Contingency Plan

The following eight steps will prepare you to handle a contingent situation and to conquer a sin pattern.

I. Recognize the danger signals.

1. Avoid putting yourself in the path of sin (**Ps. 1:1**).
2. Flee from all evil (**1 Thess. 5:22**).
3. Avoid triggers/stumbling blocks that can start you down the road to sin (**Matt. 18:7**).

II. Ask God's help immediately (Heb. 4:15-16; James 1:5-8).

III. Generate movement NOW!

1. Not in any direction but in a biblical direction (**James 4:17; Isa. 55:8-9**).
2. Not having any specific biblical alternatives can lead you onto another path of sin (**Matt. 11:43-45**).

IV. Recall Scriptures you have memorized (Ps. 119:9-11; Matt. 4:4), since actions begin in the mind (**Prov. 23:7**).

V. Implement specific biblical put-offs and put-ons while renewing the mind (**Eph. 4:22-24; Rom. 12:1-2; Phil. 4:8-9**).

VI. Seek God's strength for today (Phil. 4:6-7,13).

1. Don't look back at past failures or ahead to what we might perceive as future failures (**Matt. 6:33-34**).
2. We have God's grace to handle situations when we need it (**Heb. 4:15-16**).

VII. Solicit help from believers if necessary (Gal. 6:2; Eccl. 4:9-12).

1. Seek the support and prayers of other believers (**Heb. 10:24-25**).
2. Prearrange to call someone if you need help (**Prov. 27:17; 1 Thess. 5:11**).

VIII. Start doing the loving and responsible thing regardless of your feelings (**Gal. 5:22-25; Gen. 4:7; John 14:15,21; 1 Cor. 13:4-8a**).

A.10. Change is a Two-Factored Process

God's word says I must put off the old nature (old habits) and put on the new nature (new habits). Using the following Scriptures, list the old habits I must put off on the left column and the new habits I must put on on the right column.

Scripture For Put-off/Put-on	
Ezek. 36:25-27	2 Tim. 3:17
Matt. 16:24	Heb. 10:25
Eph. 4:17; Eph. 4:32	James 1:14-15; James 3:13-18
Col. 3:1-25	1 Pet. 3:1-17
1 Thess. 1:9	Gal. 5:13-26
Phil. 2:2-5,14	2 Tim. 2:22-3:7

Put-off/Put-on Worksheet	
God Says I Must Put-off	God Says I Must Put-on

319

A.11. Scheduling Worksheet

Use this worksheet on a weekly basis to discover existing schedule deficiency that leads to sinning patterns, and to establish new schedule for a godly lifestyle.

Scheduling Worksheet					Date: ___/___/___		
Time	Sun	Mon	Tue	Wed	Thu	Fri	Sat
5 AM							
6 AM							
7 AM							
8 AM							
9 AM							
10 AM							
11 AM							
12 Noon							
1 PM							
2 PM							
3 PM							
4 PM							
5 PM							
6 PM							
7 PM							
8 PM							
9 PM							
10 PM							
11 PM							
Midnight							
1 AM							
2 AM							

A.12. Anchor Posts

The following four anchor posts provide a method and the means to develop a firm and comprehensive foundation to support a disciplined and structured lifestyle of godliness:

Anchor Posts			
Daily Practices Plan	**Overcoming Temptations Plan**	**Forgive/ Reconcile Plan**	**Lord Alone Plan**
Devotions and self examination	Put-off and put-on in order to respond in a godly manner	List people and situations to forgive/reconcile	List offensive thoughts/images
Ps. 1:1-3; Ps. 139:23-24; Josh. 1:8; Ps. 19:14.	**Eph. 4:22-24; James 1:5; 1 John 1:9; James 1:2-4; Phil. 4:13; Ezek. 18:20.**	**Matt. 5:23-25; Matt. 18:21-35; Rom. 12:18-21; Heb. 10:17; Matt. 7:5.**	**Col. 1:10-12; Col. 3:17; Phil. 2:12-13; 2 Cor. 10:3-5.**

Appendix B. Suggested Memory Verses

Why Memorizing Bible Verses

The word of God is food for our souls. These selected verses are important extracts of the entire Bible, especially for biblical counseling purpose.

Memorizing these verses will purge and renew the intellect, the memory and the will. By the process of meditation (you speaking to God) and contemplation (God speaking to you), one will be filled with God's precepts instead of being corrupted and constantly being tossed by the swing of the world's value system.

Memory Verse List

1. (**Eph. 2:8-9**; **Matt. 7:1**; **Matt. 7:5**) You can change biblically
2. (**2 Tim. 3:16-17**; **2 Cor. 3:5-6**) Man's way and God's way
3. (**1 Cor. 10:13**) Biblical dynamics of change
4. (**Rom. 8:28-29**) Biblical basis for change
5. (**Eph. 4:22-24**) Biblical structure for change
6. (**Heb. 5:14**; **James 4:17**) Biblical practice achieves lasting change
7. (**Luke 9:23-24**; **Rom. 6:12-13**) Dealing with self
8. (**Eph. 4:31-32**; **James 1:19-20**) Anger and bitterness
9. (**Matt. 5:23-24**; **Eph. 4:29**; **Phil. 2:3-4**) Interpersonal problems (love your neighbor)
10. (**Eph. 5:21-22**; **Eph. 5:25**; **1 Pet. 3:1,7**;) Marriage relationship
11. (**Eph. 5:18-20**; **Eph. 6:4**; **Eph. 6:1-3**) Parent child relationship
12. (**Gen. 4:7**; **James 1:22**) Depression
13. (**Matt. 6:33-34**; **1 John 4:18**) Fear and worry
14. (**Rom. 6:22**; **Eph. 6:10-11**; **Eph. 5:18**; **Eph. 6:12-13**) Life dominating sins
15. (**Gal. 5:22-25**) God's standards for life
16. (**1 John 5:3-5**) Biblical counseling

Appendix C. Internet Resources

Christian links on the Internet that may prove beneficial:

- **The Bible Gateway** [http://bible.gospelcom.net/]: Comprehensive bible search engine.

- **Christian Classics Ethereal Library (CCEL)** [http://www.ccel.org/]: Large electronic library of classic saintly writings.

- **Blue Letter Bible** [http://www.blueletterbible.org/]: Bible study resources with concordances, lexicons, dictionaries and commentaries.

- **St Paul Center** [http://www.salvationhistory.com/]: Rich catholic bible study tools and resources.

- **Biblical Counseling Foundation** [http://www.bcfministries.org/]: A large portion of this book is derived from the ministry of BCF.

- **Reasons To Believe** [http://www.reasons.org/]: Discoveries in the sciences vs. the God of the Bible.

- **The NET Bible** [http://www.bible.org/netbible/index.htm]: New English Translation Bible for Internet.

Bibliography

Note: Most of these books can be purchased online at http://www.amazon.com/.

[**Adams1**] Christian Counselor's Manual. By Jay Adams. Zondervan.

[**Adams2**] Competent to Counsel. By Jay Adams. Presbyterian and Reformed Publishing Co..

[**Allender1**] Bold Love. By Dan Allender. NavPress.

[**Allender2**] Wounded Heart. By Dan Allender. NavPress.

[**BCF1**] Self-Confrontation Manual and Handbook. Biblical Counseling Foundation (http://www.bcfministries.org/), Palm Desert, CA.

[**Boehme1**] Dialogues on the Supersensual Life. By Jacob Boehme. Edited by William Law. Kessinger Publishing Company.

[**Chambers1**] Not Knowing Where. By Oswald Chambers. Christian Literature Crusade.

[**Chambers2**] My Utmost for His Highest. By Oswald Chambers. Epiphany Books.

[**Fromke1**] Unto Full Stature. By Deverne Fromke. Alfred Mainzer Inc..

[**Hammond1**] Pigs in the Parlor. By Frank and Ida Hammond. Impact Christian Books, Inc..

[**Hildebrand1**] Transformation in Christ. By Dietrich Von Hildebrand. EWTN, Irondale, Alabama.

[**Julian1**] Showings (From "The Spiritual Life" magazine). By Julian of Norwich. OSF, Washington, DC.

[**Kavanaugh1**] Collected Works of St. John of the Cross. By Kieran Kavanaugh. ICS Publications, Washington, DC.

[**Leader1**] The Preacher's Outline & Sermon Bible. Leadership Ministries Worldwide (http://www.outlinebible.org/).

[**Lloyd1**] Life in the Spirit. By D. Martyn Lloyd-Jones. Baker Book House.

[**Mack1**] Strengthening Your Marriage. By Wayne Mack. Presbyterian and Reformed Publishing Co..

[**Mack2**] Your Family, God's Way. By Wayne Mack. Presbyterian and Reformed Publishing Co..

[**Mack3**] Homework Manual for Biblical Living. By Wayne Mack. P & R Press.

[**Nee1**] The Spiritual Man. By Watchman Nee. Living Stream Ministry.

[**Payne1**] The Healing Presence. By Leanne Payne. Baker Books.

[**Payne2**] Restoring the Christian Soul Through Healing Prayer. By Leanne Payne. Crossway Books.

[**Pieper1**] Four Cardinal Virtues. By Joseph Pieper. University of Notre Dame Press.

[**Sanford1**] The Healing Gifts of the Spirit. By Agnes Sanford. Harper, San Francisco.

[**Sanford2**] Transformation of the Inner Man. By John and Paula Sandford. Victory house, Tulsa, OK.

[**Smith1**] Dealing with Self (audio tape). By Malcolm Smith. Malcolm Smith Ministries.

[**Smith2**] Fear of Unknown (audio tape). By Malcolm Smith. Malcolm Smith Ministries.

[**Smith3**] Meditation (audio tape). By Malcolm Smith. Malcolm Smith Ministries.

[**Smith4**] Freedom from Fear (audio tape). By Malcolm Smith. Malcolm Smith Ministries.

[**Smith5**] Fear of Rejection (audio tape). By Malcolm Smith. Malcolm Smith Ministries.

[**Spitzer1**] Healing the Culture. By Robert Spitzer. Ignatius Press.

[**StJohn1**] Ascent of Mount Carmel. By St John of The Cross. Paraclete Press.

[**StTeresa1**] The Interior Castle. By St Teresa of Avila. ICS Publications, Washington, DC.

[**StThomas1**] Collected Works of St Thomas Aquinas. By St Thomas Aquinas. Philosophy Documentation Center, Charlottesville, VA.

[**Willard1**] The Divine Conspiracy. By Dallas Willard. HarperCollins Publishing.

Index

This book is also available electroncially at two locations:

Immanuel's Church [http://www.immanuels.org/biblical_counseling/]
DocBook Format   [http://www.ecoin.net/bcbook/]

You can perform online keyword search (powered by Google).